Saving Our Environment

from Washington

Saving Our Environment from Washington

How Congress Grabs Power,

Shirks Responsibility,

and Shortchanges the People

David Schoenbrod

Yale University Press   New Haven & London

Set in Minion type by Keystone Typesetting, Inc.

Printed in the United States of America by Vail-Ballou Press.

Library of Congress Cataloging-in-Publication Data

Schoenbrod, David.

Saving our environment from Washington : how Congress grabs power, shirks responsibility, and shortchanges the people / David Schoenbrod.

    p.   cm.

Includes bibliographical references and index.

ISBN 0-300-10621-1 (cloth : alk. paper)

1. Environmental policy—United States. 2. Science and state—United States. 3. United States. Congress—Powers and duties. I. Title.

GE180.S374 2005

333.72′0973—dc22

2004061589

A catalogue record for this book is available from the British Library.

The paper in this book meets the guidelines for permanence and durability of the Committee on Production Guidelines for Book Longevity of the Council on Library Resources.

10 9 8 7 6 5 4 3 2 1

For Angus Macbeth and Ross Sandler,
colleagues and friends, then and now

Contents

Part III. Our Republic

Part IV. What We Lose

Preface

This book is based upon my experience as an environmental advocate and observer of the environmental scene over the past thirty-five years. The tales it tells took place in the United States, but the practices it attacks—legislators hiding behind bureaucracies and needlessly centralizing power—are of concern in Europe and beyond.

In the United States, Congress passed statutes shaped so that the legislators could claim to have guaranteed a clean earth, yet still escape blame for the subsequent disappointments and costs. The statutes ordered the Environmental Protection Agency (EPA) to solve every pollution problem, no matter how local, yet left it with the hard choices on how to do so. Every time the public's desire for a clean earth ran up against its other desires, the agency found itself in the middle. Such conflicts came with dizzying rapidity because every environmental problem was on this national agency's agenda. The United States is much cleaner today than it was thirty-five years ago, but the reason was the public's deeply felt desire for environmental quality rather than Congress's handing off the ball to the EPA.

Congress has been "political" in the worst sense of the word. Regulation is inevitably political because, no matter who makes the rules, they reflect tugging and hauling between conflicting interests in society. The system that Congress has established for making environmental regulation is political in a different and invidious sense: the legislators shaped it to make themselves look good rather than to serve the interests of their constituents.

I hope this book attracts general readers. For them, it is meant to stand on its own. Those with a special interest in regulatory politics or law should regard it as part of a trilogy on the problem of legislators shirking responsibility and needlessly centralizing power by establishing ersatz rights. The other volumes are *Power without Responsibility: How Congress Abuses the People through Delegation* (Yale University Press, 1993) and, with Ross Sandler, *Democracy by Decree: What Happens When Courts Run Government* (Yale University Press, 2003). While the earlier volumes dealt with this problem in all areas of regulation, the present volume deals with it exclusively in the environmental area. Because the present volume tells how my career in environmental advocacy opened my eyes to the problem, it is, although written last, the one to read first.

CHAPTER ONE

Introduction
Then and Now

"Then" began late in 1975 at a dusty little airfield near San Juan, Puerto Rico. My traveling companion and I got into a one-engine plane and were flown west beyond the end of land and out over the Caribbean. We spotted our destination on the watery horizon, at first only the silhouette of a distant mesa and then a huge white rock. Its cliffs plunged two hundred feet to a narrow fringe of palms surrounded by sand, clear waters, and reefs. We flew the seven-mile length of the island, banked sharply around the far tip, plunged down the cliff, and stopped with a jerk on a tiny strip of grass hidden in the palms. This was Isla de Mona.

The pilot kept the engine running as he quickly passed us the food and water. We had to bring our own because no one lived here. There were only a few campers—a Commonwealth of Puerto Rico forest ranger near the strip and a family somewhere far down the beach. The pilot said goodbye and took off, leaving us in stillness and silence. We searched out a campsite and met our neighbors, the Mona Iguanas. Tinted red and purple with spiky backs, they look like dragons but are only four feet long and eat plants, not maidens.

I had come to Mona for a reason. Lawyers from the Puerto Rico bar association had asked me—a lawyer at the Natural Resources

1. A Mona Iguana. Courtesy of Commonwealth of Puerto Rico Department of Natural and Environmental Resources.

Defense Council, a private environmental advocacy group—to bring a lawsuit to stop the island from being turned into a massive petroleum complex. Major oil companies would bring crude oil from Iran, Iraq, and other Persian Gulf countries to Mona in supertankers and refine it there. The gasoline and products would then be transshipped in regular tankers to established ports in the eastern United States. This home of the Mona Iguana and more than a hundred other endangered and unique species, rightly known as the Galapagos of the Caribbean, would become a smelly eyesore.

Mona was surely not the most appropriate site on the eastern seaboard for such a project, but newly strengthened environmental laws had made it all but impossible to build a supertanker port or refinery in anyone's backyard. Mona's attraction was that it was no one's backyard. Yet, to our Puerto Rican clients, Mona was their

Grand Canyon, and the "Superpuerto," as it was called in the Puerto Rican press, epitomized colonialism in modern guise.

American environmental laws apply in Puerto Rico. The hope of the Superpuerto's sponsors was that no one in Puerto Rico could put together sufficient legal resources to mount a serious challenge, at least until after the project was too far along to stop. They made it an elusive target by keeping the particulars of their plans secret. But our team of Puerto Rican and mainland attorneys was able to piece together enough facts to file a detailed complaint. We moved the district court judge to act, but he never responded. When we called his strange silence to the attention of the Court of Appeals in Boston, a new judge was assigned and he made it clear that he would decide. At this point the sponsors of the Superpuerto announced that it would be abandoned, but not, they said, because of our lawsuit.

Now I had come to Mona to savor what we had worked to save. We dove among the pristine coral reefs and, from under the clump of palms that was our home, watched brilliant suns and soft moons. One day I hiked to the top of the mesa and, looking out over the expanse of land and sea, I thought of my work as bringing together justice and beauty. In short, I felt altogether satisfied with myself—a sure sign of danger.

The next evening, the weather changed. Off the spit of land on which we camped, tall banks of dark clouds collided and billowed higher. The sea rose and the waves boiled. Just then, newly hatched turtles popped out of the beach and raced toward the water. Their timing felt perfect, was perfect, but I knew nothing of their natural clocks and was utterly surprised. The baby turtles struggled to surmount the ruffles in the sand and wobbled toward crashing waves. No sooner had the first few won my heart and been swept out to sea, than gulls and hawks spotted the moving feast and swarmed to eat their fill. Like a youngster watching *Bambi*, I was appalled. I tried to chase the predators away, but the task was hopeless. I could taxi this or that little turtle to the sea, but they hated being picked up and were now emerging by the thousands and most were being eaten. I stopped, took a breath, and realized that the birds and turtles had been at this for ages. Just who did I think I was to interfere? I went back to the camp and made a fire, and it grew dark.

The next morning, it was still dark and even more foreboding, the wind fierce and cold. The forest ranger came by to tell of a radio message warning of worse to come. We had been ordered to evacuate on boats that would be sent to get us at dawn the following day. That night, the tiny populace of the island camped together. It turned out the family down the beach was that of the former oil company executive who had been in charge of the Superpuerto project. Our previous opponent now had a face, and he seemed decent enough. If he knew we had been opponents, he did not say, nor did I. This was no time for a confrontation.

At the dark dawn, he and his family boarded the spiffy yacht on which they had come. The forest ranger got on a modern police launch sent out to fetch him, but not before putting us on an old trawler that had been fishing off Mona. The yacht and the police launch, with their sleek hulls and powerful motors, seemed like safer bets in a storm, but they would not take us. I remembered from researching the case that the Mona Passage was notoriously dangerous in a storm.

The winds were too fierce for the fishermen to hoist their sails. An auxiliary engine barely pushed us through the towering waves. For me, the choice was to go below deck, where the diesel fumes made me sick to my stomach, or to stay above deck, where the spray chilled me to the bone. Above I could at least see the threat. I wanted to ask the crew, "Will we make it?" but they seemed far too busy pumping water out of the creaking wooden hull. I could tell from the looks on their faces that we probably would if the engine did not quit.

As the trawler chugged along, I reflected that these fishermen had had more at stake in the Superpuerto fight than anyone. Oil spills might have ruined their fishing; oil refineries might have employed their children. But no one had ever asked them whether they wanted the project or our opposition to it. They had been treated like children, but now I was huddled on the deck at their feet, helpless as a babe, my life in their capable hands. I had fallen a long way from the heights of the Mona mesa. Sick to my stomach, I asked myself—I really did—"Isn't there some way that ordinary people such as these fishermen could have a meaningful say on environmental decisions so vital to them?" I was not enough of a romantic to believe that such matters could be decided in New England–style town meetings and too much of a skeptic to believe that sessions in which government and corporate bureaucrats hear out the locals would be more than charades.

When we landed in the little port of Mayaguez that afternoon, the piers were lined with anxious faces. Upon stepping ashore, we learned that the police launch, whose passengers I had envied, had hit a reef and had gone down with all aboard. A kind family took us to their home, gave us hot soup, and put us to bed. I was asleep before the winter sun had set.

I awoke the next morning not quite believing how near death we had come. I made my way back to New York, putting out of my mind for the moment the question posed by the Mona Passage: How could environment policy be made less elitist and more accountable to ordinary people? I believed, as I had all along, that the appointed administrator of the Environmental Protection Agency (EPA) sitting in Washington should have the power to make the environmental rules for the entire country.

That was then.

"Now" is the writing of this book. It began almost a quarter century later. If I had to pick a date and a place, it would be July 11, 1998, on a hilltop in an apple orchard in upstate New York. Dan Wilson and Susan Knapp are getting married among the apple trees they tend, as his parents did before them. In their thirties, Dan and Susan are of a cohort that says, "We are all environmentalists." They are sophisticated ones, too. She has worked for the California Coastal Commission. He chairs the board of the local natural history museum and wildlife sanctuary. His mother has a doctorate in biology, and his brother is a cancer researcher at a major medical school.

After the ceremony, the wedding party gathers down by the cider barn to toast the couple with their own cider. As almost everyone knows, the Food and Drug Administration (FDA) is considering whether to issue a rule making its sale a crime.

The FDA says the juice of apples is dangerous unless pasteurized.[1] The parents at the wedding are neither ignorant of the FDA's concerns nor uncaring about their children, who are enjoying the cider with them. Some among them can explain precisely why the risk of drinking this cider is smaller than other risks that FDA experts regularly let their own children run. We also know that Dan and Susan worry about whether an FDA mandate to pasteurize would turn the orchard into a losing proposition. The kind of pasteurization equipment they can afford would make their cider taste more like canned apple juice. There would be no future in that.

They also worry that a new federal statute , the 1996 Food Quality Protection Act,[2] has empowered regulators to control how they grow apples. Under it, the EPA has signaled that it will tightly control most of the chemicals that they use. In deciding how to use chemicals, they must take account of complex variations in weather, pests, and microclimates in order to produce a crop that is not only safe, but will also yield a decent livelihood. They could make more money if they gave up farming, but they love it. With an agency sitting in Washington setting out to issue national rules dictating how they

2. Dan Wilson and Susan Knapp at their wedding rehearsal in front of their cider barn, 1998.

deal with local conditions, what they fear will slip through their fingers is not only their livelihood, but also the enjoyment that they get from farming. A few nights before the wedding, sitting at our kitchen table, Dan said, "I can imagine the day when my closest relation to growing apples will be buying them in the supermarket." Susan nodded. What a tragedy that would be. They express their artistry and friendship through the orchard and the many activities that take place around it. They are a focus of our rural society. Their quitting farming would leave a hole bigger than a barn.

Dan and Susan's fears are widely shared. The day after their wedding, I fly down to Washington to address the state presidents of the American Farm Bureau Federation. They had supported the Food Quality Protection Act. They know that the wrong pesticides, or the right pesticides wrongly applied, can be harmful. They had been told by their representatives in Congress that the EPA would base its regulation of farmers on long-standing and commonsensical scientific practices. But, now that it has the power, the EPA, they tell me, is changing its mind about how the act will work, and the result will be that many widely used chemicals will be eliminated. These farm leaders represent a powerful constituency, yet they feel powerless to protect themselves from what they consider a regulatory juggernaut.

The farm leaders wonder, as I had in the Mona Passage, whether environment policy could be made less elitist and more accountable to ordinary people. Now I have an answer. It is twofold.

First, states and localities rather than the federal government should make the rules controlling almost all pollution sources. The federal government should step in only when states, left to their own devices, are likely to allow significant harm to be done beyond their own borders. The result would be that federal government would make the rules for only a small fraction of sources, generally the largest ones. Today, in contrast, the EPA controls the regulation of millions of farms, businesses, and government activities, regardless of how localized their impact may be. This is why the EPA, whether measured by staff, budget, or impact, now runs the nation's largest regulatory regime.[3]

Second, at every level of government, elected legislators should make the pollution control rules. Today, in contrast, appointed functionaries at the EPA and its state counterparts acting under its supervision make most of the rules.

My answer is, of course, not the least bit new. Our Constitution sought to guarantee a republic in which government would be as close to home as possible and there would be no taxation without representation or, for that matter, regulation without representation. In that republic, new rules could come only in statutes on which our elected representatives would vote. That, for our representatives, is the rub. They would be stuck with direct, personal responsibility for the costs as well as the benefits of the rules. Better for the legislators is a system in which they pass statutes ordering the EPA to make the rules necessary to clean the earth. In that way, the legislators can say they passed a "law" to clean the earth while shifting to the EPA the blame for the costs of making it so. The EPA often lacks the political muscle needed to deliver the rules that would achieve the environmental goals in the statutes, but that presents no political problem for the legislators. They can blame the EPA for the failure.

This arrangement lets members of Congress profit from the environment issue on the cheap and so gives them a personal stake in expanding the federal environmental regulation franchise to include issues plainly within the competence of state and local government. Congress will let go of local environmental problems only if its members take responsibility for the environmental laws, and they can take responsibility only if Congress lets go of local environmental problems.

When I became an environmental advocate, I regarded questions about the constitutionality of the EPA's power as the last refuge of polluters, and I litigated accordingly.[4] I wanted to uphold the public interest in the present rather than the constitutional ideals of the past. Experience has since taught me that those constitutional ideals

---

"Rules," "Laws," and "Statutes"

Congress fails to make law when it passes a statute that tells the EPA to make the rules regulating pollution. The word for a rule regulating private conduct is "law." In Britain to this day, law means rules of conduct, whether based on statute, custom, or morality, and does not mean a statute that fails to contain the rules. In the United States, we sometimes say that a statute handing off lawmaking authority to an agency is a law, but that depreciates the word and lets our elected "lawmakers" take credit for shouldering responsibility that they in fact have shirked.[5] I will use "law" to mean rules, whether made by Congress or the EPA, but not statutes telling the EPA to make rules.

---

are the safest road to the public interest, including the public's deeply felt interest in a clean earth.

Because it was experience that opened my eyes, this book starts with the experiences that persuaded me to change my mind about what Congress has done. These stories, and the essays intertwined with them, lead the reader along the following path.

Part I of the book traces the EPA's rise to power and what became of that power. Rachel Carson published *Silent Spring* in 1962. It broadened public concern about the environment. The next year Congress passed a largely symbolic statute called the Clean Air Act, which called for states and localities to regulate pollution. From 1963 to 1968, the number of states with air pollution laws went from sixteen to forty-six.[6] The burdens imposed varied greatly and were small by modern standards, but they were enough to prompt the auto industry and then the coal mining industry to try to check the state and local response to grassroots demands. The solution they hit upon was to get Congress to amend the Clean Air Act to put a national agency in charge of making air pollution laws. Congress complied in the mid-1960s. The agency, a part of the Department of Health, Education, and Welfare, made it harder for states and localities to respond to the growing environmental concern.

The grassroots movement not only survived but grew beyond all expectations. On the first Earth Day, held on April 22, 1970, twenty million Americans gathered at demonstrations in forty-two states "to challenge the corporate and government leaders who promise change" but do not deliver. Congress shut down so that the legislators could go home to show their solidarity, but it had to do something substantial. While members deliberated, President Richard Nixon established the EPA.[7] By the end of the year, the 1970 Clean Air Act endowed it with sweeping new powers to make law. It was the prototype for many subsequent statutes dealing with other kinds of pollution.

With the new Clean Air Act, the EPA, politicians said, was to be different from and better than government as usual. Power would be shifted from state and local governments to the national government and from legislators elected by voters to functionaries bound to do what science demands. No longer would the environment be vulnerable to governors, mayors, and legislators swayed by greedy corporations and voters who did not care enough about the environment.[8] Instead, a scientific elite insulated from politics would rule. Most industries went along, seemingly out of a belief that the new EPA would not accomplish much. They were correct, at least in the beginning.

Through the 1970s, the air pollution laws that the EPA made accomplished less than the laws that came directly from Congress, states, and localities. Today the air is much cleaner than it was in

1970, and the EPA deserves some of the credit, but it is simply wrong to think that the EPA imposed environmental protection on a reluctant public.

Part II examines the EPA's claim to speak for science. The well-intentioned hope that an expert national agency would base its decisions on science has foundered on the reality that the science is surprisingly uncertain, that zero risk is physically impossible, and that measures to decrease a risk have costs and sometimes actually increase other risks. There are still other considerations that science cannot possibly take into account, such as the trustworthiness of individuals and the desire of people to take pleasure from self-directed work. Take, for example, the regulation of pesticide use on farms like that of Dan Wilson and Susan Knapp. They have more at stake in safe practices in their orchard than does anyone. They and their children live among its trees and eat the fruit throughout the year. They are good people who could not sleep if they sold tainted apples or cider.

There are, of course, people unlike Dan and Susan—power-hungry entrepreneurs and the well-intentioned but heedless. We need environmental law to guard against such as them. Yet having these decisions made by the EPA does not necessarily get them resolved in a commonsense, let alone a scientific, way. After all, not all the people with influence over the EPA's laws—whether in Congress, environmental groups, trade associations, or the EPA itself—are sensible people. They too have their share of power-hungry entrepreneurs and the well-intentioned but heedless. Lawmaking by the EPA is inevitably political, but the agency is forced to dress up its politics as science.

Part III examines the conflict between the EPA and two fundamental principles of our republic—that government should be as close to home as possible and that laws should be made by elected legislators. It shows how we can honor these principles without impairing government's ability to respond to the voters' desire for a sound environment. We do not have to be ruled by the EPA for science to be given its due. Experts would still provide what information science offers, but the final judgments are political and ought to be made by elected politicians rather than appointed ones. We also do not have to be ruled by the EPA for environmental protection to get its due. It has strong support in the electorate and gets organized expression through thousands of groups at the state and local level and well-financed national organizations that are powers in Washington. Their leaders enjoy the same access to many national political figures as do the heads of the largest corporations and unions.

Part IV shows that the EPA delays good laws, imposes bad ones, and is too big, muscle-bound, and remote to consider the facts on the ground. The problem is not that it delivers too much environmental protection in the aggregate, but that sometimes it does not deliver enough, and that which it does deliver comes with unnecessary burdens on the public. The burdens on businesses and farmers are highly visible because they are direct. The burdens on wage earners, consumers, and taxpayers are all but invisible because they come circuitously, but they are large and they hurt. Such leaders of the academic left and center as Bruce Ackerman, Stephen Breyer, E. Donald Elliott, Richard Stewart, and Cass Sunstein, as well as those of the right, have argued that the EPA needlessly burdens society.[9] The burdens sap not only our monthly budgets and retirement savings but also values more precious than dollars—democracy, liberty, justice, and (I will back this up) joy. These downsides are a drag on environmental protection.

How, if I am right, could all this have been missed by the general public? The reason is that most people see environmental protection as a struggle between the EPA and big business. The perception is in many ways false. Major corporations today understand that the EPA provides them with substantial benefits. Its lawmaking is necessarily slow because of procedural requirements imposed by Congress and the courts. The EPA also buffers large corporations from competition from small and emerging businesses. The regulations are expensive to large corporations, but most of the cost can be passed on to consumers. A powerful EPA is good for many big businesses and all national legislators, but bad for small business and local flexibility—good for national advocacy organizations and industries that sell pollution-control services, but bad for civic and neighborhood associations and the rest of us.

Many major corporations want to keep the EPA in charge but have it make laws that burden them less. Under the banner of his "Contract with America" released in 1994, House Speaker Newt Gingrich backed a bill that would have required the EPA to balance costs against human health benefits in making environmental laws. It was easy for environmental advocates to picture the legislation as a macabre payback for campaign contributions. The bill did nothing to correct the delays in the EPA's issuing of laws needed to protect public health, but instead would have made them worse by requiring it to prove in advance that the law's benefits would exceed its costs. Such proof is often unavailable, even for laws that make perfectly good sense. The bill should have been defeated, as I argued at the time.[10] Gingrich's proposal was to amend the EPA's lawmaking power. Mine is to end it.

In the stylized struggle between "good" EPA and "bad" big business, most voters support the EPA because they distrust big business. In a column chiding President George W. Bush for dismissing an EPA report as written by "bureaucrats," journalist Thomas L. Friedman wrote that he wanted to be counted as having a fundamental belief in federal agencies, "not because I have no faith in ordinary Americans, but because I have no trust in ordinary Big Oil . . . to do the right thing without proper oversight."[11] I often admire Mr.

Friedman, but not here. He is, of course, right to distrust large corporations, but big oil sometimes gets what it wants from the EPA. That is only one reason to distrust the EPA. Voters should not have to take its laws on trust.

Mr. Friedman's "not . . . hav[ing] no faith in ordinary Americans" is less faith than we deserve. The great majority of ordinary Americans (68 percent) tell pollsters that the public does not care enough about the environment.[12] Think about it. *Most people* think *most people* do not care enough about the environment. We do care enough. The problem is that we have been convinced we do not. Once we get that sorted out, there will be an end to "environmental protection" without representation.

Part I

Power

CHAPTER TWO

Coming to the Environmental Movement

The draw of environmental advocacy was inevitable, but only in retrospect. My parents reared me to trust in farsighted and benevolent leaders dedicated to high-minded ideals and to aspire to be one of those leaders myself. In 1960 I made it to Yale College, where I was taught that important public decisions are best left to experts. That message went down easily because we were being trained to be those experts and President John F. Kennedy was surrounding himself with "the best and the brightest."[1] Heeding the call of that knight in tailored armor, I set out to position myself for public service. I got a succession of summer jobs with Senator and then Vice President Hubert H. Humphrey and then a Marshall Scholarship to study economics at Oxford.

After Oxford, I was at Yale Law School when Vice President Humphrey received the Democratic nomination for president. I was asked to join the campaign staff. I declined despite knowing I was passing up a chance for a White House job because Humphrey had not satisfied the requirements of my conscience by renouncing the Vietnam War. I took a clerkship instead with Judge Spottswood W. Robinson III, who had argued *Brown v. Board of Education* in tandem with Thurgood Marshall.[2] Next came a job with the community development project established by Robert F. Kennedy in the Bedford-Stuyvesant section of Brooklyn.

Up to this point, it had never dawned on me that environmental advocacy might become a profession. "Environmental Law" was not yet a course in the law school catalog, and the word "ecology" was new to common parlance. My interest in the environment had, however, been primed. My mother had been an avid reader, and the readings I most often heard her speak about accused people of ruining the earth. There was one long season during my early teens when she worried out loud that America wasted water. Just how one wasted water baffled me. Where, I wondered, could the water go that it would not come back as rain? But later, when she worried that pesticides were killing the birds, I had no trouble understanding.

She was reading Rachel Carson's *Silent Spring* as it originally appeared—as a series of essays in the *New Yorker* in 1962. The book described a country lane denuded of life except for some scraggly weeds. It then pictured the same lane, this time brimming with life, especially fluttering, singing birds. Carson warned that we will have the barren future, and not the bright one, if people continue to spray poisons to control pests and weeds. Chemicals were not only killing cock robin but, according to Carson, were a major cause of cancer in humans. The choice was simple: chemical apocalypse, yes or no?[3]

Carson called attention to the environment, but even in the mid-1960s the issue had yet to take center stage. Gallup first polled the public on the environment in 1965 and found that only 28 percent rated air pollution a serious problem. In the 1968 presidential campaign, neither Richard Nixon nor Hubert Humphrey mentioned the environment. Interest was, however, building. When an oil platform five miles off the California coast sprang a major leak in January 1969, the story made the front pages and stayed there. By 1970, 69 percent of the public rated air pollution serious.[4]

On April 22, 1970, came the first Earth Day. I did not participate, as I had in the civil rights march on Washington in 1963 and the rallies against the Vietnam War in the late 1960s. For most leftists then, the environment was a distraction from the graver problems of racism, poverty, and war. As Richard Hatcher, the black mayor of Gary, Indiana, stated, "The nation's concern for the environment has done what George Wallace was unable to do—distract the nation from the human problems of black and brown Americans." Whitney Young Jr., head of the National Urban League, argued, "The war on pollution is one that should be waged after the war on poverty is won." The then reliably left *New Republic* termed "the ecology binge . . . a cop-out."[5]

Working at Bedford-Stuyvesant Restoration made me see that the environment was a problem for the urban poor. My immediate boss, John Doar—himself one of the heroes of the civil rights struggle—told me to figure out how to improve the community's ambience and to start by helping the tenants of three particularly dilapidated buildings. Their complaints included no heat and crumbling walls. I wondered whether those crumbling walls contained lead paint. The press had just begun to break the news that ingesting small flakes of lead paint could kill or maim children.[6] We took paint samples to a laboratory, which reported that they contained enough lead to kill. When we took the landlords to court, they abandoned the buildings. The judges asked me to collect the rents and run things. The rents under New York's rent control law proved barely enough to buy heating oil and pay the janitor, let alone make basic repairs. It was taking much of my time to make only marginal improvements in three of the thousands of buildings in Bedford-Stuyvesant.

Wanting a broader impact, I set out to find some way to clean the area's garbage-littered streets. We wrote a formal proposal to the city for Bedford-Stuyvesant Restoration to collect residential trash and sweep the streets. After crunching the numbers, we figured we could do a good job for only a third of the cost it took the city to do a crummy one. Moreover, we would be giving jobs to unemployed community residents. The city's head of sanitation embraced our proposal and recommended it to Mayor John Lindsay. He was in a tough race for reelection and wanted the support of the sanitation workers union. The union, of course, nixed the deal. Fighting city hall was not an option at Bedford-Stuyvesant Restoration because the project was dependent upon government funding.

I cast about for some other way to make my mark. One day I learned from the morning paper that I lived in a newly drawn state senate district perfectly suited to a candidate of my stripe. The "Reform Democratic" leaders gave me the nod. I was, in my late twenties, a cinch to get elected, and I believed I could quickly rise from there to where I really wanted to go, Congress. Others thought so, too, and volunteered to run my campaign. But with the machinery in place, I began to ask myself if I really wanted a career as a politician, a field in which success depended on saying what goes down well and glad-handing day and night. I told my supporters, "Thanks but no thanks," and withdrew.

Wondering what to do, I thought of my friends from Yale Law School who were founding a legal advocacy organization to do for the environment what the NAACP Legal Defense Fund had done for civil rights. It was called the Natural Resources Defense Council (NRDC). They had gotten a grant from the Ford Foundation and were under way. I asked to join and was ultimately accepted. I was elated. With the NRDC, I could sue the government, something I could never do at Bed-Stuy Restoration. Yet I would not be abandoning the civil rights and anti-poverty causes because the NRDC would allow me to focus on the environmental problems of the inner city and minorities.

CHAPTER THREE

Congress Does Its Thing

In a high-profile ceremony on December 31, 1970, President Nixon signed the Clean Air Act Amendments of 1970 into law. The act's author was Senator Edmund Muskie. Having also written the previous air and water pollution legislation, he was known in Congress as Mr. Environment. He was also the front-runner for his party's presidential nomination, having been Hubert Humphrey's running mate in 1968. Muskie hoped to ride to the White House in 1972 as the environmental champion.[1]

Bad news about the environment was good news for presidential candidate Muskie. The news about air pollution was particularly bad. Earth Day in spring 1970 had been followed by a summer of air pollution emergencies regularly featured on network news. The air was so bad in Southern California that children had to be kept home from school. An acrid haze covered the East Coast from Boston to Washington. When Mayor John Lindsay had joked, "I never trust air I can't see," he could see the pollution in his city. Leave a window open for a few days and the sill would be black with soot. Air pollution episodes in New York had killed 405 people in 1963 and 168 in 1966. Earlier episodes had killed thousands in London, England, and Donora, Pennsylvania. The victims were generally old and moribund, but Rachel Carson suggested that chemical soups could give cancer to the young and healthy.[2]

Just as Muskie's hopes of winning the White House were soaring, Ralph Nader pinned the blame for the air pollution crisis on him. In 1970 a Nader book blasted Senator Muskie for selling out to the polluters because of his "preoccupation with the 1972 election." Nader wrote of "chemical . . . warfare," "corporate power that turns nature against man," and the collapse of the federal air pollution program "starting with Senator Edmund Muskie."[3]

Nader's angle of attack, like that in his other reports on federal regulatory programs,[4] was that Congress enacts high-sounding statutes that in fact pass the buck to agency regulators. They are then captured by those they should regulate. The legislators make out at both ends—by telling their constituents that they have given them regulatory protection and by getting contributions from the regulated companies to pressure the regulators into submitting to capture.

There was some truth to Nader's charge. When California had set out in the mid-1960s to regulate emissions from new cars and other states had threatened to do the same, the auto manufacturers sought help in Washington. They consulted Lloyd Cutler, an eminent Washington lawyer who later served as President Jimmy Carter's White House counsel. He suggested that the manufacturers get Congress to authorize a federal agency to regulate emissions from new cars. The companies could use their clout in Washington to keep the bureaucrats from imposing expensive requirements, but the federal agency's being on the job would dissuade states from regulating. In 1965, Senator Muskie sponsored, and Congress passed, legislation that gave the power to regulate emissions from new cars to an agency within the Department of Health, Education, and Welfare. In 1967, Congress passed legislation that barred every state except California from regulating new-car emissions. By then, coal mining companies also wanted an impotent federal agency to slow states' increasing restrictions on the use of coal. The 1967 statute granted the mining companies' wish by tangling the states in procedural requirements that would delay regulation, yet gave the federal regulators no effective power.[5]

Whatever Senator Muskie thought his statutes would accomplish, they produced through the rest of the 1960s just what industry hoped—very little expense. The federal regulators made auto manufacturers spend only a few dollars per car to control emissions and showed no aggressive tendencies toward pollution from factories. Some states did impose tough emission limits on factories, but that was despite the federal superstructure.[6]

President Nixon sought to replace Muskie as the environmental champion. In late 1969, Muskie had introduced a bill that would have made federal air pollution regulation marginally tougher, but Nixon topped him with a much tougher bill in February 1970. Then, in May, Ralph Nader issued his report damning Muskie and, in July, Nixon created the EPA. Muskie responded in August with a new air pollution bill that was still tougher than Nixon's in every respect. Muskie, as chair of the Senate subcommittee in charge of air pollution, was able to get his bill to the Senate floor, and it passed and was signed into law.[7]

The new act was Muskie's answer to Nader's charges that his previous environmental legislation had passed the buck to bureaucrats. Muskie boasted that his bill "faces the air pollution crisis with urgency and in candor. It makes hard choices."[8] To back up this claim, the act required the EPA administrator to take three steps:

- *Identify the most important air pollutants.* Specifically, the administrator was required to list each harmful pollutant that came from many sources.[9]
- *Establish ceilings for the concentration of each of these pollutants in the air we breathe.* Specifically, for each listed pollutant, the ad-

ministrator was required to set a "national primary ambient air quality standard" (from now on, "an air quality standard") adequate to protect public health with a margin of safety.[10]

- *Bring air pollution below these ceilings by controlling the emission of these pollutants.* This is the step that counted, but it was also the most challenging. The act itself contained a law requiring that new cars emit 90 percent less of three key pollutants. The act also directed the administrator to make laws requiring that new factories and other new stationary sources of pollutants reduce emissions to the extent feasible. Because these national regulations would not be enough to achieve the health-based air quality standards, the administrator was further directed to have each state adopt a "state implementation plan" containing laws sufficient to achieve the air quality standards. Should a state fail to comply, the administrator would have to promulgate a federal plan and federal laws for the state.[11]

The act imposed deadlines for each of these actions. Cumulatively, the deadlines meant that health would be protected from all pollutants coming from many sources by 1976. Should a state find that it was technologically or economically infeasible to meet the air quality standards by then, the act allowed it a little extra time, but not much. On this basis, Muskie told voters that "all Americans in all parts of the country shall have clean air to breathe within the 1970's."[12]

Muskie's statute extended this promise to all harmful pollutants, not just those coming from many sources. For these other pollutants, particularly those that were especially hazardous, the act provided analogous procedures. That way, according to Muskie's Senate committee report, "there should be no gaps" in the act's program to protect health.[13]

The bill passed by overwhelming margins. The Senate voted for Muskie's bill with seventy-three for and none against, and the House voted for its bill with a lone dissenting vote. The Senate and House passed the conference bill unanimously. The only hard fight along the way was over the only law explicitly stated in the statute—that emissions from new cars must be cut by 90 percent. This target was based not on any assessment of what the automakers could do but on what was needed to allow Muskie to claim that the public was guaranteed perfectly healthy air by the end of the 1970s. The automakers complained that they could not meet the deadline, and amendments were offered to give them extra time. Muskie countered that the EPA or Congress could allow extra time if it later turned out that they really needed it.[14]

The Clean Air Act appeared to put environmental protection in the hands of a scientific elite. No longer would pollution control be dependent on state and local politics, or, for that matter, even national politics. An environmental protection administrator was ordered to employ scientists who would determine the degree of cleanup required to protect public health and then to make it so. Congress had seemingly put the experts in charge.

An idea current at the time that the earth is a spaceship[15] explains the appeal of the thing. Like the passengers of a manufactured spaceship, inhabitants of the earth must preserve the air, water, and other supplies that we carry with us or die. Ships must, of course, be run by expert captains, not the passengers or their elected representatives. Spaceship Earth, or at least its American compartment, now had a captain (the EPA administrator) and a crew (the EPA staff).

To many of us who read the statute when it was new, all this seemed almost too good to be true. In fact, it was. The EPA had not come from Starfleet Academy but rather was an amalgam of the federal government's preexisting environmental programs, including the agency within the Department of Health, Education, and Welfare that had produced such disappointing results under Muskie's previous air pollution statutes. To this concern, however, the Clean Air Act had an innovative answer suggested by one of the NRDC's founding trustees, David Sive. Should the administrator fail at any point to do what the act commands, private citizens were authorized to bring a lawsuit, and a federal judge was empowered to make him follow the act's directives. Clean air was now a statutory right.[16]

To take effective advantage of this citizen suit provision, a citizen would, of course, need an attorney expert in environmental law and dedicated to environmental quality; that is where the environmental attorneys at the NRDC and like organizations came in. We now had honored places on the bridge of Spaceship Earth. We were not under the captain's command, but rather had the power to haul this official before a court should there be any flinching from the prime directive —to protect public health.

The NRDC's first headquarters did not look anything like a Star Trek flight deck. It was several small rooms facing an air shaft at the back of a modest office building in midtown New York and furnished with hand-me-downs. But we were making ourselves heard.

CHAPTER FOUR

Leaving the Lead In

My first case filed in 1972 charged the EPA administrator with violating the Clean Air Act by failing to protect young children from lead in gasoline. Getting the lead out occupied me and my colleagues for the rest of the decade.

The lead story starts earlier. In the 1960s physicians discovered that lead was killing many children and crippling the brains of even more. At first it was thought that the fatal lead came from house paint, in which it was a common ingredient before 1950, but suspicion also turned to the almost two hundred thousand tons of lead that refiners added to gasoline every year. This lead came out of tailpipes, settled onto streets and sidewalks, and blew through windows. The street dust in some cities was richer in lead than is lead ore. It was the toddlers in poor, urban areas such as Bedford-Stuyvesant who absorbed the biggest doses of this lead because they played on the sidewalks and slept by open windows near ground level. As news of lead poisoning spread, wealthier people too began to worry about the impact lead had on their children. Bumper stickers demanded "GET THE LEAD OUT." Lead was by consensus the most worrisome pollutant as Congress considered the Clean Air Act in 1970.[1]

The Clean Air Act offered a seemingly precise remedy for this threat. As a harmful pollutant emitted by many sources—millions of cars and thousands of mines, smelters, and factories—the administrator would put it on the list of pollutants requiring an air quality standard. That is what Muskie's Senate report said. Listing lead would force the administrator not only to set an air quality standard but to achieve it. According to the act's timetable, health would be protected by May 1976.[2]

When the Clean Air Act was signed into law on the last day of 1970, the EPA's scientists were ready to move on lead. Within a week they had issued a draft of their report providing the scientific basis for setting an air quality standard for lead. Yet when the deadline arrived three weeks later for the first EPA administrator, William Ruckelshaus, to list pollutants for which he would prepare air quality standards, lead was omitted.[3] Instead, the EPA hired the National Academy of Sciences (NAS) to study whether lead pollution is harmful.

The NAS is the citadel of science in Washington, but science in Washington is sometimes politics by other means. The NAS appointed a panel slanted in favor of the lead-additive makers and their allies in the petroleum and lead industries. According to *Science* magazine, the panel included four industry employees, but "no identifiable 'environmentalist' . . . as a counterpoise to industry's weight." The NAS claimed that industry scientists were "asked to serve as scientists and not as representatives of their organizations." The panel, according to *Science,* gave lead in gas "a clean bill of health."[4]

The EPA did, however, suggest in 1972 that it might issue a law cutting lead in gasoline in order to protect health. Industry scientists objected to the proposal, while other scientists generally supported it or called for stronger action. The EPA's medical staff concluded that the proposed law did not go far enough to protect fetuses and young children. With the NAS report in hand, industry could portray a regulation strongly favored by most independent scientists as scientifically unorthodox and unjustified.[5] The comments from the legislators in Congress, including liberal Democrats with industry connections, urged the EPA to go slow on lead. With no cover from official science or powerful politicians and with no legal duty to protect health from lead because there was no air quality standard, Administrator Ruckelshaus in late 1972 postponed the decision indefinitely.

We filed a lawsuit charging the administrator with unreasonable delay. The court of appeals, agreeing with the charge, gave him thirty days to decide whether to take some of the lead out. The court order prompted a battle behind closed doors at the Nixon White House. The upshot was that, in late 1973, the EPA issued a law requiring refiners to cut the amount of lead in gasoline by three-quarters in five years, with incremental cuts along the way.[6] The cut was smaller and slower than I thought needed but was nonetheless a step forward.

Hoping to get the EPA to take stronger action, we filed a second lawsuit in 1974 to force the administrator to put lead on the list of pollutants for which he must set an air quality standard. The standard would require him to protect health on a schedule. It took the district court judge until 1976 to sort through the agency's many rationalizations for why it need not and should not list lead. He rejected them all. The EPA, now under President Gerald Ford, appealed. After the usual delays of briefing and argument, the federal court of appeals in New York told the EPA to stop its "administrative foot-dragging."[7]

The EPA complied by adding the word "lead" to the list of pollutants requiring air quality standards. That step had taken *five years* instead of the *thirty days* that the Clean Air Act contemplated. Meanwhile, in 1976 the court of appeals in Washington, D.C., finally affirmed the EPA's law to cut the lead content of gasoline.[8] At this point the EPA delayed the start of actual cuts until 1978. Although the EPA was supposed to have fully protected health from lead by May 1976, its deliberations on lead's health effects failed to produce any reduction in emissions by then.

Meanwhile, studies were beginning to suggest that the amount of lead absorbed by many urban children was causing a measurable, though small, loss in IQ. Yet in 1976 the EPA released a document concluding, in essence, that the lead pollution in America's cities was safe. It suggested setting the air quality standard for lead at a level higher than the existing lead pollution in the most car-crowded cities.[9]

Fortunately, the EPA was required to seek advice from a science advisory board. My colleagues and I asked scientists and physicians who specialized in lead poisoning to let the board know what they thought of the agency's document. They did and the board in turn devoted a whole day to heaping scorn on the agency staff for rating current levels of lead pollution as safe.

The problem, I thought, was that the Republicans held the White House. When the Democratic candidate for president won in 1976, I hoped for a change. Candidate Jimmy Carter had stated that "I want to make clear, if there is ever a conflict [between environmental quality and economic growth], I will go for beauty, clean air, water, and landscape." But after he entered the White House in 1977, the EPA still went slowly. It took the agency two more years to issue a rather political air quality standard. Although the Clean Air Act told the agency to set it to protect health without regard to cost, it was under standing orders from President Carter to prepare a cost-benefit analysis before issuing regulations. It did so for lead, claiming all the while that cost would not influence how it set the standard. No one took the disclaimer seriously. The agency was bound to set the standard to minimize the political fallout, and that meant taking cost into account. Indeed, Senator Thomas Eagleton, a liberal Democrat who was one of Senator Muskie's lieutenants in getting the Clean Air Act passed, demanded that the EPA avoid harming the lead industry in his home state of Missouri.[10]

Like the listing of lead, the air quality standard was not a law that cut anyone's children's exposure to lead. Rather, it meant that the EPA had a duty to ensure that in four years, there would be laws to cut lead emissions sufficiently to meet the standard. Even that work was put on hold because industry challenged the standard in court.

One piece of good news was that the EPA's law to protect health from lead in gasoline required the first modest cuts in lead additives in 1978. The oil shortage of 1979 gave refiners and lead-additive makers an excuse to seek delay of further, more meaningful cuts. The excuse was spurious. Adding lead does not make a barrel of crude oil go farther; it only reduces slightly the cost of turning it into gasoline. But, the shortage of gasoline was unpopular with voters and the president needed to appear to be doing something about it. With Democrats in control, I was on a first-name basis with top officials at the EPA. Indeed, a former colleague at the NRDC was the assistant administrator for air pollution. But EPA officials made it clear that they could do nothing to stop a command from the White House to delay further cuts of lead in gasoline. In a speech to the nation, President Carter announced the delay as part of his response to the energy crisis.[11]

I left the NRDC in 1979 to become a law professor. I sought detachment and time to understand where government by an environmental captain had gone wrong. This much I knew: despite the directive in the Clean Air Act to protect health, the EPA had to bow to pressure from legislators and presidents to go easy on lead because they could slash its budget, neuter its powers, or fire its administrator.

I hoped to devise a way of keeping politicians from tampering with the experts but realized in time that this hope was vain. The legislators and the president have too many reasons and too many ways to make their power felt. The real question was, How could the legislators be made to bear responsibility? Over time it slowly dawned on me that the Constitution had already provided the answer. It contemplated that laws be made in statutes enacted by the legislators themselves.[12] But the Clean Air Act, like most other regulatory statutes, had empowered an agency to make the laws by regulation. The difference was critical. Only by delegating their lawmaking responsibility to the EPA could legislators take credit with voters for protecting health yet curry favor with the corporations that put lead in gasoline.

As it happens, the legislators did enact a law in the Clean Air Act—the provision requiring new cars to emit 90 percent less of three pollutants. Although lead was not among them, manufacturers seeking to come into conformity with the law would likely have to equip cars with pollution-control devices that would not work with leaded gas, and Congress authorized the EPA to require refiners to provide lead-free gasoline if needed to protect this anti-pollution equipment.[13] Congress had, as a practical political fact, taken responsibility for regulating lead to protect pollution-control equipment—but not to protect health.

The legislators dared not tell voters in 1970 that this provision would protect their children from lead. The cleaner cars using lead-free gasoline would not become available for five years. Even then, one hundred million older cars as well as new and old trucks would still use leaded gasoline.

The legislators were, in 1970, unwilling to enact a law to get all the lead out immediately. The petroleum refiners could have produced lead-free gas—as they now do—but at a cost. Because all refiners would have faced that cost, they could have passed it along to motorists. The cost need not have been great; eliminating lead would have increased refining costs by less than a penny per gallon. But the price at the pump would have jumped a few cents—which would have been noticeable back in 1970, when gas prices were much lower and more stable—and the legislators would have gotten the blame. The obstacle to satisfying the people's demand to get the lead out was that the people also wanted cheap gasoline. It is the job of Congress in our constitutional scheme to resolve such conflicts, but that requires legislators to make hard choices, and making hard choices is not conducive to reelection. So Congress passed the buck to the EPA by telling it to make the laws needed to protect health completely and soon.

As it happened, the amount of lead in gasoline was no lower in 1975 than it was in 1970.The Clean Air Act's requirement to protect health by May 1976 produced no reductions by this deadline. The amount of lead in gasoline was halved from 1975 to 1980, mostly because new cars using lead-free gasoline replaced old cars using leaded gasoline. The act's requirement to protect public health accounted for only about a quarter of this reduction.[14]

It was only in 1985 that the EPA really squeezed the lead out. With the demand for leaded gasoline dropping as old cars were junked, large refiners wanted to stop supplying it but feared losing market share to smaller competitors. The large refiners asked the EPA to use its mandate to protect health as a reason to ban leaded gasoline. With mounting medical evidence against lead, the EPA found that such a ban would benefit health substantially yet cost little. In 1985, with President Ronald Reagan in the White House, the agency ruled that all but a tiny bit of the remaining lead be removed from gasoline.[15] The EPA acted with resolution only after the most powerful opposition had vanished.

But what if the legislators had thought in 1970 that voters would see through the trick of fobbing off on the EPA the hard choices on lead in gasoline? Congress would have passed a law removing *most* of the lead from gasoline. This would have been an obvious and sensible compromise; it would have eliminated most, but not all, of the health threat in exchange for only a tiny increase in the price at the pump because a little bit of lead reduces refining costs almost as much as does a lot. After all, Congress did pass a law requiring automakers to cut emissions of other pollutants by 90 percent within several years and the automakers were more powerful than lead-additive makers and cared more than refiners. Besides, Congress did not know whether the automakers could comply, and lead was the pollutant that most worried voters. The problem for the legislators with voting to get most of the lead out was that they would have had to take the blame for leaving the rest of it in and for a tiny rise in gas prices. Instead of enacting such a law, which would have been good for the American people, the legislators enacted a statute that was perfect for themselves.

Such a law would have, in my estimation, removed at least half of the lead by 1975 instead of 1980 and much of the rest in the years that followed (see figure 3).

We are now in a position to gauge the harm done by Congress's passing the buck on lead. The EPA claims that the reduction in lead in gasoline in 1980 prevented:

- 6,960 deaths
- 20,100 children having their IQs reduced below 70
- 5,020,000 IQ points lost in children generally
- 3,090 cases of coronary heart disease
- 2,120 strokes.[16]

The EPA's body count came from the cut in lead that was made in 1980 alone. This cut was, however, far smaller than the amount of extra lead to which Congress had exposed the public by passing the buck to the EPA and thus delaying getting the lead out. Whatever the health benefits of the cut in lead in 1980, the legislators inflicted much greater suffering upon their constituents by delegating the lawmaking job to the EPA.

President Clinton boasted in his 1996 State of the Union address

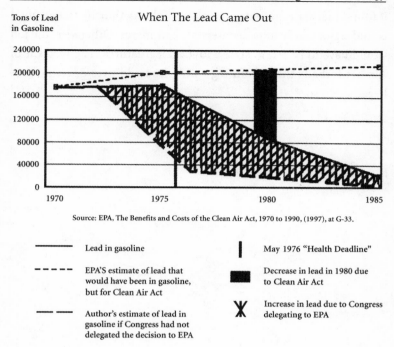

Tons of Lead
in Gasoline

When The Lead Came Out

Source: EPA, The Benefits and Costs of the Clean Air Act, 1970 to 1990, (1997), at G-33.

——— Lead in gasoline		▌ May 1976 "Health Deadline"
– – – – EPA'S estimate of lead that would have been in gasoline, but for Clean Air Act		▬ Decrease in lead in 1980 due to Clean Air Act
—— —— Author's estimate of lead in gasoline if Congress had not delegated the decision to EPA		✗ Increase in lead due to Congress delegating to EPA

3. When the lead came out.

that "lead levels in children's blood has [*sic*] been cut by 70 percent" through a "generation of bipartisan effort."[17] No, it was a bipartisan disgrace.

As the market for lead additives slowly wound down in the late 1970s, the chairman of a large additive maker, Ethyl Corporation, expressed pleasure that the government had been so slow to get the lead out. "We knew that lead was an old product when we bought [the company]. We didn't think it would last as long as it has."[18]

A word on how lead in gasoline fits into my recommendations. In my view Congress could legislate on the lead content of gasoline if it found that state-by-state regulation of this nationally traded good would significantly impede interstate commerce. Otherwise, the job would have to be left to state and local legislatures. The 1970 Clean Air Act forbade them from regulating lead additives once the EPA began to do so.[19]

CHAPTER FIVE

Failure and Success in Cleaning the Air

Lead made me doubt the wisdom of trusting in an environmental captain, but I was not yet convinced. Perhaps there was something special about lead, or we had botched the job. I began to consider how the EPA had fared with other pollutants. In 1970, the Clean Air Act had itself listed five pollutants—carbon monoxide, sulfur oxides, hydrocarbons, ozone, and particulate matter (soot and the like)—as harmful and coming from many sources. The EPA quickly added one more—nitrogen dioxides—but not lead. It issued air quality standards for these pollutants in 1971 and 1972, more or less on the statutory schedule.[1]

This seemed like a promising start, but it was the easy part. Air quality standards are goals rather than accomplishments. They impose no law limiting pollution from any source, but rather add to the administrator's "to do" list: "Get the states to adopt laws achieving the air quality standards or promulgate them myself." This is the hard part, because laws impose burdens and those burdened—whether homeowners with furnaces or businesses with big factories—may object.

The least objection is provoked by laws limiting pollution from new sources, like cars not yet bought or factories not yet planned, because such laws threaten no one's present job or investment. Regulating them is the easy bit of the hard part. On new cars, Congress mandated the 90 percent reduction in emissions. Congress was also willing to be tough on new factories. Instead of settling for a law requiring them to limit emissions to the lowest levels achieved by the cleanest existing factories, it told the EPA to set the standard lower still—at the lowest level of emissions that could practicably be achieved, even if it had never yet been achieved.[2] What is practicable is first of all a question of scientific fact (Is it technologically possible?) and secondly a question of policy (Is it economically prudent?).

The idea was that the EPA would "force technology" at a reasonable pace. The EPA proved unable to do so. It did issue laws defining acceptable levels of emissions for various categories of new plants— concrete plants, copper smelters, and others—but in reviewing the laws, the courts found that the agency had failed to show that the limits it set were feasible. The EPA ended up requiring that emissions from new plants meet the lowest levels achieved by the cleanest existing factories.[3] It would have been simpler had Congress passed a law requiring that in the first place.

Congress knew in 1970 that laws on new cars and new factories would not be enough to reach the air quality standards by the end of the 1970s. Also needed would be laws cutting pollution from *existing* sources, whether giant industrial plants, regional hospitals, corner dry cleaners, residential furnaces, or cars already on the road. Deciding which of these sources to regulate, and to what extent, was the hardest part. Congress left it to the states, under the EPA's supervision. That way, according to Senator Muskie, the states could opt for the measures "most responsive to the nature of their air pollution problem and most responsive to their needs."[4]

Many states, however, could not achieve the air quality standards by the deadline in a way that was "responsive to their needs." In Los Angeles, state officials would have to take four out of five cars off the road. If pressed to adopt implementation plans with such draconian laws, many states would have refused to adopt any state implementation plan at all. That would have left the EPA with a statutory duty to promulgate the plans and the draconian laws to go with them. To avoid that nightmare, the EPA resorted in 1972 to the plainly illegal expedient of telling states to put off dealing with those pollutants that come primarily from cars and concentrate instead on those that come primarily from factories and other stationary sources.[5] Most states adopted plans containing laws designed to meet the air quality standards for those pollutants.

Whether these laws would actually be obeyed was another question. Many states based their laws on calculations of how much large plants would have to cut emissions in order to achieve the air quality standards without considering whether such cuts were really feasible. In retrospect that sounds crazy, but before 1970 regulators generally had the power to change restrictions that proved infeasible. Not so with the Clean Air Act. It had been written to require that its goals would be met, practicalities be damned. Muskie's Senate Report stated, "Existing sources of pollutants either should meet the standard of the law or be closed down." This claim was not in the early 1970s taken seriously by the powerful. No industry even bothered to challenge in court any of the EPA's health-based air quality standards, although compliance with them eventually cost hundreds of billions of dollars.[6] The standards would have made an easy target for industry lawyers despite the pollutants' clearly being harmful because the EPA did not have the time or resources needed to do a good job of explaining the level at which it set the standards. Similarly, governors signed state implementation plans without giving serious thought to the consequences if local industries found them too tough to obey. Just like Congress, the states promised clean air, expecting to be able to decide later whether achieving it would be convenient.

This charade ran up against reality in 1975. By then the emission limits in the state plans had started to take legal effect. The key test case concerned Union Electric, the power company that served St. Louis. Complaining that the law in the state plan required emission cuts that proved impossible despite its best efforts, the company asked the courts to order the EPA to amend the law. The Supreme Court concluded that it was powerless to help because in the Clean Air Act Congress had mandated that states must achieve the air quality standards by the deadline. If the state adopted a plan that imposed an emissions limit that could not be met, that was the privilege of the state. Besides, as the Court noted, the limit could in theory be met by shutting down the plants.[7]

Turning off the power plants would, of course, have been insane. During sweltering St. Louis summers, air conditioning is literally a life-support system for many older people.[8]

No one thought the air conditioners would go off in St. Louis. There would be a fiddle. The Court put its blessing on the fiddle that the EPA proposed. It would find Union Electric in violation and order it to move toward compliance on some schedule that would not shut off the lights.

Businesses were not happy with this kind of fiddle. Even if they did their best, they could still be classified as violators, fined, and put under the close control of bureaucrats. They would moreover be sitting ducks for lawsuits brought by environmental advocates who would be less sympathetic than the EPA to claims that compliance was infeasible.[9]

Meanwhile, some of my colleagues at the NRDC brought a citizen suit claiming that the EPA had violated the statute by telling states to postpone dealing with pollutants that come primarily from cars. The court agreed, and the EPA told the states to produce plans to achieve the standards for these pollutants. Just as the EPA had feared, states generally refused to comply. New York was an exception.[10]

In 1974 New York governor Nelson Rockefeller and New York City mayor John Lindsay adopted a plan to reduce pollution from traffic in New York City. The plan called for tolls on the bridges over the Harlem and East rivers, a ban on the daytime delivery of goods in central Manhattan, and thirty-two other measures, the last of which was to bar private cars from central Manhattan altogether should the air quality standards not otherwise be achieved on schedule.[11] They were not. One might wonder how elected officials could commit to such measures. The answer: the plan called for compliance later. The same governor and mayor had also borrowed so much money (to be paid back later) that the state and city nearly went bankrupt after they left office.

When it came time to implement the clean air plan, a new governor and a new mayor refused. Bridge tolls would infuriate motorists. A ban on daytime deliveries would burden factories, stores, and offices normally closed at night. And banning cars from Manhattan would push out of the city most of the corporate headquarters that had not already moved to the suburbs or sunnier climes.

In 1975 Ross Sandler, a colleague at the NRDC, and I asked a federal judge to order the governor and mayor to implement the plan. We thought that the state and city should honor their own plan or else find some other way of achieving the air quality standard. After litigation up to the Supreme Court, we got a court order backing up our position. The governor and mayor felt wronged. The states that had failed to submit plans were let off the hook entirely. For New York, the reward for being the only state that had submitted a plan that the EPA approved was that it was the only state that had to do anything, and it had to do it with both state and city at the brink of bankruptcy. Standing on the steps of city hall flanked by key business and union leaders, Mayor Abraham Beame declared that the clean air plan would turn New York City into a "ghost town."[12]

Although we had won in court, we were not about to make the

state and city do anything destructive. Like the EPA, we knew that we would lose our power if we pushed too hard. The major area of continuing disagreement was the bridge tolls. We insisted on them because their function was to provide the money needed to fix the city's subway system, which was breaking down after decades of neglect. "Show us the money to fix the subways and we will drop the tolls" was our position. They did not, so we pressed ahead. What happened next I have told elsewhere,[13] but it bears repeating here.

Once the litigation made clear that the ultimate source of the bridge-toll requirement was Congress, Congress opposed it. Representative Elizabeth Holtzman of Brooklyn, who had been a heroine in the campaign to impeach President Nixon, led a contingent of legislators, almost all liberal Democrats, in a protest march across the Brooklyn Bridge. She and Senator Daniel Patrick Moynihan proposed amending the Clean Air Act to outlaw our lawsuit. I rushed down to Washington to look for support from other members of the New York delegation, all of whom had voted for the Clean Air Act. There were two prospects. One, Theodore Weiss, represented the Upper West Side of Manhattan, an area with few motorists. The other, Jonathan Bingham of the Bronx, would support bridge tolls, but not on the bridges to his district.[14]

Along the way, Holtzman told me she strongly supported clean air. I asked her what clean-air laws affecting her constituents she would support. She would not say. Legislators wanted to be for clean air but not for the burdens involved in cleaning it. They claimed credit for having created a federal right to healthy air but shifted the blame for the corresponding duties onto the EPA and the states. The legislators did vote to reduce emissions from new cars because they had to prove they could do something. Coming down on automakers cost them the least politically because many voters naïvely thought that the cost would be taken out of auto manufacturers' profits, not added to sticker prices. By the time new car prices went up, voters would have forgotten that the Clean Air Act was responsible and would blame the manufacturers more than they would their representatives. Legislators could also readily vote for practicable limits on emissions from new factories.

In contrast, Congress assigned to officials in the state capitals responsibility for imposing the most politically painful measures. Laws that impinged on existing factories in which voters had invested or worked and on existing cars that voters drove would come on state letterhead. These laws would not be limited to what was practicable but rather would require whatever was necessary to deliver on the federal legislators' promise of healthy air in the 1970s. They in effect told state officials, "We take the credit, you take the blame." For state officials that was a sucker's game.

The sucker of last resort was the EPA because it was required to take up any slack left by the states. Seeking to avoid the fury that would come if it did what the statute required, it proceeded gingerly except when prodded by court orders and then with all deliberate delay. Although Muskie had promised that "all Americans in all parts of the country shall have clean air to breathe within the 1970's," come the statutory deadline most Americans lived in areas that violated at least one of the air quality standards.[15]

This failure put the EPA in a bind even before the ultimate deadline had quite arrived. If it allowed new factories in an area that violated an air quality standard, the agency could be shot down in court for exacerbating the violation. If it forbade the new factories, it would be shot down in Congress for blocking new jobs. The EPA called in representatives from the leading national environmental organizations. The result was a deal announced in 1976 that allowed the EPA to approve any new plant whose emissions were more than offset by cuts in emissions from existing plants over and above those already required by the relevant state implementation plan.[16] This deal was itself illegal because the EPA was supposed to achieve the standards on schedule, even if that meant stopping new plants *and* closing existing plants. The environmental organizations agreed not to sue. The principle of clean air by a deadline and without regard to cost had been quietly bent rather than put to an open political test.

Come 1977, the final deadline for meeting the air quality standards, Congress did not return control of local environmental matters to the states. Nor did it do what had worked best—make the laws itself. It could have gone on to make the law not only for new cars but also for power plants, the steel industry, and petroleum refineries. They accounted for the lion's share of major pollutants.[17] But then legislators would actually have had to make the hard choices.

Instead, they did in 1977 what they had done in 1970. They adjusted their law limiting emissions from new cars, kept the same unmet air quality standards, and set new deadlines for the EPA and the states to achieve them through laws *they* would have to make. The deadlines were 1982 for pollutants that come primarily from stationary sources and 1987 for those that come primarily from cars. Meanwhile, the EPA was forbidden to impose bridge tolls and a host of other pollution strategies that had proved unpopular with voters.[18] How the standards would be met was a problem that Congress once again punted to the EPA and the states.

To show that it was, nonetheless, serious about achieving the air quality standards, Congress added new mechanisms to the act that supposedly would ensure that the EPA would actually do the job. States could no longer simply decline to adopt an implementation plan. The EPA was told to impose severe sanctions on states and localities that failed to cooperate. More than that, states would no longer have complete freedom to pick the way they achieved the standards. The EPA was required to instruct the states on how they should allocate the cleanup burden.[19] The costs would still be announced on state letterhead, but the EPA would have more power.

When it came to actually implementing the 1977 act, businesses and states were smarter. Businesses would never again let the EPA promulgate an air quality standard without challenging it in court. Also, having witnessed the *Union Electric* case, they would fight hard against any emissions limit that might prove infeasible. Having witnessed New York's fate, states would never again include politically unpalatable measures in implementation plans. Instead they included only politically palatable measures and then fudged the numbers to make it seem as though their plans would meet the air quality standards on schedule.[20]

It was the EPA's job to root out such cheating, but instead it joined in. To stop the cheating, the EPA would have had to sanction many states. That would have angered Congress. The EPA would also have been obligated to write its own plans and laws for the defaulting states. So the EPA helped the states to cook their implementation plans to be both politically palatable and, seemingly, legally sufficient. The fraud—it would be called criminal fraud if the IRS caught a citizen falsifying a tax return to this extent—was fully documented in a congressionally mandated study.[21] No one in the know wanted to make an issue of the cheating.

With new cars and factories gradually replacing old ones, air quality did get better, but not fast enough to meet the air quality standards everywhere by 1987. In that year, one hundred million people still lived in areas that violated at least one of the standards.[22]

So the Clean Air Act had to be revised again. That took until 1990. As in the 1977 act, Congress adjusted the law controlling new cars and extended the deadlines for attaining the air quality standards—to a whole medley of dates, depending upon the area and the pollutant, with the final date being 2010 (for achieving the ozone standard in Los Angeles). The states got more realistic deadlines, but at the expense of being under still tighter control by the EPA.[23]

The story has a surprise ending. The air quality standards on the books in 1990 will in fact be pretty nearly achieved everywhere by 2010.[24]

We should be glad that the air is so much cleaner than it was in the 1960s. The data show a truly impressive improvement in air quality. The total benefits outstrip the total costs, according to the EPA's estimates. I agree despite my sense that the EPA slants the numbers.[25]

This improvement came mostly because environmentally concerned voters demanded action from Congress and the states rather than because the EPA imposed laws on a reluctant public. According to the EPA's data, the biggest benefits came from emission limits on new vehicles. These began at the state level. Then, after a federal agency required little of automakers, Congress itself imposed a series of laws that limited auto emissions a further 90 percent and more. The EPA could have done a better job of enforcing these laws, but that is a problem with executive enforcement rather than congressional lawmaking.[26] Nonetheless, and despite increases in traffic, even gridlocked intersections in urban canyons no longer have that acrid odor that made one hesitate to take a deep breath. Credit that success mostly to lawmaking by the states and Congress.

The EPA's calculations show that the second largest source of benefits came from taking the lead out of gasoline.[27] This success too should be credited largely to Congress rather than the EPA, as the previous chapter showed.

The EPA's calculations show that much of the rest of the improvement came from reducing emissions from factories and other stationary sources.[28] These reductions were due partly to the federal emission limits on new factories, which had a significant impact over the decades as new factories slowly replaced old ones. This was a success, but not one for which we needed an environmental captain. Congress would have been willing to enact laws as tough as those that the EPA eventually imposed.

The rest of the reduction came through the emission limits imposed by the states. After 1970 the states acted under EPA supervision, so it deserves some of the credit, but how much? The states did more in the 1960s to reduce sulfur emissions than was accomplished in the 1970s, when the EPA was presiding. The states in the 1960s tended to go after the cheapest and easiest reductions, but they deserve credit for acting when support for pollution control was still building. Their accomplishment is part of the record that shows that the will for pollution reduction did not come from the EPA on high.[29]

Even more surprising is the data on air quality trends over the twentieth century. There is no single series of data on air pollution going back that far, but Indur Goklany, a former EPA engineer, managed to construct from many overlapping series a plausible index of the extent to which factories controlled their emissions of sulfur oxides and particulate matter. For these pollutants, he found considerable progress in the decades before the 1970 Clean Air Act.[30]

He also offered an explanation of how environmental improvement came about long before we think of it as beginning. He saw in the data a recurring pattern. First, there is a new technology, such as for making synthetic gas, generating electricity, or moving vehicles using internal-combustion engines. Next, pollution from the new technology grows to the extent that its ill effects are recognized. The means to control the pollution are then invented. Finally, the control technology is applied because of state or local regulations, common-law decisions by state courts, or industry's own desire to save the money wasted when valuable raw materials escape up the smokestack. For example, the increasing use of automobiles produced a new pollution problem, smog, which was first observed in Southern California. It was not until 1950 that scientists discovered that smog came from auto emissions. Then state legislators began to supply a solution.[31]

The EPA's image as being responsible for environmental improvement has had perverse effects. After 1970 science kept discovering new dangers in pollution. These dangers raised public concern, which legislators at the state and federal levels could deflect by pointing out that it was the EPA's job to deal with all air pollution dangers. Yet since its creation the EPA has added only two items to the list of harmful pollutants that come from many sources—nitrogen oxides in 1971 and lead in 1976. It said it would deal with other pollutants under another section of the act, one designed to deal with harmful pollutants that come from only a few sources but are particularly hazardous. It did not do much with that section, either. The problem was that, until 1990, the statute required it to set the regulations to protect health but doing so would result in controls that would shut down factories, and that would be unhealthy for the EPA. As Dan Farber has noted, the idealistic goals that Congress told the EPA to achieve in making its laws actually prevented sensible steps to reduce pollution. From 1970 to 1989, the EPA listed only 8 hazardous air pollutants, most under duress of court order, while various states regulated more than 700 of them. Congress finally broke the logjam at the federal level in 1990 by itself requiring that 189 pollutants be regulated to a standard pegged to the emissions of the cleanest plants in each industry.[32]

Yet probably the most dramatic reductions in such hazardous pollutants have come from an entirely different quarter, one that again demonstrates the fact that the EPA does not need to oversee the making of all pollution control laws. In 1986 Congress passed the awkwardly named Emergency Planning and Community Right-to-Know Act. It required sources of toxic pollutants to report their emissions to the EPA and required the EPA to publish them so citizens knew who emitted what in their communities. As a result, according to the EPA, "communities have more power to hold companies accountable." Sources responded by cutting emissions more than required by existing regulations, in significant part to head off regulatory and tort action at the state and local levels and maintain good community relations.[33] The engine driving the progress was again local sentiment rather than EPA fiat.

On acid rain, too, it was Congress rather than the EPA that took the decisive action. When the EPA did not resolve this long-simmering issue and public frustration grew, Congress again broke the logjam by enacting a law that cut the emissions that are the chief source of acid rain.[34]

The air got cleaner mainly because voters wanted to make it so, not because the environmental captain imposed laws on a benighted society. As Brookings Institution scholar Robert Crandall put it, "The assertions of the tremendous strides [the] EPA has made are mostly religious sentiment."[35]

CHAPTER SIX

Growing Power

The EPA was born short on power and long on responsibility. Its responsibility was to clean the air before the end of the 1970s, but that required changes in traffic management, parking, motor vehicles registration, and land use as well as emissions from existing stationary sources. These were all functions of state and local government. The EPA lacked legal authority to force them to change how they performed these functions. Its only legal authority was to assume these functions itself, but for that it lacked both the staff and political legitimacy. Its first administrator, William Ruckelshaus, pushed as hard as he could in the circumstances, telling the White House that if ordered to do less he would resign in protest.[1]

The EPA was nonetheless valuable to Congress and the president. When constituents complained that pollution control was going too far or not far enough, the EPA was there to take the blame. Declaring that its 1970 statute had been good and that the EPA and, particularly, the states had been bad for failing to implement it, Congress in the 1977 statute gave the EPA legal authority over the states; it could penalize states that failed to meet air quality standards by banning federal highway funding and new factories.[2]

These penalties served to distance legislators from the failures of the past but would so plainly have hurt the general public that they were of little use to the EPA. A ban on federal highway funds would decimate state and local budgets and mean layoffs for construction workers. A ban on new factories would mean no new jobs. If the EPA had used these weapons widely, Congress would have disarmed it.

In the years following the 1977 act, the political tide was running against the EPA. All the wrong things were on the way up—unemployment, electricity rates, and gasoline prices. Environmental regulation, often unfairly, got much of the blame. Meanwhile pollution levels were on their way down, and the killer pollution episodes of the 1950s and 1960s had faded from memory. Public opinion was coming to view the environment as a matter of aesthetics rather than survival—a passion of the "tree-huggers" and "squirrel-lovers," as environmentalists were called back then.[3]

The political tide began to turn back in the EPA's favor with a wave of press reports stating that pollution was a major cause of cancer. The idea was not new, but cancer had not been the main focus of the air quality standards initially issued under the 1970 Clean Air Act. They targeted pollutants because they hurt lung function, not because they were thought to cause cancer. In 1976, *Newsweek* ran a cover story on pollution-induced cancer. Then, in April 1978, residents of the Love Canal neighborhood in Niagara Falls, New York, learned that their homes had been built atop a toxic waste dump. On August 2 of that year, the state commissioner of health issued a report entitled "Love Canal: Public Health Time Bomb," declared an emergency, and closed the neighborhood school. Five days later President Carter also declared an emergency and provided funds to permanently relocate 239 families.[4]

The EPA, joined by environmental groups, asked Congress to enact a statute that would grant it authority and funding to clean up abandoned toxic waste sites. Such legislation would have recast the EPA's image from hugger of trees to savior of public health. Its deputy administrator asked the regional offices to produce lists of the ten most dangerous abandoned waste sites in their areas. "This request inspired deep resentment among regional officials. Like policemen assigned quotas of parking tickets, their sense of professionalism was offended by what they perceived to be an order to find a dump in every congressman's backyard. After the headlines [their bosses were] seeking had faded, these regional officials knew they would be faced with the task of calming the fears of angry residents and local officials. . . . Throughout the course of the legislative debate, EPA . . . warned that hundreds of 'Love Canals' existed across the country."[5] In 1980 Congress gave the EPA the authority it sought.

In retrospect we know that the health concerns behind this new and ultimately very expensive statute were overblown. Former residents of Love Canal have no elevated incidence of cancer or any other serious disease. An EPA staff study concluded in 1987 that the actual risks of abandoned toxic waste sites deserved lower priority than the agency gave them and that the public had an exaggerated idea of their danger.[6]

The tide that was running in the EPA's favor turned into a tidal wave with the presidency of Ronald Reagan. His environmental team with Anne Gorsuch Burford as EPA administrator came across as contemptuous of environmental concerns. One of Burford's sins was to take literally the requirement in the 1977 Clean Air Act to punish states that failed to meet their obligations. Environmental advocates complained that she was out to make the Clean Air Act look silly; she replied that she was doing precisely what Congress had instructed. Both were correct. During the early Reagan years, membership in environmental organizations soared. President Reagan had to put his environmental program into receivership by bringing back the EPA's first administrator, William Ruckelshaus, and promising to give him a free hand.[7]

Although the environmental captain was back on the bridge, the

EPA still could not carry out the prime directive—protect health at all costs—any more literally than it had under presidents Nixon, Ford, or Carter. The voters wanted to feel that they were under the care of assiduous regulators who were out to protect their health *and* their jobs *and* their driving. The EPA returned to the balancing act that had characterized its past operations. The EPA continued to bend the prime directive to serve the even more primary directive rooted in its own institutional survival—take no action that would link it unequivocally to shutting down a factory.

By the time Congress came to rewrite the Clean Air Act in 1990, the EPA finally had the strength to get statutory changes that would increase its power and reduce its responsibility. The public was more convinced than ever that an environmental captain was needed. The failure to meet the air quality standards by 1977 and then by 1982 or 1987 carried a cumulative political wallop. The air quality standards were, by definition, the U.S. government's official position on the mark society should meet. Society had fallen short. No wonder 68 percent of the public believed that most people did not care enough about the environment. Indeed, Shep Melnick has persuasively argued that, because the air quality standards do not in themselves reduce pollution, their only function is to arouse anxiety in the public.[8] Industry could no longer counter the anxiety about pollution with anxiety about unemployment. The warnings that environmental regulation would put people out of work had been repeated so often that they rang hollow and, besides, the economy was strong.

The result in 1990 was a statute that gave the EPA more power, and that in a form that could be more readily used. While the 1970 act had let Congress shift blame to the EPA, the 1990 act let the EPA pass the blame along. The EPA got sanctions that it could actually apply against states that failed to do its bidding. While the 1977 act had allowed only draconian punishments that clearly hurt the voting public, the 1990 act allowed for graduated sanctions that seemed to hurt only business. The EPA also got more control over the specifics of state air pollution control programs. What the EPA could require states to put in their plans was stated in 1 page in the 1970 act, 8 pages in the 1977 act, and 115 pages in the 1990 act.[9] These changes went far toward turning state air pollution programs into EPA branch offices.

The 1990 act also gave the EPA the power to ensure that these branch offices were funded to its satisfaction by forcing state legislatures to levy a tax to fund their state air pollution programs. Of course Congress could not say outright that it was mandating state legislatures to tax and appropriate. Instead it decreed that every source had to get a permit for which the states would charge a "fee." Prior to 1990, most sources did not need permits, yet they still had to comply with emission limitations. After 1990, they all had to have permits, and the permit fees were taxes in disguise. Although the statute calls them "fees," they must be set high enough to cover not only the relatively small cost of issuing the permit itself but also all of the costs the EPA deems necessary to running an air pollution control program.[10] Mandating such a tax did not bother Congress because the bill would come on state letterhead. The State and Territorial Air Pollution Program Administrators Association and the Association of Local Air Pollution Control Officials vigorously supported the permit fees, much of which ends up in the pockets of their members.

The EPA and the states grew more adept at crafting regulations so that the burdens appeared to fall on business rather than the broad mass of voters. Consider the scheme adopted in California for reducing emissions from old vehicles, a necessary step for meeting air quality standards in that state. One way to do that would be for the state to require that very old cars and trucks with little or no emissions controls be retrofitted with control equipment, but this would anger their owners and their owners vote. Another way would be for the state to buy the vehicles and junk them, but this would be a cost imposed on taxpayers and taxpayers vote. The environmental regulators instead came up with a way to get rid of the old vehicles that seemed to put the cost on business. California imposed impracticably tough emission standards on refiners and other large stationary sources, but with the proviso that they could buy their way out of achieving the impracticable standards by purchasing and junking old vehicles. The vehicle owners could decide whether to accept top dollar for their clunkers, and state officials would not have to spend the taxpayers' money. The refiners would in turn pass some of the cost along to all motorists by raising gasoline prices. Voters would pay in the end, but they would not blame EPA or state officials.

The EPA still cannot, as a matter of practical politics, be seen to shut down a factory or impose major inconveniences on large numbers of voters (e.g., bridge tolls). Yet it can impose major costs and inconveniences if it can hide its responsibility by acting through state officials (e.g., permit fees) or impose restrictions in ways that seem to fall on big businesses (e.g., having refiners buy old cars).

In 1997 the EPA's waxing power was threatened, ironically, by news of an impending success—that the air quality standards would generally be achieved, or almost achieved, around 2010. Violation of the standards is a precondition for the EPA to command the states and much more. In 1997 the EPA strengthened the air quality standards for particulate matter and ozone, thereby ensuring widespread, long-term violations. It was obvious why the EPA strengthened the particulate matter standard. Its analysis showed that strengthening the standard would save thousands of lives. Less obvious is why it strengthened the ozone standard. Its analysis showed that strengthening the standard would produce paltry health benefits by comparison—indeed, smaller benefits than it chose to overlook in setting the particulate matter standard. The ozone standard would, however, be violated much more widely than the particulate standard and there-fore do more to prolong the agency's power. At an informal panel on Capitol Hill, a senior EPA air pollution official, Robert Brenner, was asked by the moderator why the EPA was moving to strengthen the ozone standard when the science on ozone's health effects was essen-tially the same as it had been when the existing standard was set. His answer was that the states were moving into compliance with the existing standard.[11] The EPA had decided to move the goal posts.

CHAPTER SEVEN

The EPA Today

The Clean Air Act commands the EPA not only to protect public health—the focus of the previous chapters—but also a lot more: to preserve air that is already clean, reduce acid rain, restore stratospheric ozone, improve visibility, and protect public welfare in general. Other statutes give it sweeping duties in regard to:

- water pollution
- pesticides and food safety
- garbage disposal
- noise pollution
- ocean dumping
- oil spills
- drinking water
- new chemicals
- storage, treatment, disposal, and transportation of hazardous wastes
- abandoned hazardous waste disposal sites
- asbestos in schools
- public notice of chemical releases and
- more.[1]

The EPA regulates large numbers of persons and things. Here is a sampling:

- 1,241 hazardous waste sites that are listed for priority cleanups
- 39,961 stationary sources of air pollution
- 89,455 direct sources of water pollution
- 94,885 asbestos demolitions
- 173,272 drinking-water suppliers
- 405,657 underground injection wells
- 3,080,740 farms and other pesticide applicators
- 12,800,000 lead sites.[2]

The detailed regulation of so many things requires a highly complex system. Its complexity can be roughly gauged by looking at the length of the orders in the chain of command as it descends down from Congress to the regulated sources. Under one statute, the Clean Air Act, the commands from Congress alone grew from 8 pages in 1965 to 85 pages in 1970, 238 pages in 1977, and 450 pages in 1990.[3]

The commands that the EPA has issued in the form of regulations under the same statute now run to 7,200 pages. In addition, many documents accompany EPA regulations through the regulatory process. For example, although the air quality standard for particulate matter is only 9 pages long, the EPA's rationale for it, called in federal regulatory parlance "a concise general statement of their basis and reasons," runs more than 80 pages.[4] Most regulations are accompanied by many collateral agency documents as well as court decisions. Such documents and decisions are often necessary for interpreting the regulation itself.

The EPA also issues "guidance documents." One reason is that the regulations themselves can be unclear. Another reason is that the EPA omits controversial decisions from the regulations because the regulations themselves, and not the guidance documents, are reviewed by other federal agencies and courts. Through guidance documents, observed a federal appellate court, "law is made, without notice and comment, without public participation, and without publication." According to the same court, "Several words in a regulation may spawn hundreds of pages of text [in guidance documents] as the agency offers more and more detail regarding what its regulations demand of regulated entities." When a congressional committee asked the EPA to list all of its guidance documents, the agency produced documents issued over only a few years, yet there were 2,653 of them with a total length of 96,905 pages.[5] This suggests that the guidance issued over the EPA's thirty-three-year history may run to a million pages.

Many of the EPA's directives tell states how to issue many further commands. Under the Clean Air Act, for example, each state must adopt a state implementation plan to achieve each air quality standard in each of its air quality control regions. The plans are not documents in the ordinary sense of the word but large stacks of documents the meaning of which is changed by those that come afterward. The plans include statutes, regulations, and much more.

The states also issue additional source-specific commands in the form of permits. A major source may have dozens or even hundreds of smokestacks and vents and emit more than a few of the 6 pollutants subject to air quality standards and the 188 hazardous pollutants. Pollution limits are generally put on each smokestack and vent for each pollutant. The permits also often dictate the pollution-control technology and production processes that the company must use to achieve those results.

The permit can thus control not only the source's impact on the environment but also what it produces and how it produces it. The purpose of the EPA's regime is, of course, environmental protection, but its reach is far broader. Indeed, a new source must be denied a permit—even if it would meet all air quality requirements—unless regulators find that it would, on balance, "significantly" benefit society and the environment. The EPA's regulation "has grown to the point where it amounts to nothing less than a massive effort at Soviet-style planning of the economy to achieve environmental goals," according to Richard Stewart, one of the founding trustees of the Environmental Defense Fund.[6]

Congress was of course not thinking of Soviet economic organization in 1970. Military organization was more like it. War was a motif of the times. We had a war in Vietnam, a "War on Poverty," and a response to air pollution that was sufficiently military in organization that Congress could boast that it had assured victory as soon as it enacted the Clean Air Act. Military organization is characterized by detailed instructions from the top to the bottom of a hierarchy. A military term, "command and control," is used to describe the EPA's style of regulating.

Top-down military organization is the logical consequence of thinking that the environmental captain should be insulated from accountability to the passengers of Spaceship Earth. The EPA is built on the premise that no one below it in the chain of command, including state and local governments, can be trusted. As designed by Congress, the EPA fits novelist Herman Wouk's description of the navy: "A master plan designed by geniuses for execution by idiots."[7] Richard Stewart was nonetheless right. Military organization applied to the civilian world is Soviet-style economic planning.

No other regulatory agency has ever been given such a massive job. The Interstate Commerce Commission regulated in detail, but its reach was limited to interstate railroads and trucking. The Office of Price Administration, established in 1941, controlled prices throughout the entire economy, but its rule was confined to a short era of military crisis. The EPA has been going thirty-plus years and is meant to be permanent. And its impact is massive. Two-thirds of the cost imposed by major rules issued by all federal agencies over the past decade has come from rules issued by the EPA.[8]

One might reasonably wonder how one agency could carry out such a massive mandate. The EPA has the largest budget of any federal law-making agency, almost three times that of the agency with the next largest budget, the FDA. The EPA's staff of 17,500 is larger than those of either the FDA (10,111) or the Federal Communications Commission (2,007), to pick some well-known examples. Moreover, unlike these other regulatory agencies, the EPA has been given leave by Congress to harness the powers of state governments and the staffs of their environmental agencies. And, too, the EPA has in effect deputized employees of large public and private pollution sources to act as EPA enforcers. It has done so by adopting an explicit policy of imposing far larger penalties for violations—even paperwork violations—when a source has failed to adopt an EPA-specified program for discovering and reporting violations. Large sources must set up these self-audit programs because they can't, despite the best intentions, avoid technical violations and the statutes give the EPA broad discretion in assessing penalties.[9]

Yet even with these forces at its disposal, the EPA has been unable to complete its tasks and in its striving to get them done has often gotten them wrong. From 1993 to 2000, the court chiefly responsible for reviewing its nationally applicable laws sent back a shockingly high 62 percent of its regulations while affirming almost all of the comparable laws issued by the Occupational Safety and Health Administration (OSHA). Agencies should fare far better in court than does the EPA because judges may not reject an agency's law simply because they disagree with it; rather, they must find that the agency ignored the statute or acted without reason or explanation.[10]

The problem, simply put, is that the battle plan that Congress has told the EPA to execute is beyond its capacity. As of 1985, the EPA had met only 14 percent of the hundreds of deadlines set for it by Congress. It must choose which of its mandatory duties to fulfill. But it does not have the choice. When it decides to let a duty slide, environmental groups have an open-and-shut case against it and get paid attorney fees for winning. The environmental groups get to decide which mandatory duties to force the EPA to perform and which to let slide. The environmental groups and the courts are not simply enforcing congressional directives but rather setting environmental priorities.[11]

The EPA, according to former administrator Ruckelshaus, suffers from "battered agency syndrome." It is "not sufficiently empowered by Congress to set and pursue meaningful priorities, deluged in paper and lawsuits, and pulled on a dozen different vectors by an ill-assorted and antiquated set of statutes." As the environmental captain, the administrator has a powerful craft but is not in charge of where it goes. The result is, as Richard Stewart put it, a "self-contradictory attempt at central planning through litigation."[12]

Part II

Science

CHAPTER EIGHT

What's Science Got to Do with It?

We had forced the EPA to set an air quality standard for lead so that science would dictate how much to cut airborne lead. But what did science dictate? Everyone's scientists—the EPA's, industry's, and NRDC's—agreed that the air quality standard should be derived from the following commonsense approach: First, determine *the amount of lead children can tolerate in their blood*. Second, subtract *the amount of lead in children's blood that comes from sources other than air pollution*. The difference is the maximum amount of lead that children can safely absorb from the air. Third, divide that amount by *the rate at which children get lead in their blood from lead in the air*. The result should be the maximum amount of lead in the air that children can tolerate.[1]

The EPA decided that *the amount of lead children can tolerate in their blood* is 15 micrograms per deciliter of blood ($\mu g/dL$). It got that number by finding that adverse health effects start at 30 $\mu g/dL$ and that keeping 99.5 percent of children below that level requires getting the median child down to 15 $\mu g/dL$. The EPA also decided that *the amount of lead in children's blood that comes from sources other than air pollution* was 12 $\mu g/dL$. Subtracting 12 $\mu g/dL$ from 15 $\mu g/dL$ meant that 3 $\mu g/dL$ was the maximum amount a child could safely get from the air. Finally, as to *the rate at which children get lead in their blood from lead in the air,* the EPA decided children's blood lead goes up by 2 µg/dL for every microgram of lead per cubic meter of air ($\mu g/m^3$). Simple arithmetic produced an air quality standard of 1.5 $\mu g/m^3$. That is where the EPA set it in 1978, and that is what it is to this day.[2]

Although scientists generally agreed on the formula, there was no consensus that these were the values to plug into it. Industry scientists argued that the EPA underestimated the amount of lead children can tolerate and overestimated the rate at which lead gets into children's blood from the air. Scientists from the environmental side argued the opposite. The disagreements sprang from differences in how scientists interpreted the thousands of studies that the EPA had considered. In a book-length report published after the courts upheld the EPA's standard, the NAS concluded that there was a broad range of uncertainty regarding the values to plug into the formula, with the result that reasonable scientists could come up with radically different air quality standards. Setting all of the values at the ends of the range most favorable to the lead industry would produce a standard ten times higher than the worst lead pollution in the United States. Setting these factors at the opposite ends would produce a standard of zero, which would be widely violated even if we stopped using lead.[3]

It turns out in retrospect that the science of the 1970s was wrong. Whereas the EPA found that adverse effects of lead start at 30 µg/dL, the Centers for Disease Control and Prevention now suggests that lead poisoning starts at 10 µg/dL. The NAS found that the amount of lead that children were getting from non-air sources was somewhere between 7 and 15 µg/dL, but the blood lead level in the median child in the United States dropped from 15 µg/dL in the late 1970s to 2 in 2000. Most of this drop came from removing lead from gasoline; reducing exposure to deteriorating lead paint has had a dramatic impact on the blood lead levels of many children but cannot account for the dramatic drop in *median* lead levels. Getting this level down to 2 µg/dL suggests that children got even less than 7 µg/dL from non-air sources.[4]

By overestimating the amount of lead that children get from non-air sources, the EPA and the NAS were underestimating the rate at which air lead gets into children. Back when the EPA was setting the air quality standard, it struck me as implausible that the *median* child could get a blood lead of 12 µg/dL from background levels of lead in food and drinking water. There was relatively little lead in the biosphere before the industrial revolution. Children living in the Himalayas, high above industrial pollution, had blood lead levels around 3 µg/dL.[5] The lead that scientists thought came from food actually came, I thought, mainly from air pollution, particularly lead in gasoline. My intuition was, however, only an intuition and was backed by no measurements. Neither I nor my experts knew of any way to put my amateur's speculations on a scientifically credible basis, at least not soon enough to make a difference in the air quality standard.

I had stumbled on an important truth about science—its finely calibrated techniques provide no right answer to many questions of the greatest policy consequence. There is inevitably uncertainty in describing risks. Besides, even if the risks can be described precisely, deciding on the extent to which to reduce them requires policy judgments. Science's inability to produce a right answer for lead is no aberration. According to a distinguished scientist, the late Dr. Alvin Weinberg, "when the concern was subtle . . . science was being asked a question that lay beyond its power to answer; the question was trans-scientific. Yet the regulator, by law, is expected to regulate, even though science could hardly help in the process. This is the regulator's dilemma."[6]

Regulators respond to this dilemma in different ways. The EPA assesses risks differently than do other federal regulatory agencies. According to a study prepared for a national commission, these "awkward" differences arise not only from different statutory mandates but also from "different institutional judgments about the most appropriate methods," "different scientific judgments about matters with high scientific uncertainty," and "simple policy choices made for the sake of consistency within each organization (which, owing to independent histories, becomes inconsistent among organizations)."[7]

Thus the hope for environmental regulation based on science rather than politics turned out to be in vain for two reasons: (1) politics cannot be kept out, as chapters 4–6 showed, and (2) science cannot step in to provide definitive answers. The hope that it can is "a sweet old-fashioned notion," to borrow a phrase from the song "What's Love Got to Do With It" yet it is a hope that still tugs on many hearts today.[8]

Elected politicians use this hope to avoid responsibility for policy choices by pretending that such choices are questions of science to be resolved by scientists at the EPA. In commanding the EPA administrator to use science to set air quality standards to "protect health," Congress failed to state a coherent command. The implication of such language is that there is some clear line between safety and danger. Not only does science often lack the knowledge of what is safe, but for lead and many other pollutants no such line exists. Any lead is bad. As Senator Muskie acknowledged in 1977, after the responsibility for setting air quality standards was safely in the EPA's lap, "Our public health scientists and doctors have told us [in 1970] that there is no threshold, that any air pollution is harmful. The Clean Air Act is based on the assumption, although we knew at the time it was inaccurate, that there is a threshold."[9]

The legislative pretense to the contrary put EPA scientists in a strange position. As one former EPA researcher put it, "This is the problem with ambient air quality standards. What you're trying to do is ludicrous—set the level below which the most sensitive person in the population will have no adverse health effects."[10]

The EPA would be paralyzed if it really tried to bottom its laws on pure science, but it does not. EPA dutifully claims that its air quality standards are based solely on considerations of health rather than cost, but that simply is not the truth, as observers from a wide range of political perspectives have noted. EPA is a political agency in scientific disguise. According to a Resources for the Future study, *Science at EPA,*

> EPA's norms, staffing patterns, and incentives subordinate science. Instead, EPA is a regulatory agency dominated by a legalistic culture. . . . Unlike the leaders of the public health agencies (that is, Centers for Disease Control and Prevention, Food and Drug Administration, and National Institutes of Health) who are traditionally doctors and scientists, EPA policymakers are typically attorneys who lack formal scientific training. . . . The agency . . . does not support the level and type of in-house research and analysis necessary to attract or retain a large cadre of high-caliber scientists. Communications between scientists and policymakers within EPA are often poor or missing, and scientists do not always have a "seat at the table" when regulatory decisions are being hammered out.
>
> On the other hand, the current state of environmental science is such that it often invites decisions to be based on economic, political, administrative, or technological criteria.[11]

According to former EPA general counsel E. Donald Elliott, "Science did not play a significant role in the policymaking conversation at EPA during the years that I was there, and I do not believe that has changed much in subsequent administrations. In my experience, scientific issues were rarely mentioned, and very few of the participants in the policymaking dialogue at high levels within the Agency were scientifically trained. . . . Every EPA Administrator I know of has invited his or her general counsel and his or her political adviser to be present at his or her daily personal staff meeting, thereby symbolizing that law and politics have a seat at the table. I know of only one administrator (Lee Thomas), however, who met regularly with his science advisor."[12] Elliott was at the EPA under Administrator William Reilly (1989–93), which was, according to the Resources for the Future study, the "peak of science at EPA." (In 2002 the EPA created the post of agency science advisor, a staff member who is supposed to ensure that "science is better integrated into the Agency's programs, policies and decisions.")[13]

The EPA plays on the "sweet old-fashioned notion" for all it is worth. In order to shield itself from political criticism and judicial review, the agency pretends that choices driven by politics and policy preferences are in fact driven by science. This pretense was aptly dubbed "the science charade" in an article in which Wendy Wagner documented it at length. Her conclusion is shared by many close observers of the EPA from across the political spectrum.[14]

Although science can't dictate answers, it should play a role. It can define reality in general terms. For instance, it can tell us today that a blood lead level in children of 20 μg/dL does have certain effects that most people would think significant. What it cannot tell us is at precisely what lower level the effects become small enough to be acceptable. Science can also help structure the policy discussion, letting us know that some arguments are inconsistent with the science.

For that reason, science can be inconvenient for politically driven policy making of any stripe. President Reagan's first EPA administrator, Anne Gorsuch Burford, allegedly got rid of many of the scientists on the EPA's science advisory panels whose names were on a "hit list" of those with the wrong policy proclivities. According to the Resources for the Future study published in 1999, EPA lawyers kept its scientists from "acknowledging the scientific uncertainty in estimates of the toxic potency of chemicals." The same Resources for the Future study also describes private organizations that "count many eminent scientists and physicians among their number, [but whose] policy prescriptions arguably reflect their environmental values more than their scientific credentials. Their 'science-policy' positions can also create a political climate within the scientific community that makes it difficult for scientists to challenge the more 'politically correct' views of the prominent scientist-activists."[15]

The pressure to produce favorable peer reviews of EPA science is especially great on scientists who receive research grants from it or gain standing by serving for long periods on its scientific advisory panels. Law professor and geneticist Gary Marchant reports that three such scientists expressed concern about adverse consequences should they sign an amicus brief to the Supreme Court arguing that the EPA exaggerates the extent to which its laws are dictated by science.[16] Whether they would in fact have suffered retaliation was one experiment they did not wish to run.

CHAPTER NINE

Lois Swirsky Gold, Chemicals, and Cancer

Lois Swirsky Gold was in a bind. She needed pajamas for her daughter, but the only ones for sale contained the chemical "TRIS," and it was known to cause cancer in laboratory animals. Federal regulators required children's sleepwear to contain a flame retardant, and TRIS was the only one then available. To keep her little girl safe, she ordered TRIS-free long johns from Italy.[1]

Later, after regulators banned TRIS in 1977, Gold was left wondering how they had previously tucked the nation's children into bed for the night with a carcinogen. She decided to write an article on the subject. To that end, she sought a meeting with Professor Bruce Ames, an expert on cancer at the University of California at Berkeley. In 1974 Ames had developed a simple but ingenious test to determine whether a chemical causes mutations. The chemical is put into a colony of salmonella bacteria to see if they mutate. If the chemical proves to be a mutagen in the "Ames test," as it is known to cancer researchers, then it is more likely to be a carcinogen and should be tested on laboratory animals. The Ames test showed TRIS to be a mutagen, it was tested on animals, and Ames pushed for its ban.

Ames told Gold that it was difficult to answer her questions about the size of the risk to people from a chemical such as TRIS. It did cause cancer in laboratory animals, but, he explained, it is difficult to evaluate the results of laboratory tests on many different chemicals because the tests are done and reported in so many different ways. There was, he told her, a pressing need to put the results of these tests into a standardized format so that they could be more readily used to evaluate the risk to humans. He asked her to come to work in his laboratory and help to develop such a database. She was initially reluctant to commit to this long-term project but did agree to sign on for several short-term ones. One study sought to gauge the dose of TRIS that children get from sleepwear by collecting urine from children wearing TRIS-treated hand-me-downs in UC Berkeley graduate student housing. No TRIS was detected in the urine. Another was to work with the Oil, Chemical, and Atomic Workers' Union to survey members exposed to chemicals similar to TRIS. In working on these smaller projects, Gold came "to understand the importance of having the laboratory animal tests available in a single repository and presented in a standardized format." She signed on to develop the database.

Now, a quarter-century later, Dr. Gold is still the director of the Carcinogenic Potency Project at the University of California at Berkeley and Lawrence Berkeley Laboratory. Her Carcinogenic Potency Database includes fifty-six hundred chronic, long-term cancer tests on fourteen hundred synthetic and natural chemicals. The database shows, surprisingly, that about half of the synthetic chemicals come out as rodent carcinogens; even more surprisingly, about half of the natural chemicals tested also come out as rodent carcinogens.[2] In short, chemicals that cause cancer in laboratory animals are everywhere.

Lois Swirsky Gold knows other surprising things about environmental carcinogens. To a standard handbook on environmental risk assessment, she, Thomas Slone, and Bruce Ames recently contributed a chapter that neatly punctures several misconceptions about pollution and cancer.[3]

"*Misconception #1: Cancer rates are soaring.*" "Overall cancer death rates in the U.S. (excluding lung cancer due to smoking) have declined 19% since 1950. . . . The rise in incidence rates in older age groups for some cancers can be explained by known factors such as improved screening."[4]

"*Misconception #2: Environmental synthetic chemicals are an important cause of human cancer.*"[5] They are not. Smoking accounts for about a third of U.S. cancer deaths. Dietary imbalances, such as failure to eat enough fruits and vegetables, account for another third. Chronic infections, sun exposure, and hormonal factors influenced by reproductive history, lack of exercise, obesity, and alcohol intake account for most of the rest. Age and genes, of course, also play a role. As for synthetic chemicals,

> Although some epidemiological studies find an association between cancer and low levels of industrial pollutants, the associations are usually weak, the results are usually conflicting, and the studies do not correct for potentially large confounding factors such as diet. Moreover, exposures to synthetic pollutants are very low and rarely seem toxicologically plausible as a causal factor, particularly when compared to the [high] background of natural chemicals that are rodent carcinogens. Even assuming that worst-case risk estimates . . . are true risks, the proportion of cancer that [the EPA] could prevent by regulation would be tiny. Occupational exposures to some carcinogens cause cancer, though exactly how much has been a controversial issue: a few percent seems a reasonable estimate, much of this from asbestos in smokers. Exposures to substances in the workplace can be much higher than the exposure to chemicals in food, air, or water. . . . Since occupational cancer is concentrated among small groups with high levels of exposure, there is an opportunity to control or eliminate risks once they are identified.[6]

"*Misconception #3: Reducing pesticide residues is an effective way to prevent diet-related cancer.*" Studies in people repeatedly show that eating fruits and vegetables, most of which contain synthetic residues, substantially reduces cancer risk. "The quarter of the population with the lowest dietary intake of fruits and vegetables vs. the quarter with the highest intake has roughly twice the cancer rate for most types of cancer." Most Americans eat fewer fruits and vegetables than recommended by the National Cancer Institute. "Less use of synthetic pesticides would increase costs of fruits and vegetables and thus reduce consumption, especially among people with low incomes, who eat fewer fruits and vegetables and spend a higher percentage of their income on food."[7]

Most startling of all is "*Misconception #4: Human exposures to carcinogens . . . are primarily to synthetic chemicals.*" Only a tiny proportion of our exposure to carcinogens is from synthetic chemicals. Some carcinogens come from cooking food. Other carcinogens are made by plants. Americans eat roughly five to ten thousand chemicals that plants produce to defend themselves from pests. We consume ten thousand times more of these "natural pesticides" than of synthetic pesticide residues. Half of the seventy-one natural pesticides tested so far (52 percent) show up as rodent carcinogens, while a similar proportion of synthetic pesticides (41 percent) shows up as rodent carcinogens. "In a single cup of coffee, the natural chemicals that are rodent carcinogens are about equal in weight to an entire year's worth of synthetic pesticide residues that are rodent carcinogens, even though only 3% of the natural chemicals in roasted coffee have been adequately tested for carcinogenicity."[8]

The point is not that foods with natural pesticides are necessarily dangerous, but rather that we need to rethink whether chemicals that at high doses cause cancer in lab animals are necessarily dangerous to humans. Rachel Carson argued that synthetic chemicals are more dangerous than those found in the natural environment because humans have adapted to them through evolution. That, according to Dr. Gold and colleagues, is wrong. "Various natural toxins that have been present throughout vertebrate evolutionary history nevertheless cause cancer in vertebrates." Besides, our hunter-gatherer forebears did not eat many of the plants that we eat today such as coffee, cocoa, tea, potatoes, tomatoes, corn, olives, to name just a few. "Natural selection works far too slowly for humans to have evolved specific resistance to the [natural chemicals] in these relatively newly introduced plants."[9]

All plants must have defenses against pests. Those grown without synthetic protection taste better to some people, but whether they pose less risk to health is another question. There is a trade-off between natural pesticides and the use of synthetic ones. "When a major grower introduced a new variety of highly insect-resistant celery into commerce, people who handled the celery developed rashes when they were subsequently exposed to sunlight. Some detective work found that the pest-resistant celery contained 6200 parts per billion (ppb) of carcinogenic (and mutagenic) psoralens instead of the 800 ppb present in common celery." The celery came from standard plant breeding techniques rather than genetic modification and is only one instance of many instances in which efforts to reduce exposure to synthetic pesticides have increased exposure to carcinogens. "[I]f the same methodology were used [by the EPA] for both naturally occurring and synthetic chemicals, most ordinary foods would not pass the default regulatory criteria that have been used for synthetic chemicals."[10] And the shelves of both supermarkets and organic food stores would be bare.

"*Misconception #5: Cancer risks to humans can be assessed by standard high-dose animal cancer tests.*" Such tests show that high proportions of both synthetic and natural chemicals are carcinogens because "rodents are given chronic, near-toxic doses," consuming huge amounts of the chemical every day for a lifetime. "High doses can cause chronic wounding of tissues, cell death, and consequent chronic cell division of neighboring cells, which is a risk factor for cancer. Each time a cell divides the probability increases that a mutation will occur, thereby increasing the risk for cancer. At the low levels to which humans are usually exposed, such increased cell division does not occur. . . . Therefore, the very low levels of chemicals to which humans are exposed through water pollution or synthetic pesticide residues may pose no or only minimal cancer risks."[11]

There is much more to Bruce Ames and Lois Swirsky Gold's analysis, and it is worth reading in full, but the key point is that the research results they have examined have convinced them to abandon the opinion they held in the 1970s—that chemicals that cause cancer in lab tests are rare and should be banned. As Dr. Gold put it, "Animal tests give you some information, but one needs more data, from epidemiology and about the mechanism by which a chemical causes cancer in animal tests." They began to spell out this analysis in a series of articles written in the late 1980s.[12]

By this time Americans had received a decade's worth of reports that pollution, pesticides, and other synthetic chemicals were causing a cancer epidemic. For example, secretary of the Department of Health, Education, and Welfare Joseph Califano stated in 1978 that up to 38 percent of future cancers would come from occupational exposures. Most cancer researchers, however, came to agree with Ames and Gold. Polling of members of the American Association of Cancer Researchers by the Roper Institute in 1993 showed that they agreed by substantial margins that the United States does not face a cancer epidemic and that human cancer risks should not be assessed by giving animals the maximum tolerated doses of suspect chemicals. The researchers disagreed sharply with the position of environmental advocates that industry is causing cancer rates to rise. These researchers generally identified themselves on the Democratic and liberal end of the political spectrum and worked predominately in universities, government agencies, and medical practices.[13]

Also in 1993, Judge Stephen Breyer, soon to be nominated to the Supreme Court by President Clinton, published a book that declared that the "leading authorities," among whom he includes Ames and Gold, believed that "pollution and industrial products account for under 3 percent" of all cancer deaths. "[T]he more widely accepted view is that only a relatively small portion of these are 'regulatable.' " We should of course do what we reasonably can to reduce cancer from any cause, but the science, he concluded, showed that the EPA had gone overboard in regulating against cancer risks.[14]

Neither Justice Breyer nor Dr. Gold are "soft" on cancer. She has been hard on OSHA for failing to move faster to control workplace chemicals that pose significant cancer risks and on the FDA for failing to control Internet sales of herbal products that contain similarly risky carcinogens. She and Dr. Ames are also hard on the EPA, whose well-intentioned efforts, in their opinion, perversely "distract from the major task of improving public health through increasing scientific understanding about how to prevent cancer (e.g., the role of diet), increasing public understanding of how lifestyle influences health, and improving our ability to help individuals alter lifestyle."[15]

The EPA has begun, albeit slowly, to respond to scientific criticism. The National Research Council recommended in 1983 that agencies such as the EPA open themselves to new science on cancer by easing the conservatively health-protective assumptions they make in assessing cancer risk when the evidence warrants. One assumption that the EPA makes is that the cancer risk to humans at low doses of a chemical is linearly proportional to the cancer risk to animals at high doses. In other words, if the maximum tolerated dose of a chemical causes cancer in one out of ten mice, then, the EPA reasoned, exposing people to the human equivalent of one-thousandth of that dose would cause cancer in one out of ten thousand people. That is a conservative assumption, and one which is, in fact, considered unlikely by Gold and Ames and most cancer researchers, as noted above. This and other conservative assumptions were supposed to be *default* assumptions but became absolute rules in practice. As a 1994 NAS report noted, the EPA "has never articulated clearly its criteria for a departure." The agency has responded to this criticism and others in a series of drafts for new guidelines for assessing cancer risk issued in 1996, 1998, 1999, and 2003. These guidelines open the door in principle to more scientifically grounded regulation.[16] Time will tell the extent to which there is a change in practice.

The message that has hopefully begun to get through to the EPA has not gotten through to the public. The American Cancer Society reports, for example, that 68 percent of the public believes that the risk of dying from cancer is increasing and that, astonishingly, 40 percent believes that living in a polluted city puts one at greater risk for lung cancer than does smoking a pack of cigarettes a day.[17]

The disparity between what mainstream scientists know and what the public believes is so striking that it spawned a book, *Environmental Cancer—A Political Disease?* The book presented the Roper Institute poll of cancer researchers discussed above. The poll reported that researchers ranked Bruce Ames as the most credible scientist on the subject of environmental cancer.[18] The book then correlated the polling data with a detailed analysis of press coverage of the issue. The conclusion: most mainstream cancer researchers had relatively little respect for those scientists who speak for environmental organizations, and they had little respect for the expertise of the organizations themselves. Indeed they rated the Environmental Defense Fund only slightly higher on a scale of reliability than the Tobacco Institute. "They also give relatively low ratings to newspaper coverage of environmental issues, including the coverage offered by the *New York Times*. And no wonder. Newspapers tend to report views of environmental activists as if they represented the views of the expert scientific community. So the scientists are correct in their assessment. The accuracy of newspaper coverage of the scientific issues involved in environmental cancer is, by any measure, quite poor."[19] (After the polling was conducted, some *New York Times* reporters have written excellent articles on chemicals and cancer.[20])

Although the EPA has begun to correct its cancer guidelines, it has done little to correct the public's belief that pollution and pesticides cause much cancer, a belief from which the agency has derived public support since the late 1970s. "The public believes it," as Gold said, "and EPA does not tell us differently." The EPA does not forcefully acknowledge to the public in regulating specific chemicals that the true risk may be zero. Its reports provoke headlines such as "STUDY PUTS CANCER SCARE IN AIR."[21] No wonder 40 percent of the public believes that "living in a polluted city is a greater risk for lung cancer than smoking a pack of cigarettes a day," a misconception which the American Cancer Society deplores. When I recently asked an EPA scientist where I could find the agency's estimate of the extent to which cancer comes from pollution and pesticides, he said, "The agency does not talk about that."[22] Actually, sometimes it does. The following is from a speech that Administrator Carol Browner gave in 1997:

> We need to know more about whether environmental factors are in any way responsible for the alarming increase in new incidences of childhood cancer.
> The good news is that the death rate from childhood cancer has declined dramatically.
> But an equally dramatic rise in the overall number of kids who get cancer threatens to overshadow the gains we have made.
> For the past two decades, the incidence of new cancer cases in children has been rising at the rate of one percent each year.
> And we don't know exactly why. But many leading health experts believe that the environmental factors very well may play a role.[23]

Consider in contrast how the American Cancer Society analyzed the same data: "The incidence rate of all childhood cancers combined increased from the early 1970s—when rates were first measured . . . until 1991 and then leveled off and declined slightly through 1996. . . . Small increases in the incidence of several childhood cancer types . . . have been attributed to changes in diagnostic technology, reporting, and classification. Similarly, observed increases in cancers among infants . . . may be due to earlier diagnosis and better case identification. . . . Reasons for modest increases in retinoblastomas and small declines in Hodgkin's disease remain unclear."[24] The report went on to point out that genetics, certain medicines, and certain viruses are known to contribute to childhood cancers. It also mentioned many factors that might contribute to childhood cancer. It discussed pollution and pesticides much the way Lois Swirsky Gold and Bruce Ames discuss them.[25]

CHAPTER TEN

Angus Macbeth and the Hudson River

Angus Macbeth and I go way back—Yale College, Oxford, Yale Law School, the NRDC—but his essence is captured by a single episode. When the newspapers were publishing transcripts of President Nixon's conversations about covering up Watergate, NRDC's New York office staff would squeeze into the reception room early in the morning to hear Angus read that day's installment. We could have read it on our own. Most of us had. But it was good to hear Angus read it. Even for us Nixon-haters, the transcripts were a depressing blow to the high-minded expectations we had for the Oval Office. Angus's rendition lifted the gloom. He laughed and we laughed with him, not at the office or its occupant, but at the ridiculousness of human frailty. Angus is a buoyant man.

At the NRDC in the early 1970s, Angus had represented the Hudson River Fishermen's Association in litigation against several electric power companies. The companies had had the bad fortune to site their generating plants on the stretch of the river where the striped bass spawn. In sucking in river water for cooling, the plants would kill the eggs and hatchlings of a fish much prized for sport and valuable commercially. The power companies could not stop

4. Angus Macbeth, drawn by an admiring fisherman-client in the early 1970s. The caption, "Amicus Piscatoris" (friend of the fisherman), alludes to the legal term "amicus curiae" (friend of the court). The drawing hung in Angus's office at the NRDC.

using the river water without abandoning the plants or building huge air-cooling towers that would cost a fortune and mar a spectacularly beautiful stretch of the river valley. Regulatory authorities had found it convenient to skirt this thorny problem, but Angus fought successfully in the courts to make them weigh the impact on the fish under new environmental statutes.[1]

Angus left the NRDC in 1975 to become a federal prosecutor and rose to be deputy assistant attorney general in charge of environmental cases in the Carter administration. He also directed the staff of the federal commission that convinced Congress to pay reparations to the Japanese Americans put in camps during World War II.

He now heads the environmental department of a nationally prominent law firm. On the side, he sometimes teaches law school classes with me from a casebook on which we are co-authors.[2]

Angus still litigates about the Hudson River, but in a much different capacity. His client is General Electric (GE), which discharged PCBs—polychlorinated biphenyls—into the river until the mid-1970s. Since the first outcry about PCBs in the Hudson in 1975, they have been accused of causing cancer, birth defects, neurological disorders, and more. In August 2001 Christine Todd Whitman, appointed by President George W. Bush to head the EPA, decided to dredge PCBs from the upper reaches of the Hudson River at GE's expense. The cleanup was necessary, Whitman declared, to reduce "risks to humans and ecological receptors" in the Hudson River Valley all the way from GE's facilities to New York City, two hundred miles to the south. Although the EPA is still pondering the exact scope of the operation, it will entail, at a minimum, dredging 2.65 million cubic yards of sediment along a forty-mile stretch of the river. The EPA expects the project to take five years and cost GE close to $500 million; the eventual cost could well be much larger.[3]

Most people would assume that if any EPA decision had a strong basis in science, it would be the decision to force GE to pay for cleansing the river of PCBs. The Bush administration is often charged with being a tool of corporate America and a reckless steward of the environment, so if its EPA imposed a big expense on the likes of GE, the scientific case would presumably be ironclad. But Angus told me over dinner shortly after Administrator Whitman had issued her decision that it was all political. Lawyers who identify with the problems of their clients are not impartial judges, but the way he laughed in describing the EPA decision prompted me to check it out for myself.

GE began using PCBs at its two plants north of Albany in the 1940s. The plants made capacitors: metal cans, some as large as barrels, whose electrical innards must be submerged in a coolant. Mineral oil had served this purpose, but it was dangerously flammable. To save lives, GE switched to the more expensive but nonflammable PCBs.

Located on low cliffs above the Hudson, the plants operated according to the lax environmental standards of the day. Workers would send the dregs from a container of PCBs out with the waste water. The oily chemical often spilled out onto the factory's rock floors and disappeared into the interstices of the cliffs. No one at the plants gave much thought to where the PCBs were going. They did not come marked with skull and crossbones, and, at the time, chemicals were presumed innocuous unless labeled otherwise. A neighbor of mine in upstate New York worked at one of the GE plants during this era, and he and his colleagues toiled up to their elbows in PCBs, sometimes not bothering to wash before sitting down for lunch.

When the EPA began regulating water pollution in the early 1970s, GE informed regulators that it was discharging PCBs into the Hudson and received permits to continue doing so. Because the chemical is heavier than water and clings to soil particles, most of it had come to rest in sediment piled up behind a dam just downstream from the GE plants. When the owner of the dam tore it down in 1973 with the approval of federal and state agencies, more than a million cubic yards of PCB-contaminated sediment spread downriver. Two years later came reports that the substance had contaminated fish caught far downstream.

With environmental concern on the rise, scientists made it a priority to investigate the health effects of PCBs, whose chemical structure is similar to that of DDT (dichloro-diphenyl-trichloroethane), the insecticide that Rachel Carson had declared public enemy number one in *Silent Spring*. One of the first studies of PCBs, done in 1975 by Dr. Renate Kimbrough, then a scientist at the federal

Centers for Disease Control, showed that heavy doses caused liver tumors in rodents. Not long after, Congress banned the use of the chemical and then in 1980 passed the toxic waste cleanup statute discussed in chapter 6. It gave the EPA sweeping authority to force polluters, including those who had no reason at the time to know they were doing anything dangerous, to clean up toxic waste sites.[4]

It took the EPA another twenty years to decide to dredge PCBs in the Hudson. One reason was that the scientific evidence turned out to be less ironclad than it had first appeared. No one questioned the finding that PCBs produced cancer in laboratory animals. But such tests are often poor predictors of the threat to humans, as the reader already knows. Far more conclusive is information about long-term impacts on a large human population. But here the data on PCBs told a very different story. Because of her reputation for independence Dr. Kimbrough was funded by GE in the mid-1990s to do an epidemiological survey of the employees who, more than twenty years earlier, had worked with the chemical at the company's plants on the Hudson. She found that they died from cancer no more often than did other Americans. The scientist hired by the EPA to evaluate Dr. Kimbrough's study concluded that it was well designed and executed: "I think that it is appropriate to downgrade the priority given to PCBs. . . . I'm sure this has not been particularly useful for you, but it's the best I can do."[5]

Only one abnormality has been uncovered by the many studies of GE workers: a small percentage of those exposed to massive doses of PCBs developed chloracne, an acnelike skin condition that goes away in time. Taken as a whole, studies of workers exposed to PCBs elsewhere also show no greater incidence of cancer (or other serious diseases) than would be expected in a randomly chosen group of people.[6]

As for the EPA's own scientists, they concluded in 2000 that PCBs at high doses present considerable risk, but that the doses found in the Hudson River made its water safe to drink all day, every day: "Cancer risks and non-cancer health hazards from being exposed to PCBs in the river through skin contact with contaminated sediments and river water, incidental ingestion of sediments, inhalation of PCBs in air, and *consumption of river water as a drinking water source* are generally within or below [the EPA's] levels of concern."[7]

The EPA's giving a clean bill of health to the cities that draw their drinking water from the Hudson is particularly striking given the EPA's highly precautionary approach to assessing cancer risk. The EPA's track record on PCBs illustrates the lengths to which it was willing to go to build precaution into its analysis. The agency of course assumed that the risks to humans at very low doses are linearly proportional to the risk to laboratory animals at very high doses. Yet in promulgating one law on PCBs, it also exaggerated the impact on animals at high doses by using an old and discredited analysis. When its bad science was challenged in court, it decided not to defend its law. It then, on two succeeding occasions, promulgated other laws based on exaggerations of PCBs' cancer impact on animals, claiming that this was necessary to take account of non-cancer risks it had not yet adequately analyzed. When this claim was challenged in court as scientifically groundless, the EPA again decided in the end not to defend its laws. Having had to back down three times in court, the agency then tried to avoid judicial review altogether by posting its criteria for evaluating the risk from PCBs on a Web site used by regulators in ruling on specific controversies. A court set aside this ploy.[8]

Although they found the Hudson River's water safe to drink, the EPA's scientists found that some Hudson River fish were unsafe to eat. Though the level of PCBs in the fish had dropped over the previous quarter century, it was still high. But even here, the threat was hardly dire, despite the EPA's highly precautionary approach. The EPA concluded that the risk was acceptable for those who ate fish taken from the Hudson north of Albany (where PCB concentrations are highest) up to six times a year.[9] Dredging would make the fish in these upper reaches safe to eat again, according to the EPA, but not for four decades. New York State, it should be noted, bans the consumption of fish caught in the Hudson north of Albany.

And yet, despite the evidence of research and despite the EPA's own scientific analysis, the agency told the public that PCBs in the Hudson were a grave danger. In 1998, EPA administrator Carol Browner told a committee of the New York State legislature that "we do not have every single answer, nor every single piece of data. But clearly, the science has spoken: PCBs [in the Hudson] are a serious threat." When the risk assessment quoted above was issued under her auspices in 2000, the accompanying press release included the passage quoted above, *but with the omission of the phrase indicating that the water had been found safe to drink*. And when Browner formally proposed later in 2000 that the river be dredged, the EPA's press release failed to mention that the only unacceptable risk came from regularly eating the fish caught north of Albany in defiance of a state ban. Browner's successor, Christine Whitman, has similarly omitted any mention of this critical fact.[10]

The EPA thus ignored and misrepresented its own highly precautionary scientific analysis. Nonetheless, General Electric, after years of resisting dredging, threw in the towel. The statute as written by Congress forbids it to challenge the EPA's decision. Its only recourse is to sit back, defy any orders that the EPA directs at it, and wait to be sued by the EPA at a time of the EPA's choosing, which might be a decade or more hence. In any such litigation, GE would be at a steep disadvantage because the statutes tell the courts to defer to agencies, especially when agencies claim to act on the basis of science. And if GE lost the appeal, the price would be high—the relevant statutory provision imposes a penalty three times higher than the already large cost of the cleanup operation itself.[11]

But GE is not the only interested party here. The dredging will also affect the people who live in this forty-mile stretch of the Hudson River Valley. They will reap the greatest benefits—such as they are likely to be. Sometime after 2040, locally caught fish will be safe to eat. Since, however, there has never been a commercial fishery in this stretch of the river, the chief beneficiaries will be the state's amateur anglers, who catch-and-release more than they catch-and-eat.[12]

As for the local burdens, they will be heavy. A massive excavation project will center on the river, which is to the local communities what Central Park is to Manhattan. The dredging will remove from the river bottom enough sediment to fill a line of rail cars stretching almost from New York to Chicago. Those who live nearby oppose dredging by more than two to one. Were such a massive construction project to be proposed in Central Park to placate upstate voters, urban environmentalists would take to the barricades, claiming that the EPA cannot prove that it would not create more hazard than it abates. A group of farmers sought to enjoin the dredging on the theory that the EPA had illegally hidden information on its harmful local impacts. The EPA thwarted the suit by invoking the same statutory provision that prevented GE from getting a court to review the EPA's decision before it was carried out.[13]

Why did the Bush administration go along with a decision vehemently opposed by a major corporation and the local voters? Like Angus, I have come to believe that the answer has nothing to do with science and everything to do with politics and, in particular, the desire of the Bush administration to deprive its opponents of political ammunition. As a former official in President Clinton's Department of the Interior observed, "Environmental issues are sapping the life out of Bush's political viability, and the White House is trying to stop the bloodletting by allowing the dredging in the Hudson."[14]

The press had painted a picture of the risks presented by PCBs in the Hudson that would have made any explanation President Bush offered for *not* dredging look like an excuse for killing people to enrich his corporate contributors. From the discovery of PCBs in the Hudson in 1975 through the EPA's final decision on dredging, the *New York Times* published 150 articles and editorials linking the chemicals' presence in the river to one or another serious disease. Of these 150 items, a full 145 mentioned cancer, and not a single one tried to disabuse the presumption of most readers that chemicals causing cancer in lab animals pose a serious cancer threat to people. Of the 150 articles, only 34 mentioned that the science on PCBs was inconclusive, and then generally only as a weak qualification to the allegation that PCBs were dangerous; for example, "PCB's have been linked to cancer in animals in laboratory tests. EPA officials said PCB's, or polychlorinated biphenyls, were probably also carcinogenic to humans, although scientific evidence on the theory is conflicting." Only one, concerning Renate Kimbrough's critically important study of GE workers, mentioned up front the possibility that PCBs in the river might not be dangerous, and then it added the insinuation that this was "not the first time that the cancer risks of PCB's . . . have been *played down* by scientific studies." Most startling of all, none of the articles in the *Times* mentioned that the EPA's own risk assessment found the water in the river safe to drink. Yet, one article reported that the agency had found that drinking the water is risky. The *Times* has occasionally given a more balanced account of PCBs when GE was not the target.[15]

Such flawed reporting helped to produce a decision based on bad science and worse politics. In 1980, Congress voted for a proposition with immense popular support: that the EPA should rely on scientific analysis to identify dangerous toxic wastes and clean them up at the expense of those who were to blame. The legislation instructed the agency to assess honestly what science showed was necessary to protect public health and the environment. In the case of PCBs in the Hudson, the EPA gave the public an exaggerated account of what its own scientific analysis showed. It falsely suggested that dredging was necessary to protect not only the locals who opposed it but the tens of millions of people living downstream. The upshot was a purely political decision that was dressed up as a scientific decision in order to silence critics.

Reasonable people might think that, even if PCBs pose no significant risk to health, good environmental housekeeping demands getting them out of a great river. I understand that sentiment, but it leads to removing all of the PCBs. The EPA, in contrast, decided to remove only the 10 percent or so occurring at the highest concentrations directly downstream from the plants.

Reasonable people might also think that GE deserves a thumping great punishment even if the PCBs pose no danger and even if the company did not know of PCBs' possible danger when it released them. It took decades before the evidence on PCBs came in, and, in the meantime, many people went through much worry. I understand this sentiment too, but it ought to lead to assessing a large fine on GE rather than digging up the chief environmental asset of an innocent community.

The federal government should have left New York State to decide what to do about PCBs in the Hudson. The overwhelming majority of the exposure to PCBs takes place within the state. Indeed, the stated basis of the EPA's action was primarily worry over exposure north of Albany, a hundred miles upstream from where the river touches any other state. The state could not have left the decision to local government because so many local governments were involved. Yet in a world in which home rule plays a bigger part in environmental decisions than it does today, the state might have paid more attention to the wishes of the communities most affected.

What the state would have done in the end is difficult to predict.

Its environmental department twice sought to dredge, but was stopped when residents of the area filed legal challenges. Knowing that the federal EPA can dredge without prior judicial review, state environmental officials asked the EPA in 1989 to take over.[16]

What the Hudson River story shows is that putting power in the hands of the EPA does not guarantee decisions based on good science. That is important because bad science can be used to justify doing too much or too little in the name of environmental protection.

CHAPTER ELEVEN

Precaution and Policy

Put in its best light, the EPA's insistence that GE dredge the Hudson can be seen as precautionary. Precaution makes sense in environmental regulation as it does in everyday life. Just as we should lock our doors against thieves who probably will not come in the night, so too should environmental regulators take sensible precautions on our behalf against harms that are potential but not proven. My own career as an environmental activist was inspired by this notion. In working to reduce lead in gasoline, my colleagues and I suspected on the basis of emerging scientific evidence that these additives were causing permanent brain damage to children, but we could not prove it. But to its credit the EPA eventually decided not to wait, and it was upheld in a landmark decision by a federal court, which ruled that "the statutes—and common sense—demand regulatory action . . . even if the regulator is less than certain that harm is otherwise inevitable."[1]

A measure of precaution makes sense in dealing with chemicals that cause cancer in laboratory tests on animals but for which no data exist showing whether they cause cancer in humans over several decades. PCBs, however, are one of the few sets of chemicals for which we do have such data, and we know the effects are not grave.

This does not mean that they should go unregulated. PCBs do cause chloracne, suspicions have been raised that they pose other threats to humans, and at very high doses they have interfered with the breeding of mink. Moreover, there is no avoiding the fact that, however extraordinary the experimental conditions, PCBs have caused cancer in laboratory animals. Though no link to cancer rates in humans has been established, one cannot be ruled out; perhaps it exists at a level too slight to be detected by the research conducted so far.[2]

The problem lies not in identifying such threats but in treating them with a sense of proportion. After all, PCBs are hardly the only substances that, delivered in sufficiently large quantities, have produced cancer in laboratory animals. Mainstream cancer researchers believe that the EPA should factor precaution into its regulation of potential carcinogens. It does and then some, as the previous chapters demonstrated.

But why did the EPA not reduce the measure of precaution on PCBs once subsequent research showed that the risk was smaller than originally feared? That was the recommendation of the consultant it hired to review Dr. Kimbrough's work. That was a question posed even earlier by Don Elliott when he became EPA general counsel in 1989. The staffer to ask, he was told, was a certain lawyer in the agency's enforcement division. When that lawyer applied for a job with him, he popped the question. As he recounts the exchange, the job applicant explained: "PCBs are present in the chemical plumes coming from many toxic waste sites. We can test for PCBs in a soil sample for a dollar. So it's cheap to use them to trace the contamination that needs to be cleaned up. If we announced that PCBs were not particularly dangerous, we would probably have to use TCE [trichloroethylene] to trace the contamination, and testing a soil sample for it costs much more."[3] Elliott hired the lawyer.

A better-known example of precaution run amok is the federal government's 1986 initiative on asbestos in school buildings. No one disputed that it made sense to clear away any loose asbestos that children might inhale. But, the program has triggered removal of much intact or encapsulated asbestos. As a study published in *Science* pointed out, the risks from asbestos in schools were "magnitudes lower than commonplace risks in modern-day society" and "panic," induced in part by the EPA-run program, has resulted in actually increasing asbestos levels in many schools.[4] For no obvious net gain in public health, the asbestos removal program diverted billions of dollars from educating children to paying environmental contractors. The EPA will soon rain money on contractors dredging the Hudson.

Some environmentalists rationalize those of their policy preferences that have no direct basis in science by invoking the scientific-sounding "precautionary principle." In its most rigid form, it goes beyond the prudent dose of precaution that sensible people take in dealing with suspected dangers. It dictates leaving things "natural" unless there is proof positive that the unnatural way is safe.[5]

The problem with this form of the "precautionary principle," according to Cass Sunstein, is *not* that it "leads in the wrong direction, but that if it is taken for all that it is worth, it leads in no direction at all" because there are inevitably risks in regulating against risk. For example, leaving PCBs at the bottom of the Hudson presents a risk, but so does stirring them up by dredging, as the NAS has found. Moreover, digging up the bottom of a river and moving it long distances subjects the workers to the risk of industrial accidents. Many peer-reviewed studies have suggested that the EPA's toxic waste cleanup program often does more to shorten life through accidents in the cleanup operation and handling the waste than to lengthen life through removing wastes from where they lay. There are other risks from taking disproportionate precautions. As Jane E. Brody wrote in the *New York Times*, the millions or billions spent in compliance and enforcement might be better used in ways that would save many more lives, and sometimes the cost is not worth the potential benefit. I say "potential" because in many cases, the risks involved are only hypothetical, extrapolations from studies in laboratory animals that may have little or no bearing on people.

. . . Not every regulation is a good investment. For example, for each premature death averted, the regulation that lists petroleum refining sludge as a hazardous waste costs $27.6 million while the rule that does the same for wood preserving chemicals costs $5.7 trillion per death avoided, according to estimates from the Office of Management and Budget.

. . . Remember, too, that "natural" is not necessarily safer, and just because something is manufactured does not make it a potential hazard. Nature is hardly benign. Arsenic, hemlock and, despite its current medical applications, botulism toxin are wholly natural but also deadly.

Those who wish to take strong precautions against slight "unnatural" risks also ignore that "a great deal of evidence suggests," in Sunstein's words, "an expensive regulation can have adverse effects on life and health simply by reducing income."[6]

The real point of this rigid brand of precaution is to stop actions that offend its proponents' sense of the "natural." Otherwise, many of them show slight interest in health or safety. Take the abandoned mine shafts that have been killing about twenty people a year in the United States. Under a statute passed in 1977, the federal government levies a tax to pay for sealing them up, but pockets most of the proceeds. If the government used the money now on hand plus the tax receipts over the next few years, it would have enough money to stop this annual death toll forever. Such mundane risks fail to trigger action by activists.[7] It would be more honest to call the "precautionary principle" the "natural principle."

There is much to be said for caution in altering natural systems. They are difficult to understand. Misunderstanding can produce grave harm. The harm can be irreversible. Besides, nature inspires awe. As Isiah put it, "Holy, holy, holy is the Lord of hosts: the whole earth is full of his glory."[8]

When the Age of Reason made it unfashionable in some circles to believe in a god on high, many people skipped "the Lord" and deemed the earth holy. They had shifted their religious attachment from a transcendent deity to nature.[9]

Religion deserves respect whether the object of devotion is called God, Gaia, or nature. Nonetheless, no religious cohort is entitled to insist that its dogma trumps the policy preferences of the rest of us. A tolerant society necessarily leaves room for differences of religious convictions, not only between places of worship but also in councils of government. The doctrine behind the precautionary principle in its rigid form is that we humans left nature's ways and now stand in peril unless we return to them. It is similar to that of the older western religions in which humans were exiled from a paradise (a word derived from an ancient word for a protected garden) because of our evil activities and can hope to escape hellfire and regain paradise only by obeying God.

The key question in the case of the environmental doctrine is, What is "natural"? Apparently it does not include human society as we have it today, for otherwise everything would be natural. The natural is either the earth before *Homo sapiens* appeared (which tells our species nothing about how to behave) or before it improved on Stone Age technology (which tells us to get rid of modern dentistry and central heating, both of which entail risks). The nature concept on its own fails to answer such questions as whether to remove PCBs from the river or asbestos from the schools. The answer comes from augmenting it with a story like one in the Bible. Just as Adam and Eve fell prey to the serpent that tempted them to eat from the tree of knowledge, modern humans have fallen prey to the industrial serpent that has tempted us to eat from the tree of technical knowledge.[10] There is thus a moral imperative to bruise the head of the industrial serpent. GE must be made to suffer, regardless of whether science shows that the dredging does any good.

Adherents of the rigid precautionary principle are entitled to their beliefs, but most people, including many environmentalists of my acquaintance, do not agree. It is not at all inevitable that the entire blame should be assigned to the industrial serpent. We all want "better living through chemistry," as the old Dupont ad put it, and that is not simply because we have been seduced. The utility workers had a good reason to prefer PCBs to mineral oil—avoiding the risk of being burned to a crisp. Peer-reviewed research shows that PCBs saved many people from burning. Yet GE is judged guilty without regard to whether it knew that PCBs might be dangerous. The regulators are not blamed, although they explicitly permitted GE's release of PCBs, authorized the removal of the dam in 1973 that sent a flood of the chemical downstream, and were found by a New York State hearing officer in 1975 to be equally culpable.[11]

GE alone is consigned to hell. The president of the Sierra Club fanned the flames by writing a letter to every member of Congress stating that because of the company, "more than two hundred miles of river are virtually a 'dead zone.'" The executive director of Riverkeeper, according to the *New York Times*, "said he did his best to demonize the giant corporation."[12]

Environmentalists get demonized too—as misanthropes and Luddites. The problem with basing policy on religious doctrine of the natural kind or its industrial opposite is that the arguments never end and have no right answers. We cannot even agree on which side introduced religion into the policy discussion. Some environmentalists, after all, claim that the Bible perpetuated environmental degradation through its injunction to "subdue [the

Earth]: and have dominion over the fish of the sea, and over the fowl of the air."[13] Meanwhile, government necessarily makes policy.

Whether to dredge the Hudson and many other environmental questions cannot be definitively decided by either science or the scientific pretense of the precautionary principle in its rigid form.

Part III

Our Republic

CHAPTER TWELVE

Coming Down to Earth

Before Rachel Carson, there was Aldo Leopold. Born in 1887, he was an early graduate of what was then called the Yale Forest School. It was dedicated to teaching how to make the supply of timber last, but his work in the field as a member of the U.S. Forest Service broadened his horizons. He came to believe that the United States should save some forests from logging altogether and forever. He worked successfully to get the Forest Service to establish wilderness areas.

He is best known today for a book of enduring beauty, *Sand County Almanac and Sketches Here and There*. In it he gently urged people to regard themselves as members of the biological community rather than as its lords and masterful consumers. Although its initial sales were small, it is now, according to the *New York Times,* "a bible of the environmental movement every bit as much as Rachel Carson's *Silent Spring*" and within the movement Leopold is "a titan."[1]

"Sand County"[2] was a scrubby section of Wisconsin where he had bought a farm in 1935. The farm had been abandoned because it yielded a poor crop, but to Leopold's eye it was rich in the wonders of nature. *Sand County Almanac* describes those wonders in their yearly round and along the way makes its readers understand that we

5. Aldo Leopold in front of his "Sand County" home. Courtesy of the Aldo Leopold Foundation Archives, Baraboo, Wisconsin.

can find the wonder for ourselves, even in seemingly prosaic bits of land, if only we see the creation as well as the crop.

I read the book in 1970 and the next year bought an abandoned farm of my own, in upstate New York. Sumacs as thick as thighs had sprung up in the farmyard, and the little cabin was sagging at the edges. What attracted me was the woods. The tiny fields and ridges had long since sprouted into a promising forest of oak, maple, birch, and evergreens. The trees stood in a blanket of snow framed by jutting rocks and stone fences. It was a bucolic Christmas card, and I wanted to be in it.

I had come to join the biological community on this land, not the human community around it. My neighbors—none closer than a quarter mile—were unlike my circle in New York City. All had been born in the area, few had been away to school, and most made their living with their hands. I thought them, truth be told, small people in a small town and myself a person who mattered in national affairs. Yet being a proper liberal I wanted to think of myself as a "man of the people." Desiring the psychic rewards of both superiority and equality, I kept quiet about my doings in the big city.

One of my neighbors was Everest Morrow. Born down the road on his parents' dairy farm, he was in the mid-1970s a small-scale logger, cutting firewood and fence posts with his three sons. He was tall and wiry strong, his face weathered by half a century in the outdoors. Although a generation my senior, he was boyish and bashful. But when he felt accepted his face broke into a big crooked smile and his eyes lifted from the ground and danced.

What brought us together was a piece of work. A colleague at the NRDC who ran a program to encourage owners of small wood lots like mine to manage them properly had suggested that I consult the state forester in my area. The forester advised cutting the sickly and bent trees to make more room for the better ones. The local grapevine told me that Everest was the fellow to do the job. On a cold, damp day we walked the woods, surveying the trees marked for cutting, and then sat by my wood stove. I told him the state forester had told me to ask him how he was going to dispose of branches too spindly to be worth cutting into firewood.

Everest responded by describing a recent dictate requiring that branches of trees cut in state-owned forest be piled in an exactingly specified way. He went on to point out that, although he did not have much education or put on airs, he knew a thing or two about cutting wood, and in his opinion this edict from the desk jockeys in the state office buildings made no sense in the woods. He enumerated the possible reasons for their rule—such as providing wildlife habitat, controlling fire, and easing passage around the forest floor—and argued in detail that there were better ways to serve those ends.

Once I got over my surprise at being presented with a lecture, it began to dawn on me that it was a good one. The argument was well structured and took account of the full range of interests at stake, not just his own. It would have made a solid draft of a lawyer's written presentation to an administrative agency. When the room finally fell silent, I told him to dispose of the branches as he saw fit. The results were splendid.

After the cutting was done, Everest took to dropping by on a Sunday afternoon to neighbor. I learned more about him. One brother was a professor of forestry at Cornell; another was an airline pilot in Chicago. Their father had reared Everest to stay near his parents as they grew old. He was taught to think of himself as not bright enough to go places. Perhaps this teaching stuck because he had a slight speech impediment, or perhaps it was the other way round. In any event, after Everest married and had a family of his own, his father leased him the farm. Everest's dairy operation went bust, as did most upland dairy farms in the area. His father evicted him and sold the family farm to the airline pilot brother. Everest felt short-changed, but took it out on himself, not the world.

On one of Everest's visits, we were standing in my yard when he happened to look across the little field toward a birch grove just as the sun made the trees' bright white bark glisten against the dark-green pines behind. "That view is worth a million dollars," he said with one of his smiles. "Well, maybe twenty-five thousand," I responded. The smile vanished. What I had really wanted to say was that I myself had cut brush with my little chain saw to make the most of that view and was proud of it. Instead, my wise-ass remark had thrown cold water on his epiphany.

In the elite environmental circles from which I came, it was never assumed that loggers could look at a forest and see anything but a commodity. One textbook in environmental law includes a Gary Larson cartoon that makes that point. In it, two loggers are eating their lunch in a forest they had leveled to stumps. One says to the other: "You know what I'm saying? Me, for example, I couldn't work in some stuffy little office. . . . The outdoors just calls to me." The outdoors did call to Everest. If money had been all that mattered to him, he could have earned more of it with less strain on his tired body down at the local furniture factory.

The state environmental department now uses my little forest, to which Everest periodically gave a trim, to show farmers what they can accomplish with theirs. The state forester who has helped me over the years comments on the craft of Everest's work by noting that some of his colleagues with degrees in forestry find it hard to believe that the forest was cut in modern times. When I told Everest a few years ago that the state environmental department was making a film of his work for instruction across the state, he was pleased but with his characteristic modesty just nodded.

In his feeling for the land and his keen awareness of what happens on it, Everest was typical of many country people. Of this I was reminded on a recent Sunday morning when several hundred people gathered in an upstate hotel ballroom to thank three state foresters for their long service in providing advice to private wood lot owners. Many owners, most of whom were truly unaccustomed to public speaking, got to their feet to testify to how the foresters had helped improve their land and their appreciation of it. Some were tearful. Yet the most fitting tribute of all came from a young logger. At first he tried to be humorous, but he was ill at ease and it did not come off. Then he gulped and said what was really on his mind—that these three foresters had educated wood-lot owners to think of themselves "not as users of the land but as stewards of it." This logger may not have known the name Aldo Leopold, but he had absorbed Leopold's message and believed in it profoundly. This message is to be heard not just in wood lots in upstate New York but in schoolrooms across America and in every nature documentary.

Aldo Leopold was concerned that people failed to understand nature, but his response was to educate people to take care of it.[3] That is why, after becoming a professor, he wrote for magazines read by gardeners, hunters, farmers, and lay conservationists instead of solely for elite scientists and high officials. Leopold's message has reached the people. This success undercuts the assumption that ordinary people are too short-sighted to care about the environment. Thinking that way today would be arrogant.

I see instances of such arrogance all around me. For example, the *New York Times* wrote off my neighbors who opposed dredging the Hudson as some loopy fringe. It failed to report the polls showing that a substantial majority of the locals opposed dredging and gave the impression that the opposition was marginal and stupid. It presented the opponents as being blind to the EPA's science showing the dangers of PCBs, "confused," gulled by GE, and prejudiced by "disdain . . . for big government" and dislike of "people from New York City." It was the *Times*'s reporters, however, who had blinders on.[4] The locals had reason to pay close attention to the science because they and their children have the greatest exposure to whatever danger there is. The neighbor who had worked with his hands in pure PCBs knew the specifics of the epidemiology.

The local opponents of dredging were concerned with preserving their local *environment*. The *Times*, however, never dignified this opposition or its concerns with the approving adjective "environmental." Instead it characterized it as putting selfish concerns above public health in the entire Hudson River Valley. In fact, however, the EPA's actual scientific rationale focused primarily on *local* public-health impacts.[5]

Another country person who did not fit my city stereotypes was Mr. Hughes. That was what I always called William Hughes. I saw him regularly at his service station/bicycle shop down in the village that is seven miles away. The reason was an old icebox that I found buried under the hay in my barn. In the back-to-basics spirit of a hippie-environmentalist of the early 1970s, I used it for a while to cool my food instead of buying a refrigerator. He was the only one around who sold block ice. After years of perfunctory conversations about ice and gas, I decided to engage Mr. Hughes in real conversation. This was back in 1977, when the bridge tolls were doomed and I was wondering where the money might come from to rescue New York City's subway system. One possibility was to tap the state's revenues from its gas tax. This, I thought, ought to be attractive to the state government because improving the subway would help to preserve the tax base of the city and thus of the state. A gas station owner, I thought, might give me some insight into the reaction upstate, and I decided to use him as a miniature focus group. I mentioned that there was a proposal to use the state gas tax for transit improvement in New York City and asked what he thought of it.

He pondered and then expressed wonder at why people upstate should pay for a service in the city. I explained that most of the state's transportation funds went to roads rather than urban transit. He pointed out that most of these funds came from the gas taxes paid by people who used the roads. By this point, I had blown my cover as a disinterested questioner and found myself in an argument with an opponent with points in his favor and the will to use them. I countered by invoking the need to conserve energy. He said kindly but insistently that if people in the big city want to use less energy, let them take transit and, if they wanted better transit, let them pay for it themselves just as local motorists had paid for their own cars and trucks. Glancing at some of those motorists then driving by, I realized that it was absurd to make them subsidize transit riders and transit workers in the city, the lowest paid of whom earned more than most of my upstate neighbors.

My encounters with Everest Morrow, Mr. Hughes, and many

6. William Hughes at his service station/bicycle store in the 1970s.

others forced me to see that in this upstate community people believed that they were entitled to the dignity of their own opinions on public affairs and that their opinions should get equal respect in the sense that everyone has one vote on election day. The Clean Air Act was, however, pointedly aimed at shifting power from ordinary voters to those of us on the command deck of Spaceship Earth. In becoming a part of the upstate community, I was gradually realizing that the pride I felt in my position as a national environmental advocate came at the expense of my upstate neighbors.

I was also coming to realize that the rationales for my elevation and their subjugation were bogus. Our respective positions could not be justified by a need to follow the dictates of science because science fails to provide right answers. They could not be justified by a need for an environmental captain to command progress from on high because progress often comes from politicians accountable to ordinary people.

The facts in front of my face kept showing me that ordinary politics can succeed where the EPA fails. Take the case about pollution and transit in New York City about which I had asked Mr. Hughes. When the state and city had exhausted their final appeal in the courts, the governor's and mayor's people told Ross Sandler and me, in effect, "You won, so tell us what we have to do." That forced us to switch roles—from excoriating them for failing to achieve the air quality standards to figuring out what we really wanted them to do about it. We realized that there really was not much to be done, given practical and political realities. We did require them to put more traffic agents on the street, create bus lanes, and more, but none of this would have much impact on air quality. A *New York Times* editorial pointed out that the case was not really about air quality but about traffic and transit policy, which, in its opinion at the time, should be left to state and local officials, not the EPA and the federal courts.[6]

Working with the city's and state's traffic and transit officials rather than against them in court created mutual respect and, eventually, the idea that we could accomplish more working together than apart. It was agreed that the city and state would supply the real facts about the transit system and we would supply the rhetorical skills that we had previously used against them in court and the press. The system was falling apart. Back then, many of the subway cars either had no air conditioning or the air conditioner was broken or malfunctioning. Sealed shut and packed with strap hangers, these cars got as hot as warming ovens in summer. Commuters could count on being ordered off a train about once a week because it was broken or, worse yet, stuck in a tunnel. The stations were a disgrace—crumbling masonry, exposed wires, and worse still. When the transit people told us the full story, we realized that we had seen only the superficial problems. The basic structure of the system—the transformers, tracks, and signals—was in shambles. Critical equipment—such as the fans needed to save passengers from lethal smoke in case of a major fire—was inoperative. It was a miracle that the system worked as well as it did.

The book we helped write, *A New Direction in Transit* (1978), provided a blueprint for making the system functional and tolerably comfortable.[7] Although the price tag was steep, we argued that the city and state had to pay it despite their financial woes. Without a reliable subway, the city would, indeed, become a ghost town. Together with Mayor Edward I. Koch we released the report at a press conference at city hall. Editorials in all the city's dailies endorsed it and the incoming chairman of the Metropolitan Transportation Authority said he would implement it if he could get the money. Elected officials have gradually provided the money, $22 billion so far.

This was a success that dwarfs any victories we won in court. It came not because we called for enforcement of the prime directive from the command deck of the Spaceship Earth, but because we entered the field of ordinary politics and convinced state and local officials on matters for which they are still largely accountable to ordinary voters.

CHAPTER THIRTEEN

A Government of the People

The respect that my upstate neighbors demand for their opinions on public affairs is a remnant of an age in which all voters got such respect. There was a time in America when high officials were meaningfully accountable to ordinary voters and those voters were proud of their role and took it seriously.[1] This was the "government of the people" that Abraham Lincoln celebrated in the Gettysburg Address. How did this country get such a government and what happened to it?

Those who gathered in Philadelphia in 1787 to design a new government came with heavy hearts. In 1776 they had pinned their hopes on state legislatures because they believed American voters were a noble lot who would elect the best among them as their representatives. Instead, state legislatures did many selfish and stupid things. In 1787, the framers of the Constitution came to Philadelphia chagrined for forgetting how vile man can be.[2] Yet having fueled their revolution with the cry "No taxation without representation," they could not abandon representative government. Instead they built a government that was representative, yet checked against the sins of the past by dividing power.

They built in representation by requiring that all legislation be passed by a house of representatives but sought to check the rashness that would come from representation of the people by requiring also that legislation be passed by a senate and subject to veto by a president. In contrast to the representatives directly elected by the people to two-year terms, the senators and president would not be directly elected and would serve longer terms. The idea was to insulate them from popular sentiment.[3]

Through an elected house of representatives on a short leash the people could protect themselves from federal officials. The federal government could impose no new tax or law nor appropriate public money without a majority of these representatives voting "Aye." The people would know whether their representative voted "Aye." The Constitution required Congress to publish how each member voted on controversial matters. In contrast, in Britain at that time, Parliament could cloak its doings.[4]

Because the new federal government could not enlarge its power over the people without the people's representatives' accepting direct, individual responsibility, it was the public's government, not the king's or the *officials'*. That is why it was called a republic—"re" for thing, "public" for the people—the people's thing.[5] This was no perfect republic. Slaves were slaves, and women had no vote, but the officials with the power were truly accountable to ordinary people. That was, indeed, revolutionary.

The Constitution further divided power and made government more accountable to the people by limiting the federal government to the kinds of tasks for which the individual states lacked institutional competence. Such tasks included waging war, conducting foreign relations, and regulating commerce among the states. A limited government at the federal level meant that most government would be closer to home and thus easier for voters to understand, control, and even participate in. The Constitution left the states the power to decide how to allocate authority between themselves and their local subdivisions, but it did require that each state have "a *republican* form of government."[6]

The government of the people promised on paper became a vibrant reality. When the threat from overseas subsided following the War of 1812 and the heroes of the Revolutionary War grew old, the voters opted for new sorts of leaders, such as President Andrew Jackson, who was born in a log cabin and came riding in from the frontier. This changing of the guard reflected the attitudes of ordinary people. They believed they could get along without elite leaders telling them how to arrange their affairs, whether governmental, commercial, or domestic. After all, most families, whether on the frontier or in the rural areas closer to the seaboard, took care of most of their own needs in voluntary association with their neighbors. Aristocratic tourists from Europe found that ordinary Americans, even the porters and maids in hotels, thought their opinions worth as much as those of the visiting gentry and told them so to their faces. The visitors were shocked that the common people in America failed to accord proper respect to their betters. Frances Trollope, mother of the famous British novelist Anthony Trollope and a successful writer herself, wrote home about "the total and universal want of manners and the coarse familiarity, untempered by any show of respect."[7]

The American republic in the mid-1800s was closely linked to a class structure in which, unlike in Europe, there was no aristocracy and no dishonor in work. The white-gloved visitors were also aghast that all Americans seemed to get their hands dirty—if not with soil and grease, then with the ink and dust of the counting house and the warehouse. There was no idle upper class except for a few scattered plantation owners in the south. Historian Robert Wiebe, on whose work this chapter heavily relies, described free men in the United States in this era as being divided, roughly speaking, into a lower class and a middle class, but with a sense that through hard work, readily available credit, and land grants, it was possible for a lower-class free man to achieve middle-class status. Whether of the middle or lower class, white men were full citizens and could vote, the property qualifications for the vote having been eliminated here long before they were in Britain.[8] It was not property, birth, or expertise but self-sufficiency that was thought to entitle voters to hold their opinions and exercise their franchise.

Voter turnouts were high by modern standards. Four out of five citizens cast ballots in presidential elections at a time when many voters had to travel long distances on poor roads to get to the polls. Voters also considered keeping informed to be essential to their role as the ultimate sovereigns in their land. They learned to read, and they bought newspapers. By 1840, 95 percent of the white males in the north had somehow learned to read despite public education not yet being widely available.[9]

Toward the end of the nineteenth century, dramatic improvements in transportation and communications brought to prominence businesses, such as railroads and banks, that operated on a national scale. To serve their needs and cabin their powers came a bigger federal government as well as national unions, trade associations, and periodicals. Also essential were nationally prominent universities. They equipped leaders of these national institutions with the new skills and perspectives needed to run things nationally. Wiebe calls these leaders the "national class."[10]

Thinking of themselves as sophisticated because they were schooled in the Ivy League, members of the national class looked down on the old middle class that centered on the Main Streets of America. The national class thought of these Main Streeters as essentially uneducated, since provincial colleges and low-prestige universities no longer counted as "real" higher education. The Main Streeters were also thought to be mired in the past because they were content to sit on the platform of the local bank or on the local school board rather than exercising power on a national scale from an underwriting firm on Wall Street or an agency in Washington, D.C.

The national class believed that control of government should be based on what it had to offer—specialized knowledge—and not on self-sufficiency as before. The knowledge that had the national class and everyone else all agog at the turn of the century was science. Into the era of the horse and buggy came the telephone (1876), electric light (1879), automobile (1893), x-ray (1895), radio (1895), airplane (1903), and more.[11] No one knew quite how this dizzying succession of inventions would change everyday life, but the uncertainty undercut people's self-confidence at a time when it was already on the wane. Fewer people fended for themselves on a frontier. Inhabitants of farms and villages were moving to bewildering cities. Everywhere, new manufacturing techniques—as well as immigrants and freed slaves, who were willing to work for less—threatened traditional means of livelihood.

To a shaken people, the national class offered the hope that experts would use science to restore order. The message conveyed to ordinary people was that they should distrust their common sense and instead follow the lead of the national class and its experts, not only in government policy but in their personal lives. A prominent professor warned, "No one today knows enough to raise a child."[12]

In government, the national class built its power through basic changes in the political process. It got government to impose poll taxes and voter qualifications to exclude from the voting booth not only African Americans but also the Italian laborers, Jewish peddlers, and poor folk of all races who were pouring in from southern and eastern Europe. Laws were changed to discourage electioneering by the parties and other fraternal organizations that had been integral to the robust but raucous electioneering that had previously attracted the less-fancy segments of society to the polls in droves.[13]

In addition to preventing and discouraging voting by ordinary people, the national class sought to insulate critical decisions from those who still did vote. Believing that lay people should not sit in judgment of the experts, the national class pushed for transferring power away from the institutions most accountable to ordinary voters and toward those most in the hold of experts. Power was transferred from the states to the federal government and, within the federal government, from Congress to unelected officials in administrative agencies and the judiciary.[14]

For example, Congress in 1887 transferred regulation of railroads from state legislatures to a federal commission, the Interstate Commerce Commission (ICC). The railroads were the nation's life lines. They carried the farmers' crops and the merchants' goods. Legislators billed the ICC as the means to protect the people from rapacious railroads charging high rates. Yet also favoring the ICC were J. P. Morgan and other magnates of the national class who had a stake in the established railroads. They wanted the ICC to protect their investments from the low freight rates that could result from aggressive state regulation (demanded by Main Street businesses and farmers) or competition from upstart railroads (likely to be owned by Main Streeters). Morgan sincerely believed that regulation by experts insulated from the wishes of ordinary voters would benefit the nation as a whole because the experts would bring order to the unruly marketplace and therefore encourage more investment (which he would underwrite).[15]

During the early decades of the twentieth century, under a succession of largely Republican presidents from Teddy Roosevelt to Herbert Hoover, new federal agencies were created. The drift overall was toward more federal regulation and less responsibility by legislators. The administration of President Franklin Roosevelt sharply accelerated this trend. The most prominent legislation of the early New Deal, the National Industrial Recovery Act, responded to the crisis of the Great Depression by endowing a federal agency with

sweeping power to set prices and allocate the market among established suppliers. It imposed order on all markets as the ICC had
done for railroads, again often at the expense of consumers. The
businessmen who pleaded for the legislation included not only J. P.
Morgan but also John Rockefeller.[16] His Standard Oil of New Jersey
was plagued not only by falling demand but also by increasing supplies of oil from wildcat oilmen, themselves creatures of Main Street.
The trend continued under every succeeding president, Democratic
and Republican alike.

So then, the EPA's rise to power continued this trend in which
the federal government took control of controversial topics and
transferred responsibility for them to an agency acting in the name
of expertise. Not only many environmentalists in the 1960s but also
some captains of industry favored a federal environmental agency
taking control of the pollution issue, but that too was a continuation
of the same trend. Not only would-be beneficiaries of regulation but
also those to be regulated had in the past supported transferring
power to a federal agency. Although the concept of the "national
class" explains much about the rise of the EPA, it does not explain
everything. The national class, after all, includes not only nationally
prominent environmentalists and corporate leaders but also people
like myself. All along, there had been plenty of fights about in whose
interest federal agencies such as the EPA should be run.[17]

It should have come as no surprise that business interests had the
best of pollution control by federal agencies in the 1960s. After all,
J. P. Morgan had been right about the ICC; it ended up protecting
the railroads from competing railroads more than protecting the
public from the railroads. It similarly perverted regulation of interstate trucking. Despite the ICC's eventually costing the public $20
billion annually, it was not stripped of its power until recently because the railroads and trucking lines as well as their unions fought
to maintain ICC regulation.[18] But with pollution, the businesses that

sought rule by a federal agency failed to foresee the strong feelings of voters. The regulatory lap dog grew up to be an ox.

These few pages tracing events from 1776 to the present have surely not succeeded in giving a rounded rendition of a rich history. But they do serve I hope to provide a context for posing the questions upon which I want to focus: how does Congress's empowerment of the EPA square with the constitutional ideal of a republic in which ordinary citizens can hold the people they elect accountable for the laws and how does this powerful EPA square with the Constitution?

The Supreme Court affirms that the Constitution prohibits Congress from leaving the lawmaking to others. "Article I, § 1, of the Constitution vests 'all legislative Powers herein granted . . . in a Congress of the United States.' This text permits no delegation of those powers."[19] This prohibition, according to the Court, serves vital constitutional purposes. "Article I's precise rules of representation, member qualifications, bicameralism, and voting procedure make Congress the branch most capable of responsive and deliberative lawmaking. Ill suited to that task are the Presidency . . . and the Judiciary. . . . The clear assignment of power to a branch [in this case lawmaking by Congress], furthermore, allows the citizen to know who may be called to answer for making, or not making, those delicate and necessary decisions essential to governance. . . . [T]he delegation doctrine, has developed to prevent Congress from forsaking its duties."[20] The Supreme Court also affirms that the Constitution limits Congress to protecting interstate commerce and other federal powers specifically enumerated in the Constitution. "The Constitution creates a Federal Government of enumerated powers." This limitation too, according to the Court, serves vital constitutional purposes. "Just as the separation and independence of the coordinate branches of the Federal Government serve to prevent the accumulation of excessive power in any one branch, a healthy balance of power between the States and the Federal Government will reduce the risk of tyranny and abuse from either front."[21]

In practice, however, the Court has interpreted these requirements in ways that have allowed Congress to do what is necessary to serve legitimate constitutional ends and, of critical importance, has decided that legislators are the best judges of what is really necessary.[22]

The Court has *not* told the legislators that they can forget about these constitutional requirements when it suits them. The oath they took to uphold the Constitution includes upholding its spirit. Even if the Supreme Court was correct in deferring to the legislators, the legislators should not put the federal government in charge of pollution in cases where the states will not hurt other states and should not delegate lawmaking power to the EPA unless that is truly necessary. They should not enlarge federal jurisdiction simply to aggrandize themselves and should not leave the lawmaking to the EPA so that they can escape accountability to the voters.

The justices of the Supreme Court refrain from judging whether the legislators have honored their oaths, but we the people are free to judge for ourselves. The question we should ask is whether, in empowering a federal agency to make pollution laws, supposedly because doing so was necessary to protect us, the legislators have dodged the constitutional safeguards designed to protect us from them?

CHAPTER FOURTEEN

Home Rule

> In 1969, we took a top-down approach; now we must encourage innovative bottom-up, grass roots approaches. So let 1000 flowers bloom! And let us create an environment where success can go to scale.
> In 1969, we were too elitist.
> —JAMES GUSTAVE SPETH, co-founder of the NRDC and dean of the Yale School of Forestry and Environmental Studies, "A New Paradigm: Bring It On!"

At their annual meeting in 1997, state environmental commissioners handed out T-shirts with the slogan "The states are not branches of the federal government."[1] Environmental commissioners had not previously been known as champions of state sovereignty. Some of their predecessors had supported the federal mandates that forced state legislatures to give them bigger budgets and more power. The federal boons came at a price. The states were stuck with carrying out the EPA's dictates even when they made no sense to those on the scene, and it fell to the commissioners to impose the EPA's way of doing things. Angry at the EPA-commissioner axis, legislatures in many states enacted statutes denying state environmental departments any power not absolutely and specifically required by federal mandates.

Uncomfortable with having to take the heat for decisions made in Washington, the state commissioners seized upon President Bill

Clinton and Vice President Al Gore's promise to let state regulators and pollution sources find smarter, cheaper ways of protecting the environment. Their promise followed from their embrace of the "reinventing government" concept that those closer to a problem can solve it better. With the 1996 presidential campaign still under way, the commissioners asked EPA administrator Carol Browner to turn the promise into official EPA policy and she called for negotiations. Four months of hard bargaining produced a sixteen-page draft agreement under which the EPA would permit states to depart from rigid federal requirements, but only where it finds in advance that environmental standards would still be achieved and money saved.[2]

Meeting environmental standards at lower cost sounded great, but national environmental organizations urged the EPA not to sign the agreement.[3] If it worked, environmental policy might go the way of welfare, where the success of federally sanctioned experiments in state flexibility led to a wholesale shift of power to the states. Although the EPA would have ceded not an inch of environmental quality in the agreement, its success would be a powerful argument for Washington's losing power.

After President Clinton won re-election, the EPA deputy administrator in charge of the negotiations sent his state counterparts "Dear Reinvention Ombudsperson" letters declaring that the states would be allowed to try only "minor, and I stress minor, changes."[4] Even with these, the EPA reserved the right to choose how to spend the savings. So if a city found a less-expensive way for its waste-treatment plant to comply with federal water quality standards, it could not devote the savings to more teachers, tax cuts, or some other purpose chosen by local officials. Instead, the savings would have to go to an environmental project approved by the EPA. The EPA was thus insisting that it retain control of its present share of spending by states, cities, and businesses, even though environmental standards could be met for less.

The next day, state commissioners fired back a letter about "damaged trust" and "gross error."[5] The next month, they handed out their T-shirts.

Before donning such T-shirts ourselves, we need to see why in the 1970 Clean Air Act Congress had determined to "tak[e] a stick to the states," as the Supreme Court put it. One rationale for the federal takeover was that pollution has no respect for state borders.[6] A source that wafts pollution across a state line cannot be controlled by the state downwind, but the downwind state's citizens do not get to vote for the officials in the polluting state. So, the argument goes, federal officials must take control.

This logic is irresistible, but it bears little relationship to what the EPA actually has done. The 1970 Clean Air Act required each state to implement a plan to attain the EPA's air quality standards in the state and to avoid interfering with such attainment by downwind states. For the next three decades, the EPA routinely enforced the *intrastate* requirement, but not the *interstate* requirement. It refused to help the states that appealed to it to moderate pollution coming from upwind states.[7]

By enforcing only the intrastate requirement, the EPA actually increased interstate pollution. Many states found that electric generating plants could most cheaply cure intrastate violations of the air quality standards by building smoke stacks so tall that the pollution would not come down to the ground until it had crossed the state line. Making the stacks taller was cheaper than reducing the pollution coming out of them. The result was a binge of tall-stack building. As Richard Revesz found, there had been only 2 stacks taller than five hundred feet before 1970, but by 1985 the number leaped to 180; 23 were more than a thousand feet tall.[8] The states had responded logically to the federal government's illogically imposing strict deadlines to correct intrastate violations while failing to cut interstate pollution. The tall stacks, paid for by consumers, did nothing to reduce emissions, but rather turned local pollution into acid rain that fell hundreds of miles away in other states.

Congress decreed in 1977 that the EPA could not count reductions in intrastate pollution achieved by tall stacks built in the future in deciding whether a state met the ambient air quality standards. That removed the federally created incentive to construct more tall stacks, but it did nothing to get the EPA to cut interstate pollution. In 1989, a Senate report acknowledged that "implementation of the Clean Air Act . . . created a substantial number of the interstate pollution problems" and that "the law remains today largely what it was when written in 1970, keyed almost entirely to achieving local ambient air quality standards." In 1990, Congress did take responsibility for a law cutting acid rain. The EPA itself took no action to cut other instances of interstate pollution until 1998, almost three decades after it was put in business to do so.[9]

Congress predictably blamed the failure on the EPA,[10] but its people were neither slothful nor unaware that interstate pollution was the primary justification for their power. Rather, interstate pollution is a problem so fraught with high-stakes political controversy that it cannot be papered over with pseudo-scientific rationales; Congress must take the lead.

Not only has the EPA been a poor guardian against interstate pollution, the states are actually more accountable than the pollution-has-no-respect-for-state-boundaries argument suggests. All sources, even the home heating furnace, put some particles across state lines, but most sources, even large factories, do most of their harm in their own state. That makes state officials accountable for most of the harm. That should be enough in a world where local, state, and federal actions routinely affect those voting elsewhere.

Cross-boundary pollution does justify federal regulation, but only of the small minority of sources that do much of their harm in other states and are not adequately controlled. Yet the national government has taken control of all sources rather than limiting itself to instances where the states would significantly harm other states. Many federal environmental statutes focus primarily on pollution that stays within one state. For example, the statute on abandoned toxic waste sites seeks mostly to protect groundwater and soil from pollution that only rarely travels across state lines. Likewise, the Safe Drinking Water Act deals primarily with the local distribution of tap water.[11]

"Pollution has no respect for state borders" is thus a good reason for a federal role, but a more limited one than we have today. Even where much cross-border pollution is possible, as where two states border on the same lake, states may cooperate to protect a shared resource through an interstate compact or less-formal means. Congress could encourage such cooperation by enacting a judicially enforceable "golden rule for transboundary pollution,"[12] which would obligate states to protect citizens of other states as they protect their own. If unacceptable problems remain, the federal government should tailor its response to them. Congress should, moreover, enact the laws itself rather than forcing the states to do so. That way, federal legislators would have to take responsibility for the laws that they deem necessary, rather than foisting responsibility for the costs onto their state counterparts.

Another reason for a federal role in controlling pollution is to protect federally owned parks and wilderness areas of nationwide importance that have special pollution-control needs. Citizens from all states want the air around the Grand Canyon so pristine that we can see from rim to rim and far beyond. This is a reason for a federal role, but again a limited one.

Still another reason for a federal role is that state-by-state regulation can sometimes hinder interstate travel and trade. Each state having its own limits on emissions from cars driven in that state could make it difficult to drive far. Fortunately, however, the states have stuck to regulating cars that should be registered in the state, rather than any car passing through. After California began in 1964 to limit emissions from cars registered in the state, car manufacturers urged Congress to enact federal limits that would preempt state regulation on the theory that it would result in dozens of different state standards requiring different cars to be made for many states. In response, Congress established federal standards but gave California alone the right to impose tougher ones. Today, states must choose between living under the federal standards or adopting the standards imposed by California. Whether leaving the states to develop their own auto emissions standards would have significantly burdened interstate commerce is a question for Congress. If the answer is yes, Congress should regulate emissions from new cars. A similar determination could justify its regulating other nationally traded goods, for example, by limiting the lead content of gasoline.[13]

To pick up the theme with which the previous chapter ended, Congress should honor the spirit of the Constitution by limiting federal regulation of pollution to instances where the states, left to their own devices, would hurt other states. I have identified three instances of this danger: (1) states would fail to control adequately sources that do much of their harm in downwind states, (2) states would fail to protect adequately such critical national assets as our great national parks, and (3) state-by-state regulation of goods would substantially burden interstate commerce. There may be other instances. The point is that Congress should intervene only where the states are not situated to make a decision based on the full range of important interests. In other words, Congress should not intervene simply because it disagrees with decisions that the states have made.[14] Equally important, and helpful in discouraging Congress from stretching these somewhat elastic tests, if Congress decides the federal government should make the decision, Congress itself should impose the laws rather than mandating that the states

Local, State, National, and International

The principles for allocating power to the federal government can also justify its ceding power through treaties. Where, for example, regulation by nations acting alone cannot adequately control pollution with important effects beyond their borders, it makes sense to employ international arrangements, as was done in the treaty to control emissions that damage stratospheric ozone.

Similar thinking should guide states in allocating power between themselves and their municipalities. The relationship between state and municipality is, of course, not precisely parallel to that between nation and state. Most of the land area of the nation is outside the borders of any municipality. Many very small municipalities have no environmental agency. Where, however, a municipality is staffed to deal with local pollution, it should rule.

do so (chapter 16 explains why). These limitations would not and should not stop the federal government from continuing to develop information on pollution and providing it to the states and the public.

These proposals apply only to pollution control, the subject of this book, and not to other environmental-protection activities conducted by federal agencies. Where, for example, species are endangered, different considerations are at work. Although a state may deal with air pollution in a valley within its borders without significant impact on other states, if the last remaining herd of American buffalo resides in that valley, the state ought not be able to allow these beasts to be turned into trophies. That would harm the citizens of all states.[15] My proposals would not prevent the federal government from saving wild places of national importance such as Mona

Island by making them into national parks or protecting the Mona Iguana.

When it comes to pollution control, however, the federal government needs radical weight loss. The EPA runs a regime that commands and controls the regulation of all pollution sources, no matter how local their impact. A milder alternative to this rigid federal control is that the federal government set mandatory pollution-control objectives, such as air quality standards, but give states, localities, and businesses flexibility in how they are to be achieved. There is little such flexibility now. President Clinton and Vice President Gore were hinting at giving more during the 1996 election. So too now is the current EPA administrator, Mike Leavitt.[16] Yet both the command-and-control system and the more flexible alternative hold that the federal government should define and enforce national rights to clean air, clean water, and so on. I disagree. The states should be free to go their own way on environmental quality, except in those instances where they would harm other states.

For Congress to create national statutory rights to a clean environment seemed in 1970 to follow logically from its having created national statutory rights against racial discrimination.[17] The environmental movement saw itself as like the civil rights movement. As this analogy went, the environmental interests were politically powerless, up against established forces of reaction backed up by state and local government, and thus entitled to be rescued by the national government creating rights enforceable against state and local government in federal court.

This analogy between environmental rights and civil rights breaks down at several points. Congress was in keeping with both the letter and the spirit of the Constitution when it created national laws against racial discrimination by state and local governments because the Fourteenth Amendment specifically authorizes Congress to make laws to enforce constitutional rights and there is a constitutional right against such discrimination. There is, however, no constitutional right against pollution. (Racial discrimination in pollution control is, in contrast, unconstitutional and will be discussed in the next chapter. Claims of environmental injustice had nothing to do with empowering the EPA in the 1970s.) The limits on the power of Congress under the Fourteenth Amendment gave it no pause because the Supreme Court allowed Congress, at least at that time, to regulate anything that affected interstate commerce, no matter how tangentially.[18] The federal government should not, as I have argued, regulate every aspect of pollution that it can get away with controlling, but only those where states would harm other states.

Based partly on our experience as environmental advocates, Ross Sandler (my litigation partner at the NRDC and now my colleague at New York Law School) and I published in 2003 a book in which we reject the analogy between the civil rights in the Constitution and the environmental rights and other aspirational rights that Congress creates by statute.[19] The rights in the Constitution prohibit states from committing specific wrongs. The rights in the statutes require states to pursue desirable goals that necessarily must be balanced against other legitimate objectives. The good intentions, Sandler and I argue, often miscarry in the long chain of command stretching from the statutory aspirations to the facts on the ground.

The justification for Congress intervening is that state and local governments will fail because, as with civil rights, they are lined up with the supposed forces of reaction—in this instance, polluters. But the states had been making progress in controlling pollution—progress that was significant compared with what the federal government later accomplished—and the auto and coal-mining industries asked Congress to establish a federal regulatory agency to slow down the states. This argument can be overstated. Other industries wanted the states to remain in control, and the states had not been perfect environmental guardians before 1970. Many, in fact, were quite bad. But the federal government itself was often a stinker. It had a whole program to pave wild streams into concrete gutters, flogged logging rights in virgin forests at fire-sale prices, allowed destructive over-grazing of federal grasslands, and, as Rachel Carson documented, participated fully in the reckless use of pesticides.[20]

Why, then, should there be national rights to environmental quality? Environmentalists argue that the states are incapable of making good decisions because they weaken environmental standards in vying to attract business. They are thus doomed to "race to the bottom" in environmental quality if left to their own devices.

States do compete to attract business, environmental standards are sometimes part of the competition, and lower standards may make a difference to companies in pollution-intensive industries. Such competition does not mean, however, that states would forgo their citizens' environmental concerns any more than price competition among manufacturers would mean that they would forgo their profit motive. Just as manufacturers want customers *and* profitable prices, the voters who elect state officials want new businesses *and* a healthy environment. States thus have abundant reason to find less-expensive ways for companies to satisfy the environmental desires of voters, but not to ignore those desires. Studies of state behavior before 1970 and on other occasions since when states had the latitude to cut environmental standards "do not," according to Resources for the Future economist Wallace Oates, "provide much overall support for the existence of a race to the bottom. In fact, one can reasonably argue that they point more in the opposite direction —to a race to the top rather than the bottom."[21]

Since competition between manufacturers turns out to be good for the public, is not competition among states to attract new plants also good? Revesz showed in 1992 that Washington had taken control without examining this question: "Race-to-the-bottom arguments in the environmental area have been made for the last two decades with essentially no theoretical foundation." Washington, moreover, took control of many environmental issues for which there can be no race to the bottom because the problem is uniquely local and cannot be moved to another state—for example, abandoned waste sites. Environmentalists responded to Revesz by constructing theoretical scenarios in which interstate competition could result in environmental standards that are weaker than what the public wants, but Revesz showed that the same sort of theorizing could result in environmental standards that are tougher than what the public wants. Commenting on the now-massive scholarly literature, Oates observes that even if the environmentalists are correct, there is no reason to suppose that the adverse effects of the supposed race to the bottom would be any larger than the adverse effects on the public from top-heavy national control.[22] (Why national control has adverse effects is explained in chapters 18–20.)

The states would now feel even less temptation than they felt in 1970 to race to the bottom for a profoundly important reason: environmental protection has become a potent political force. Polls show that public support for pollution control has grown stronger over the long haul and is strong now. The feelings of pro-environmental voters find well-organized expression. The NRDC did not exist in 1970 and had only a few thousand members in 1972 but now claims the "support of more than 1 million members and online activists." On one hot-button environmental issue it generated a million emails to Congress within two days. The twelve largest environmental organizations have total annual budgets of nearly $2 billion. Environmental organizations have also developed close working relationships with labor unions, civil rights organizations, trial lawyer organizations, and other powerful groups.[23] The environmental movement is now part of the political establishment.

There are now also financial interests on the environmental side.

With EPA laws requiring the expenditure of more than $100 billion annually,[24] a good slice of which goes for purchasing environmental cleanup services and pollution control equipment, firms that provide environmental goods and services weigh in on the environmentalist side.

Environmental concerns are represented by large numbers of organizations at the state and local levels as well. There are some twelve thousand local environmental organizations, plus many civic and neighborhood associations with environmental interests.[25] The Audubon Society alone has 510 local chapters and 19 field offices, while the Sierra Club has 65 regional chapters and 265 local groups.

Environmental interests often win at the state and local levels. They are so frequently successful in getting state or local governments to block socially necessary but locally undesirable land uses that their prowess has acquired a name: NIMBY, for "not in my backyard." The law review of the deeply green Pace University School of Law devoted an entire issue to exploring "a remarkable and unnoticed trend among local governments to adopt laws that protect natural resources," especially when environmental problems are left unsolved by federal and state statutes. During the early 1980s, when the EPA was making little progress, many state and local governments stepped into the gap. As Evan Ringquist wrote, "many states have tossed away their recalcitrant stance toward strong environmental programs, and in many instances state governments, not the 'feds,' are at the forefront in efforts to protect the environment." A Resources for the Future study found that "[a]ll observers agree that the capability of state environmental agencies has improved significantly since 1970." States, not the "feds," bring the bulk of enforcement actions.[26]

With the public support for pollution control, state and local governments have come to prefer businesses whose employees sit at computer terminals making light goods to those whose employees hump heavy loads around gaping furnaces. To attract high-tech, high-growth companies, states need good environmental quality.[27]

One of the EPA's biggest successes of recent years has come precisely because citizen sentiment at the state and local level does matter. Its annual Toxic Release Inventories, discussed in chapter 5, have prompted companies to cut emissions because they fear provoking the community. EPA administrator Browner told the press, in releasing one of these inventories, "We believe that local residents know what is best for their own communities and, given the facts, they will determine the best course of action to protect public health and the environment."[28] Exactly so, which is why we do not need national rights to environmental quality.

Producing information on pollution and its control is one of the things the EPA should continue to do. No state could hope to duplicate the scientific staff now on the federal payroll. Most of those scientists are at institutions other than the EPA, such as the Centers for Disease Control and Prevention and the National Cancer Institute. The EPA draws on the science produced by these and other federal institutions as well as universities and hospitals to summarize a pollutant's environmental impact. Another group within the EPA summarizes information on means of control. These summaries go to the lawmakers at the EPA, but they should go instead to the lawmakers in state capitals and city halls. They should also go to the press and be posted on the Internet, available to anyone, including the incumbents' opponents in the next election.

The problem with local control, wrote Arthur Schlesinger Jr. in opposing devolution of federal authority to the states on any subject, is that it is controlled by the "locally powerful."[29] But the national government is controlled by the locally powerful of Washington, D.C. Those who look at Washington through the emerald-tinted glasses that the Wizard of Oz prescribed for his subjects deplore the "clout" of the powerful at the state capitol yet accept buying "access" in Washington. They also deplore "logrolling" at the state level but applaud "coalition building" at the national level. But when the laws come from state and local legislatures rather than EPA functionaries, we are a little better placed to know just whom to blame if we do not like the results. Arkansans know that the Tyson poultry folks have clout in Little Rock. But at the federal level the workings of the many concentrated interests are shrouded by the remoteness, size, and complexity of the federal government. Besides, it generally costs a lot less to unseat state and local legislators than to defeat their national counterparts.

One might admit that states and their subdivisions can protect the local environment but still argue for control by the federal government because it has convinced voters that it can do a better job. But the federal government stacked the competition for the public's allegiance in its own favor. Congress set up the states for failure by creating national environmental rights that they could not possibly honor, such as healthy air by the end of the 1970s. In so doing, legislators took credit for bestowing environmental benefits but shifted the blame to city hall and the state capitol for the inevitable costs and disappointments. When protests against such "unfunded mandates" led Congress to pass the Unfunded Mandate Relief Act, President Clinton observed in signing it that "today . . . we are making history. We are recognizing that the pendulum had swung too far [toward Washington.]" The act, however, does not stop the EPA from enforcing old unfunded mandates and issuing new ones under existing environmental statutes. The Unfunded Mandate Relief Act was yet another sleight of the congressional hand.[30]

With members of Congress having set up themselves as heroes and the states as scapegoats, many Americans have come to believe that only the federal government can guarantee environmental quality. History gets rewritten to fit this myth. The bit of history most frequently invoked to justify national environmental rights is the fire that burned on the Cuyahoga River in 1969. EPA administrator Carol Browner reports, "I will never forget a photograph of flames, fire, shooting right out of the water in downtown Cleveland. It was the summer of 1969 and the Cuyahoga River was burning." The leader of a national environmental organization writes, "My kids . . . can hardly remember a time when our rivers caught fire." The facts do not, however, jibe with our collective memory of a local government so indifferent to a river filling up with goop that it, in the words of Robert F. Kennedy Jr., "exploded in colossal infernos." In 1969 sparks from a locomotive settled on some kerosene and oil floating in the river and ignited picnic benches and wood stuck under a railway bridge. The debris burned for twenty-four minutes. There was little local press coverage. After all, the fire was minor compared to previous fires in 1936 and 1952, and significant progress was being made in cleaning the river. More was about to be made. In 1968 voters in Cleveland had approved a substantial bond issue to clean up water pollution, but expected federal matching funds had yet to come through. No photograph of the 1969 fire was taken. The photograph that Browner saw was probably of the much bigger 1952 fire, which *Time* magazine ran without disclaimer in its coverage of the 1969 event.[31]

The national government does not look so wonderful and the states do not look so pathetic in those rare instances where Congress has not set them up for failure. Under the toxic waste cleanup statute, the federal government had the primary duty to fund environmental improvements, and states regularly pressed the feds to do more. While the Commonwealth of Puerto Rico pursued until 1975 a project that would have ruined Mona Island despite federal laws, only a few years later it began fighting the federal government to save Vieques Island from bombing by a federal agency, the navy. The bombing continued until 2003.[32]

I must acknowledge that some states would, absent national

rights, fall short of my own hopes for environmental protection. The risk can, however, be exaggerated. When federal control of welfare devolved to the states, many devotees of federal power predicted disaster for the poor. But as the *New Republic* now notes, "Contrary to liberal assumptions, the states did not seize upon the opportunity of reduced federal mandates to starve their citizens." The assumption that states would be lopsidedly regressive made more sense in 1960. Most state legislatures then were malapportioned, but today all are apportioned according to one person, one vote. Many southern states then kept African Americans from voting, but today voting is opened to all. Southeastern states then were much poorer than the rest of the country, but the disparity in income has markedly narrowed. This is important because higher incomes bring greater concern with environmental quality. A leading student of state legislatures, Alan Rosenthal, wrote in 1998 that these legislatures are "portrayed in the press and perceived by the public to be essentially undemocratic—unrepresentative, unresponsive, unethical, serving special interests, and controlled by a few. That is not the legislature I have been observing for all these years, and it is surely not the legislature now in place. The legislature is a much more democratic institution, operating in a much more democratic environment than is popularly conceived."[33]

Different states will still have different environmental priorities, but the Constitution suggests that such differences should be celebrated rather than deplored. In a state that opted for low environmental standards, I might well side with the losers, but that's the democracy that Winston Churchill called "the worst form of Government except all those others that have been tried from time to time." American politics beyond the Beltway is no nirvana, but within the Beltway it is not perfect either.

Democracies, of course, sometimes fail, but so does our system of national environmental rights. While some state and local governments will move too slowly to protect the environment for my taste, national rights can slow protection everywhere. Implementing a national right is a slow process, as airborne lead illustrates. The lugubrious pace at which the EPA tackles new risks is the inevitable result of how Congress and the president have built the agency. As President Carter's EPA administrator, Douglas Costle, argued, EPA lawmaking requires multiple steps with multiple requirements that produce protracted deliberations at the agency and in the courts. The research that prompted the EPA to set an air quality standard for fine particles was published in 1993, but its new air quality standard did not come out until 1997. The standard did not clear court review until 2002. Years more will elapse before the standard results in federally approved state plans to cut emissions. The Clean Air Act, as the *New York Times* editorial board put it, is a prescription for "stalemate." An article in the same paper, entitled "Environmentalists Head for the States," reports that "States have long been considered 'policy laboratories,' but the reason that they often lead the way in the closely linked areas of energy and pollution, experts say, is because the federal government moves so slowly."[34] Yet the federal stalemates sometimes slow down the states. It does not make sense to impose new controls on local sources if a later EPA law might require the control equipment to be replaced.

Moreover, the sad truth is that the lofty goals that Congress builds into national rights paralyze the EPA. It often prefers to do nothing than to suffer public fury at the burdens required to achieve such high goals, as both Justice Stephen Breyer and scholar Dan Farber have pointed out.[35] Were the EPA simply providing information to the states and Congress rather than promulgating laws with nationwide effect, it could get the latest science peer-reviewed quickly and promptly produce credible reports.

If the federal government left states and localities to deal with pollution problems within their competence, the federal government would do a better job with the pollution problems that it is uniquely competent to solve. Its record on restricting interstate pollution and protecting the great national parks is poor. If federal legislators could not earn their environmental brownie points by usurping the role of states and cities, they would have to do their own jobs better. Before becoming President Clinton's director of the Office of Management and Budget, Alice Rivlin wrote a book arguing that Congress should return many programs, including some environmental ones, to the states in order to "focus the energies of the federal government on the parts of the task for which it has a distinct advantage, and rely on the states for activities they are more likely to carry out successfully."[36]

For national environmental groups, the key problem with decentralizing environmental lawmaking is institutional rather than environmental. Many such groups are centrally controlled and, like large, centrally controlled business corporations, find it easier to deal with a single national government than with the fifty states and their subdivisions. To work with these governments, national environmental groups might look to their state and local environmental counterparts, which now generally lack the money they need to hire the kind of talent on the national payrolls. The national groups have the money because they have sophisticated systems for raising it through direct mail, the Internet, government grants, and appeals to foundations and wealthy individuals. Because of economies of scale in fund-raising, the many state and local organizations would find it difficult to replicate this success. Yet it is at the state and local level that more of the money would be needed. That is the institutional problem.

The American Civil Liberties Union (ACLU) has shown how to solve it in a way that would make the environmental movement stronger. The ACLU has separately incorporated affiliates in every state, as well as in many locales, with their own boards and paid staffs. Membership in the ACLU means membership in both the national organization and a state affiliate. The members of the state affiliates elect the state boards, and the state board members have the biggest say in picking the national board. The state affiliates have considerable autonomy on local civil liberties issues, sometimes to the point of taking divergent positions in court. The group's motto is "Unity without absolute uniformity."

The ACLU has tackled the resource question head on. Money raised is shared between the national organization and the state affiliates, regardless of who solicited the funds. Between 65 and 70 percent of all funds raised are allocated to state affiliates. In addition, the national organization and the richest affiliates underwrite subsidies for affiliates in states with the least support for the ACLU. In addition, the national organization has a department with more than ten full-time employees whose sole function is to help affiliates with recruiting and training board members and staff and with running programs.

Nadine Strossen, ACLU president and a colleague on the faculty of New York Law School, observes that the saying " 'all politics are local' is certainly true for civil liberties. We have found that locally run programs are extremely helpful on national issues and essential on local ones." She points out how state and local affiliates can generate support that carries more weight with politicians in Washington than do mass mailings orchestrated from the center.[37]

Many national environmental groups have large membership rolls but only weak connections to their members. While some national environmental organizations, such as the Audubon Society and the Sierra Club, have some of the decentralized features of the ACLU,[38] many others are highly centralized. They have a few centrally controlled branch offices rather than many independent affiliates, and their boards are self-perpetuating rather than elected by the membership. They are run from the top down rather than the bottom up, like environmental regulation under the EPA.

Although national environmental organizations would have to regroup, more home rule on pollution control would be in the public interest, as I will show. First, however, I must finish showing that in pollution control, Congress has lost touch with the spirit of the Constitution.

CHAPTER FIFTEEN

Vicki Been and Environmental Justice

Vicki Been was a law student that a professor does not forget. To the seminar on public interest litigation taught by Angus Macbeth and myself in 1983 she brought not only high intelligence and earnest purpose but also work experience with the American Civil Liberties Union. After graduation she clerked for Justice Harry Blackmun and is now a professor with a national reputation in land-use law.

Been specializes in how government decides where to locate facilities, such as bus garages, that society needs but neighborhoods shun. Her interest in the subject comes naturally. She grew up in a uranium-mining town where the families were poor and the men seemed to die young. Later, after the mine closed, there came a proposal to use it to store low-level nuclear waste. Some citizens desperately wanted the jobs the facility would bring. Others thought it would be safer than the mine tailings lying around the countryside. Still others worried about the facility's long-term risks. Her mother, then the mayor, was caught in the middle. So Been paid close attention when, in 1994, President Clinton ordered the EPA and other federal agencies to stop inflicting "environmental injustice" on racial minorities and the poor.[1]

If environmental injustice is that the poor live in worse neigh-

7. Professor Vicki Been (center) with her grandmother, son, and mother, Mayor Carolyn "Cookie" Been. The picture was taken in 1992, when Been was beginning her work on environmental justice.

borhoods, it is bad news, but not new news. The poor (most of whom are white, but many of whom are minorities) have long gotten the last choice in not only neighborhoods but also housing, health care, food, and much else of consequence for health. Whether this is unjust and how we should respond has long been a staple of politics.

"Environmental injustice," however, carries a more invidious connotation—that pollution sources are steered to minority neighborhoods. In response to charges of "environmental racism," EPA administrator Browner told a group of angry community activists in 1994 that she sometimes "is not proud to be part of the EPA." When government at any level seeks to inflict pollution on a racial minority, the federal government should intervene because of its constitutional mandate to stop racial discrimination. If, however, "environmental injustice" means only disparities between rich and poor, it is no more an argument for the federal government to run pollution control than for it to run everything else.[2]

The charge of environmental racism got legs in 1987 when the United Church of Christ published *Toxic Waste and Race in the US*.[3] The study found that communities with hazardous waste facilities were disproportionately African American.

Vicki Been wanted something done about such disparities but knew that changing the method of siting waste facilities would be no solution if African Americans were moving to communities with waste facilities rather than waste facilities were moving to African American communities. In 1994, the EPA funded her to do a nationwide empirical study of whether communities with waste facilities were disproportionately African American *when the facilities were sited*. The Church of Christ study, in contrast, looked at demographic characteristics of the communities only in the present. Also, while the Church of Christ study defined communities by zip code, Been defined them by census tract. Census tracts change less than zip codes, are chosen to reflect community identity rather than the convenience of the postal service, and are more uniform in population. Besides, the zip codes listed for waste sites sometimes reflect distant mailing addresses rather than their actual locations. Been and her co-author write, "[We] found no substantial evidence that the facilities that began operating between 1970 and 1990 were sited in areas that were disproportionately African American. Nor did we find any evidence that these facilities were sited in areas with high concentrations of the poor; indeed, the evidence indicates that poverty is negatively correlated with sitings. We did find evidence that the facilities were sited in areas that were disproportionately Hispanic at the time of the siting." Such a correlation, they note, provides no evidence that the disproportionate impact on Hispanics was intentional. They also found little evidence to support the hypothesis that racial minorities or the poor come to communities with waste facilities. But they did find that "the areas surrounding [the waste facilities] currently are disproportionately populated by African Americans and Hispanics." Much of the disproportionate impact on African Americans came, they explain, from waste facilities sited before 1970.[4] Back then, minorities had less political power than they do today.

The studies by the Church of Christ and Been stand for a plethora of studies cited by advocates on both sides of the environmental justice debate. My own reading of the evidence accords with the conclusion of Christopher H. Foreman, a liberal African American whose book published by the Brookings Institution found that "taken as a whole [the environmental justice] research offers, at best, only tenuous support for the hypothesis of racial inequity in siting or exposure, and no insight into the crucial issues of risk and health impact." The Centers for Disease Control and Prevention's *National Report on Human Exposure to Environmental Chemicals,* released in 2003, found that minorities were, compared to whites, exposed more to some chemicals, exposed less to others, and exposed about the same to many others.[5]

On the question of whether any disproportionate exposure came from discrimination in making environmental decisions, a study conducted under the auspices of the National Research Council asks the right questions: "Were waste sites purposely located in these communities because of discriminatory motivations, because of the lack of politically effective opposition, because land was cheap, or because of a combination of these and other factors? Were the communities characterized by the same socioeconomic and racial or ethnic indicators when the waste sites were originally established, or did the composition of the communities evolve later, as a result of economic or other factors? The economics of land values, job opportunities, and transportation undoubtedly assert a strong influence on these outcomes, and the circumstances undoubtedly vary greatly from locale to locale."[6] The study left these questions unanswered, but subsequent research lends credence to some of the nondiscriminatory explanations, though without necessarily disproving the discriminatory ones. A study on the siting of environmental hazards in Chicago suggests that their location was influenced far more by proximity to transportation facilities than by the racial composition of the area at the time of the siting. A 2003 draft study by the United States Commission on Civil Rights points out that minority communities were once not as active as they now are in resisting the location of environmental hazards in their midst.[7]

Environmental quality is sometimes worse in areas in which minorities predominate for many reasons that have nothing to do with current siting decisions by pollution-control agencies. Many examples come to mind from my own career as an advocate who focused on environmental problems of the poor and minorities before the term "environmental justice" was coined. The substandard air quality and poor subway service which was the target of our litigation in New York City disproportionately affected minorities (as well as the elites who inhabit the metropolitan area). The lead from deteriorating paint in old housing, such as the apartment buildings we sought to improve in Bedford-Stuyvesant, disproportionately afflicted the children of minorities. The Superpuerto was to be placed in Puerto Rico because little effective opposition was expected. Large-lot zoning and other exclusionary land-use controls make it prohibitively expensive for private developers to build housing for people of modest means in many suburbs with the best environments, as I pointed out before I became an environmental advocate.[8] The beneficiaries of large-lot zoning tend to think of themselves as strongly pro-environment and antiracist and thus strong foes of environmental injustice, but one does not hear them crying for an end to the land-use controls that keep their communities exclusive.

I know of only one empirical study that claims to show that systematic discrimination in making environmental decisions is at the root of higher exposures for minorities. In 1992, the *National Law Journal* published a twelve-page analysis concluding that the EPA had discriminated against minorities. Specifically, the report claimed to find in the EPA's own data evidence that it collected lower fines and was slower in cleaning up abandoned waste sites in minority areas. In the several years after the report was published, it was cited approvingly in dozens of articles and books. Eventually, researchers sought to verify the analysis that lay behind the *Journal*'s findings. Two of them reported that they "requested the data set upon which these findings were based but were told that such data would not be released because the findings were 'too controversial.'" Independent efforts to replicate the *Journal* study using the same raw statistics from which it claimed to have derived its data set ended in heaping scorn upon its work. A recent article in the *Law and Society Review*, for example, found that "empirical analyses demonstrate the unreliability of [its] methods and conclusions and indicate that minorities have not been discriminated against in these enforcement actions."[9]

If the EPA's dominance comes to an end, federal constitutional and statutory law would still allow citizens to sue any state or locality for making pollution control decisions on the basis of race. It is easy to see the limitations of this arrangement. These lawsuits require proof of an intent to discriminate,[10] and such proof can be difficult to come by, even in those cases where the intent is there. But it is easy to overestimate the danger—the desire to discriminate is still about, but once-disenfranchised minorities now have the vote and politicians eagerly seek their support.

It is also easy, in the hunger for the "environmental justice" that the EPA ringingly promises, to overestimate its ability to deliver. Its performance falls well short of its promise. The EPA says that it is not good enough that environmental quality in minority neighborhoods meets environmental standards, but that it must also compare favorably with environmental quality in other neighborhoods. The agency promises it will use its administrative power to produce "fair treatment" even when there is no proof of discrimination. It then defines "fair treatment" to mean that "no group of people, including a racial, ethnic, or a socioeconomic group, should bear a disproportionate share of the negative environmental consequences resulting from industrial, municipal, and commercial operations or the execution of federal, state, local, and tribal programs and policies."[11] Read carefully, this does not mean that every group would experience the same share of environmental consequences. Nor could it without rural pasture lands getting environments equivalent to those in industrial cities. What the EPA actually promises is that there should be no "disproportionate" differences.

The promise was easy, and popular, to make, but is hard to keep. What is disproportionate is the kind of starkly political question that the EPA cannot readily answer. In announcing generally applicable pollution control laws, the EPA can at least pretend that science gave it the answer. In applying those laws in particular situations, the EPA can also point out that the law being applied is applicable to all. But in deciding what is disproportionate, the EPA can pretend neither that science defines the term nor that its decisions are generally applicable. In ruling on particular complaints of environmental injustice, it would find itself in the midst of hotly contested local political squabbles all across the country with neither science nor generality as a shield. We know from the EPA's record in dealing with interstate pollution and states that fail to adopt legally adequate clean air implementation plans that the agency will try to put off making the politically controversial choices.

Although the EPA announced it would accept environmental

justice complaints starting in 1993, the agency has yet to uphold a single one of the 58 complaints filed with it from 1993 to 1998. No wonder. The agency had failed to define what it took to bring a successful case. Finally, in 1998, it issued its *Interim Guidance*. As the Commission on Civil Rights recently noted, the *Interim Guidance* ducked the critical questions. Congress stepped in by passing an appropriations bill with a rider prohibiting processing of such complaints until the EPA published its final guidance. In mid-2000, the EPA produced *Revised Draft Guidance*. It too "is not specific enough to determine when violations . . . occur," according to the Commission on Civil Rights. Congress then relaxed its rider so that the EPA could process the cases, but it still failed to come up with an operational definition of a violation. Of the 136 environmental justice complaints that it has received over the past decade, the EPA has so far decided none in favor of the complainant. Two were informally settled and 31 are still pending. These 31 are not the most recently filed cases, but rather the hardest. It dismissed those that could be rejected on formalistic grounds.[12]

The Commission on Civil Rights study found that the EPA and other federal agencies have "failed to incorporate environmental justice into their core missions" and that "[w]hile EPA has support from its top leadership, it has been difficult for the agency to change its culture and attitudes about environmental justice."[13] The commission underestimates the problem. It is that, absent intentional discrimination, environmental justice is a political question that cannot be answered on the basis of rights. Rights must be stated in terms of abstractions, and there is no abstraction to steer a middle ground between the heartfelt desire for equality of outcome and the brass-tacks reality that environmental consequences cannot be made the same everywhere.

It is actually easier to discuss environmental justice in the concrete contest over a particular facility, such as a bus garage. At the concrete level, accommodation, amelioration, and compromise are possible. So it is not surprising that while the EPA's environmental justice program is in a long-term stall, state and local governments have been making real progress. Since 1993 "more than 30 states have expressly addressed environmental justice, demonstrating increased attention to the issue at a political level," according to a study by the Section of Individual Rights and Responsibilities of the American Bar Association and University of California's Hastings School of Law. A National Academy of Public Administration report funded by the EPA looked at how four states (California, Florida, Indiana, and New Jersey) deal with environmental justice issues: "The Panel has uncovered heartening evidence of leadership to address them on the part of state legislators, agency managers and staff, universities, businesses, community residents, and local governments."[14] Yet the state and local programs are works in progress, in need of further development.

National control of pollution control actually works at cross-purposes to the environmental justice movement, which seeks community empowerment as well as good environmental results. According to Leslie Lowe, executive director of the New York City Environmental Justice Alliance, "We may shut down a waste transfer station here or power plants there. But if the community isn't empowered, how can it prevent it the next time?" Kemba Johnson reported that "as these national [environmental] groups have begun to get involved in urban neighborhoods, [environmental justice] activists say they are getting pushed aside." Johnson quoted Lowe as saying, "White mainstream organizations are going into communities of color without working in respectful cooperation with community organizations. That's reprehensible."[15]

The EPA's paralyzed bureaucracy can actually frustrate community wishes. Take, for example, the proposal by a Japanese company, Shintech, to build a $700 million plant in a poor and largely African

American area in Louisiana. According to the Commission on Civil Rights, the local chapter of the NAACP and the Black Chamber of Commerce wanted the plant for the many jobs it would bring, and so too did a majority of local residents. But some local opponents, backed by a law school clinical program, filed an environmental justice complaint with the EPA. The case got stuck in the EPA's backlog, which meant that Shintech did not know when or even whether it could proceed. It decided instead to build the plant in a predominately white, middle-class community.[16] The local opponents would have counted for little in state and local politics, but they had the power through the EPA to stymie a plant that most of their neighbors wanted. Environmental justice started with the idea that poor minority communities are not sufficiently empowered. In the Shintech case, the leaders of such a community were disempowered.

The EPA deserves credit for recognizing the discontent about disparities in exposure to pollution, but also deserves blame for making the problem seem simpler and more invidious than it is and by holding out the illusory promise that it can be settled by declaring an abstract right. It thus further polarized an issue that was already deeply disturbing and divisive. This has consequences for the communities that feel afflicted, for pollution sources, and for people like Vicki Been, who could help design processes that would help bring mutual understanding.

Been sought to shed light on the issue, but took heat. She was told she was being invited to a law school conference on the subject because the sponsors needed a speaker who was *against* environmental justice. When participating in a panel on the subject at the annual meeting of the American Association of Law Schools, she was accused of being like a person who finds someone dying in the middle of the street yet wastes time asking who caused the accident rather than taking life-saving action. No one in the room objected. Thereafter, as she explains it, "I was shunned and shut out of the conversations over environmental justice policy—the environmental justice advocacy community and environmental justice office of EPA simply refused to engage my work."[17] "Because life is too short," she redirected her environmental justice work away from the aspects run by the EPA and toward the land-use questions that are largely the domain of state and local government.

The EPA's promise of environmental justice, like the Clean Air Act's promise of healthy air by the end of the 1970s, raises expectations of perfection that the agency is bound to dash, yet fails to deliver the practical results that a more overtly political system could deliver. The winner is the EPA. The *Law and Society* article concludes with the perplexed observation that "EPA—who presumably should have had a vested interest in rebutting [the *National Law Journal*'s conclusions]— . . . did not make aggressive efforts to do so."[18] While many EPA staffers were upset at such allegations, Administrator Browner instead issued a *mea culpa* on behalf of the agency, claiming its record on this issue made her feel ashamed. She thus co-opted rather corrected the agency's critics. The environmental justice advocacy groups that the agency now legitimates and funds give it a new constituency that supports it in other fights. The EPA once again succeeds by failing. "Environmental justice" is no reason to keep the EPA on top.

CHAPTER SIXTEEN

Legislative Responsibility

Congress enacts all federal environmental *statutes,* but these statutes leave the making of most federal environmental *laws* to the EPA. When the EPA makes laws, they are called "regulations."

The difference between Congress making laws and leaving that job to the EPA is critical. *Laws* are the rules that control private conduct, such as a requirement that electric power plants meet certain emission limits.[1] In voting on such a law themselves, legislators would inevitably anger those voters who want a stricter, more protective law as well as those who want a weaker, less burdensome one. In leaving lawmaking to the EPA, legislators sashay away from such responsibility. They bestow a right to protection without themselves imposing any burden. The anger falls on the EPA because it is left with allocating the burdens among pollution sources. It takes the blame for denying rights and imposing burdens.

Congress does sometimes impose the laws itself, but generally as a last resort. In 1970, having lost credibility because their previous air pollution legislation achieved so little, the members passed the law cutting emissions from new cars by 90 percent. Here was a simple law that covered massive numbers of sources. Similarly, in the 1990 Clean Air Act, with the EPA paralyzed in dealing with hazardous air pollutants, Congress decreed that existing sources meet "the average emission limitation achieved by the best performing 12 percent of the existing sources" in their industries. The EPA was left with the task of giving this concept operational meaning by calculating the emissions limits for particular industries. If that had been all that Congress had done, it would have taken responsibility for drawing the line between permissible and impermissible conduct and so would have made the law. Interpreting and enforcing the law are, as we were taught in grade school civics, proper jobs of the executive branch. Congress, however, gave the EPA additional latitude, thus obscuring the legislators' responsibility for the results. For another example, in 1990, with the EPA paralyzed on acid rain, Congress decreed a 50 percent reduction in emissions from certain electric power plants, but gave the plants the prerogative of trading emission rights among themselves. This trading allowed the greatest emission reductions to be made at the plants that could do so most economically and, by so doing, saved $1 billion per year.[2] Congress can thus make laws applicable to large numbers of sources without micromanaging.

Congress, however, generally leaves the lawmaking to the EPA. It tells it to set emission limits that are "reasonable" or to set air quality standards to "protect health" "with a reasonable margin of safety," knowing full well that these supposed standards are as elastic as a rubber band.[3] So the EPA is left to decide how clean is clean enough and how to allocate the cleanup burden.

The scope of the EPA's discretion is in some ways even broader today than it was in the early 1970s. Then, the pollution problems, such as raw sewage in rivers and black soot from factories, seemed obvious. Now, science can detect vanishing small levels of pollution, hypothesize equivalently small risks, and get rid of them at costs that are as high as the risks are small. So the EPA is confronted with a wider range of possibilities in deciding how clean is clean enough.

The Supreme Court today squares such delegation of lawmaking power with the Constitution by claiming that Congress is making the laws and the EPA is only implementing them, but the justices know this is a pretext.[4] They let Congress decide whether to delegate.

Legislators' excuses for leaving the lawmaking to agencies have changed over time. At the dawn of the twentieth century, it was said that Congress had not really left any policy-making discretion to the experts in the agencies because the statutes had instructed the experts to use scientific methods to deduce the correct laws. After endowing many agencies with lawmaking power, Congress had a new excuse: it did not have the time to do all of the lawmaking work of these agencies.[5] More recently, still another reason, special to the environmental context, is given: Congress should leave making pollution laws to the EPA because it produces stronger laws than does Congress.

None of these excuses withstand scrutiny. Science does not dictate uniquely correct environmental laws. It should nonetheless play a role in lawmaking and would do so were the laws made by elected legislators. Having to answer for their laws at the polls, legislators would want all the support they could get from scientists. National legislators would require EPA scientists and policy analysts to provide them with the information about health effects and control technologies that they now provide to EPA lawmakers and would also require these officials to propose statutory language. State and local legislators would seek similar help from their environmental agencies. The laws that would come from legislators would not necessarily be the same as those that would come from the EPA, but elected legislators would be accountable for the laws at the polls.

The public could be given an opportunity to comment on the agency's proposed recommendations as it now comments on proposed agency laws. There would thus be no loss in public participation. What would be lost is agency rationalization. And good riddance, because the elaborate rationalization needed for agency laws to survive judicial review slows the EPA's response to new science.

Lack of time is also no excuse for Congress to delegate its responsibility. In an average year the EPA now issues five "major" rules, officially defined as rules with benefits or costs greater than $100 million. Our legislators can surely take the time to vote on five pollution-control laws per year. The EPA of course also issues many minor pollution laws, but these present no practical impediment to the legislators' taking responsibility. The number of minor laws would drop precipitously were Congress to limit federal involvement to those pollution-control issues truly requiring federal attention. The balance could be handled expeditiously, yet in a way that would leave the legislators responsible. Justice Stephen Breyer pointed out in an article he wrote before becoming a judge that Congress could enact a statute requiring that all agencies stop issuing laws by fiat and instead submit them for enactment through the legislative process.[6]

Congress never accepted Justice Breyer's idea (or the responsibility that would have come with it), but we had a recent impromptu experiment with it when a federal district court judge held in 2003 that the Federal Trade Commission lacked authority to promulgate its "Do Not Call" law. The next day the House and the Senate passed legislation authorizing the program. The legislators are capable of accepting responsibility when they want to and can arrange to do so even for run-of-the-mill regulatory laws. Justice Breyer offered many variations on this approach, including an expedited legislative process for agency recommendations, but with the provision that a set fraction of the legislators could require that an agency law be ejected from the expedited process and sent to committee for consideration.[7]

Justice Breyer's idea is not an ideal solution—that will come only with a smaller federal role—but it is better than what we have now. In his scheme, power would shift from unelected agency staffers to unelected congressional staffers, but with a critical difference: elected legislators would have to take responsibility for the laws in the end.

The need for strong environmental laws is also no excuse for Congress to delegate its responsibility. In fact, delegation can lead in precisely the opposite direction. The EPA often deals with controversial issues by stalling, as it did with lead in gasoline and interstate pollution. Some of the largest reductions in pollution have come when legislators intervened to push pollution control at a much faster pace than the EPA had previously achieved. Examples include emission controls on new cars in 1970, acid rain in 1990, and hazardous air pollutants, also in 1990. In commenting on a Senate vote on global warming that "environmental groups hailed," the president of Environmental Defense, Fred Krupp, stated, "When these things come out of the back room into the sunshine, we tend to win."[8]

Such legislative strides often take place at times when the public has focused on a highly visible environmental issue. It is therefore reasonable to worry about whether legislatures would do as well on lesser issues. Surely voters will not educate themselves about every issue and be vigilant that legislators take appropriate action. True, but we do not have to become environmental experts and lobbying *nudges* to keep legislators on the mark. They know that we are free to vote them out of office at the next election, even if we have not warned them of our concerns in advance. It is the legislators and not the voters who will need to be vigilant. It is those who dog them— advocacy groups, medical societies, journalists, and their opponents at the next election—who will need to be knowledgeable. What legislators will respond to in the end is not the grade that the public gets in science, but the grade that we give them in protecting our health.[9] Their anxiety for our approval will extend not only to bills covered on the front page but also to any vote that their opponents can make an issue of in the next election. Legislators fear the charge that they failed to pass a bill that would have protected the public from some hazard. Voters can understand that charge far more readily than they can the charges about the acronym-labeled links in the chain of command from congressional mandates to source-specific permits.

The problem with Congress, according to Justice Breyer, is that it is *too* responsive to public anxieties about environmental risks and so pushes the EPA to carry precaution to an unreasonable extreme. In a book written after he went on the bench, he describes a "vicious circle" in which

- the public gets alarmed by reports of risks and comes to distrust the EPA,
- Congress tells the EPA to regulate by assuming the worst about risks and ignoring or largely ignoring costs,
- the EPA analyzes the risks in that spirit, but still hesitates to impose laws that get rid of small risks at high costs,
- environmental groups cry foul,
- Congress calls hearings,
- the public comes to distrust the EPA all the more, and
- Congress passes a new statute telling the EPA to be still more precautionary.

The vicious circle thus repeats itself. To this analysis, Cass Sunstein adds that such hypervigilant risk regulation can actually cost lives.[10]

In his book, Justice Breyer proposes a solution quite unlike his previous idea in which Congress would take responsibility. His book calls for a "centralized bureaucratic group" that would review laws proposed by the EPA and other regulatory agencies and make the final trade-offs. This group would, in his scheme, be politically insulated from voters, who distrust regulatory agencies, and would thus be able to base its decisions on science.[11]

But wait. The EPA was supposed to be insulated from popular politics, yet a vicious circle was the result. Justice Breyer's new "centralized bureaucratic group" would have to tackle politically explosive questions with no clearly right answers: How many lives will be lost through exposure to chemical X? How much is a life worth in dollars? Is a life saved now worth the same as a life saved forty years from now? Is the life of an elderly person worth the same as the life of a child?

The list of questions goes on and on. How certain are the risk estimates? How much will it really cost to limit exposure to chemical X? Will the limits on chemical X produce collateral benefits, such as reducing the use of other nasty chemicals? Or will such limits mean that other nasty chemicals are used in greater quantities? As the answers were debated, the distrust would grow, and the vicious circle would begin anew.

Justice Breyer was right that there is a problem, but wrong about its source. It is not that Congress is too responsive to the public's desire to be protected from risk, but that it is largely unaccountable when it delegates to the EPA for the burdens of providing that protection. If the legislators themselves made the laws, they would be personally responsible for the health hazards to which the public remained exposed *and* the burdens imposed on the public. Take for example what happened under a law Congress enacted to prohibit all carcinogens in food. When the FDA determined that saccharin was a carcinogen and therefore had to be removed from the market, there was a public outcry. The outcry was aimed at Congress rather than the FDA because the FDA was enforcing a law that Congress had written. Critics pointed out that saccharin was at worst a very weak carcinogen but was very important for protecting the lives of diabetics who cannot tolerate sugar. Credible experts predicted that the ban on saccharin would shorten more lives than it would extend. Congress responded by allowing saccharin to be sold.[12]

As the saccharin story illustrates, representation in our republic is supposed to be a two-way street. The Framers intended to force representatives not only to hear the demands of the people but also to explain to the people why their every demand cannot be satisfied. If legislators made the laws themselves, they would have to explain why some risks cannot be eliminated. Legislators understandably prefer to tell the EPA to make laws to get rid of all risks. The EPA cannot do this, and that is the source of the public distrust that fuels the vicious circle.

My solution is totally different from that in Justice Breyer's book and, for that matter, from that in former Speaker of the House Newt Gingrich's Contract with America (described in chapter 1). Both call for risk-regulation laws to be made by an elite using cost-benefit analysis.[13] Mine calls for them to be made by elected legislators. The legislators would necessarily have to consider the costs and benefits and might well ask for formal cost-benefit analyses to help structure their consideration. In the end, however, the decisions would be based on the free-form cost-benefit analysis that is representative government.

It is possible for legislators to take responsibility for all national environmental laws. When my book *Power without Responsibility: How Congress Abuses the People through Delegation* (Yale, 1993) prompted some legislators to seek a way to stop delegating to agencies, I suggested that they introduce a bill based on Justice Breyer's idea of barring any agency law from going into effect unless approved by Congress. The result was a bill titled the Congressional Responsibility Act. It would have required agency laws to be voted on quickly unless 20 percent of the members of either house called for a law to be referred to a committee. This threshold is the same as that required by the Constitution for a roll-call vote.[14] Noncontroversial laws would have sped through Congress, and controversial ones would have gotten plenary consideration. Either way, legislators would have had to take responsibility because they would have enacted the laws themselves rather than merely reviewing the EPA's work for gross error. The Republican leadership decided to block the bill from coming to a vote. Republicans, like Democrats, profit from delegation.

I am now suggesting a bill different from the Congressional Responsibility Act. It would be limited to lawmaking by the EPA, and all major rules would automatically be referred to committee.

Although such a statute would put the EPA out of the lawmaking business, the agency would still have important responsibilities in packaging information on the benefits and burdens of controlling pollution. Given all of the criticisms I have leveled at the EPA, why would I trust it with this important work? There is no shortage of dedicated and intelligent people in the agency. Its problem is that it gets impossible orders from Congress. Congress orders it to achieve environmental-protection goals that are so high that the public is sure to balk at the burdens. Congress has told it to regulate more things in more ways than it possibly can with the resources and time available. If Congress gave it more resources and time, the results would be even worse, because no one agency can handle so much complexity.

The problem, in short, is Congress rather than the EPA. Congress itself has gone through a learning process. It has made the Clean Air Act more realistic as time has gone by. Yet meanwhile it has piled new, equally impossible tasks on the EPA. The ultimate genesis of the problem is that we, the public, want a clean environment without the burdens of producing it. If it made the laws, Congress would have to tell us that it cannot be so.

A statute like the Congressional Responsibility Act would do wonders for reducing national control of pollution control. Once members of Congress found that they actually had to take responsibility for the laws imposed by the federal government, they would see the wisdom of the federal government's sticking to its proper role under the Constitution.

My proposal is limited to the EPA and pollution-control laws. Whether Congress should take more responsibility for the hard choices involved in running the national parks and forests is another question. Professor John Leshy thinks it should. Leshy, a former

NRDC colleague who went on to serve as solicitor of the U.S. Department of the Interior in the Clinton administration, deplores Congress's leaving these hard choices to agencies: "Congress is more directly accountable, and better able to resolve the tension between local and national interests, than unelected officials in the executive branch. . . . Congressional recapture is not without costs. . . . [Yet], our political tradition tells us that inefficiency in governmental decisionmaking is itself a positive value; it's an important reason why we've managed to survive for two hundred years."[15] Congress does sometimes take responsibility for important decisions about public lands, such as whether to allow drilling for oil in the Arctic National Wildlife Refuge. Environmental groups would be very upset if Congress left such decisions up to the presidentially appointed secretary of the interior. They should, as a matter of principle, also be upset that it leaves the making of pollution-control laws to a presidentially appointed EPA administrator.

Limited as they are to pollution control, my recommendations do not correct the violations of the principles of federalism and lawmaking by legislators that occur in other areas of government operations. I would have to call for correcting all such violations if my appeal were to a court, because courts are supposed to apply their principles across the board. My appeal is, however, to the people and their representatives, and they can take account of differences of degree. Although other federal agencies deal with matters on which the states are competent, the EPA goes much further than do other agencies. The activities of the Federal Communications Commission and the FDA, for example, are at their core appropriate to the federal government, but the core of the EPA's activities is essentially local. Although other federal agencies make laws, the EPA commands the largest regulatory apparatus, and, as the next part of the book will show, does great harm to all of us. As Senator Muskie wrote in 1973, "[f]ew other areas of public policy require the balancing of conflicting interests and the consideration of trade-offs in such agonizing detail, but that detail should not be an excuse for deferring to the courts or to the executive. Congress must define the extent of those substantive rights no matter how broad or how narrow they may be, for their economic, political, and social effects will be felt in every phase of national life."[16]

Members of Congress would have to find new ways of establishing their environmental credentials if they could no longer do so by telling the EPA and the states to make the hard choices. They might even be driven to face those environmental problems that they alone can solve. For example, Congress is uniquely placed to help cities deal with traffic congestion by requiring manufacturers to build into vehicles devices that cities could use to charge motorists automatically for using roads in congested areas. The equipment would add little to the cost of trucks and cars but make it much easier for localities to reduce the traffic jams that pollute, waste energy, and fray the nerves of drivers and city residents. Let us stop federal legislators from buying their environmental credentials with chump change.

Part IV

_____

What We Lose

CHAPTER SEVENTEEN

The Rights of Citizens

Leopold had a Jeffersonian faith in democracy: the only sure cure for
democracy's ills was still more democracy.
— CURT MEINE, *Aldo Leopold: His Life and Work*

On January 17, 2001, Carol Browner announced that she had decided
to adopt a new law lowering the limit on arsenic in public drinking-
water systems. It would become official the next month but would
give the water systems until 2006 to comply. Three days after her
announcement, George W. Bush took office and immediately put on
hold agency laws that had yet to become official so that his administration could reconsider them. Environmental groups charged that
he had killed the arsenic law in return for campaign contributions
from big mining and smelting companies. The press took up the
charge and ran with it. The arsenic law became the first and most
formidable count in an indictment of President Bush for ruining the
environment to satisfy corporate greed. Many months later, he and
his EPA administrator, Christine Todd Whitman, announced that
the drinking-water systems would have to comply with the arsenic
limit by 2006 after all.[1] A fuller telling of this story sheds light on
how the EPA's dominance subverts our rights as citizens.

Browner got the power to make the arsenic law from the Safe
Drinking Water Act of 1974. It instructed EPA administrators to set
nationally uniform limits on dangerous substances in drinking water. Arsenic can, of course, be dangerous. A stiff dose kills outright,

and smaller doses administered over time can cause heart attacks. In 1942 the Public Health Service proposed a limit of 50 parts per billion (ppb) but then suggested in 1962 that 10 ppb might be more appropriate. In 1974 the EPA issued a law limiting arsenic in drinking water to 50 ppb but promised to consider whether to lower the limit.[2]

The consideration the EPA promised took from 1974 to 2001. In 1986 Congress passed a statute requiring the agency to make up its mind by 1989. That deadline came and went. Another statute, this one passed in 1996, set a new deadline of January 1, 2001. That statute plus a lawsuit prompted the EPA to announce the new arsenic limit in January 2001. Today 5 percent of the U.S. population drinks water that exceeds the new limit of 10 ppb, mainly because arsenic occurs naturally in wells in much of New Mexico and in parts of other states.[3]

The EPA predicted that the new standard would prevent twenty-one to twenty-nine deaths from bladder and lung cancer per year. This prediction got full play in the press, but a few of the EPA's ninety-three thousand words of fine print in the *Federal Register* acknowledged the prediction's speculative nature. It was based principally on data showing that some poor rural villages in Taiwan where the average concentration of arsenic in the well water ranged from 300 to 600 ppb had abnormally high incidences of bladder and lung cancer. The agency had based its calculations on the assumption that the incidence of cancers at the lower levels of arsenic found in the United States would be linearly proportional to the incidence at the higher levels seen in Taiwan. In other words, exposure to water with 50 ppb of arsenic would cause a tenth as many cancers as did exposure to water with 500 ppb of arsenic. The fine print, to the EPA's credit, acknowledged a number of difficulties with its calculations. Many of the Taiwanese villagers studied were actually exposed to far more arsenic than the 300–600 ppb in their water because their food, unlike that in the United States, also contained substantial amounts of arsenic. Moreover, some of the villagers actually drank water with much more than 300–600 ppb arsenic. The Taiwanese study had masked these super-high exposures because it reported only the average level of arsenic in all of a village's wells. Taking this average as the actual exposure would exaggerate any conservatism in the linear proportionality hypothesis. In addition, the villagers had dietary deficiencies that made them susceptible to cancer.[4]

Representative Bernie Sanders, some of whose Vermont constituents drink water with naturally occurring arsenic, called in March 2001 for the EPA to set the limit at 3 ppb. The EPA's analysis predicted that a standard of 3 ppb rather than 10 ppb would save an additional eight to twenty lives per year. Moreover, a majority of the members of an NAS panel pointed out that we did not have hard data on whether arsenic causes cancers other than bladder and lung cancer.[5]

In contrast, many people in New Mexico wish the EPA had left the standard at 50 ppb. Leading newspapers in the state had reacted favorably in 1996 to Congress's imposing a deadline on the EPA but changed their tune when it became clear that the cost of removing the arsenic would fall mainly on the general public. Los Lunas, a village along the Rio Grande with a population of ten thousand whose municipal drinking water comes from wells with 12–19 ppb of arsenic, estimated it would have to spend $14 million to comply with the EPA's 10-ppb standard. The New Mexico papers pointed out that the state, which had the highest concentrations of arsenic in drinking water, had close to the lowest incidence of bladder cancer (forty-eighth out of fifty) and that a study had found no connection between cancer and arsenic in drinking water in the United States.[6]

Any decision on arsenic was thus bound to be controversial. No wonder the EPA could not put the issue to rest from early in the Ford administration, through those of Carter, Reagan, and the first Bush, until all but the last three days of the Clinton administration.

There is more to the story, but I will save it for later because in the making of most EPA laws the administrator's signature is the last step in the political process. Administrator Browner's signing of the arsenic law is thus the appropriate point at which to ask how law-making by the EPA affects our right as citizens to hold elected legis-lators responsible for the laws under which we must live.

Those who wanted the standard set at 3 ppb as well as those who wanted the standard left at 50 ppb could not blame any one legislator or group of legislators for the EPA's new arsenic law. In neither 1974, 1986, nor 1996 had Congress voted for 10 ppb. In 1996 it had directed the EPA administrator to pick the standard by going through a four-step process.[7]

1. *Decide how much of the substance is safe.* Browner decided, or rather assumed, that only 0 ppb is safe because there is no defini-tive evidence showing that any amount of arsenic is safe.[8]
2. *Decide how feasible it is to achieve this safe level with present technology.* She decided that the lowest level that could feasibly be attained was 3 ppb.[9]
3. *Estimate the benefits and costs of various limits on the substance.* She found that reducing arsenic from 50 ppb to 10 ppb would bring benefits valued at $170 million per year (as well as various unquantified benefits) at a cost of $210 million per year.[10]
4. *Make a law that places a nationally uniform limit on the substance.* She set the limit at 10 ppb.

Voters who wanted the limit set at 3 ppb could not blame legisla-tors because the statute did not stop her from setting it there and told her to protect health. Nor could voters who wanted the limit left at 50 ppb blame legislators because the statute had given the admin-istrator the opportunity to consider the costs. The legislators took responsibility for only two propositions—(1) health is important and (2) cost is important—and that took zero political courage. No wonder the statute passed by overwhelming margins.[11]

Even if legislators had in 1996 required the administrator to base the law on the cost-benefit analysis, they would have taken little responsibility. They could convincingly deny that they knew then how the administrator would later assess the costs and benefits. One reason is the uncertainty in the science on predicting the health benefits of a law. Another is that calculating benefits requires placing a dollar amount on the value of a life saved. (Browner chose $6.1 million.) Given these difficulties and others, Cass Sunstein estimates that the plausible estimates of the annual benefits of the arsenic law cover a large range (from $23 million to $650 million) and that a much broader range is conceivable (from $0 to $3.4 billion).[12] When Browner put her signature on the arsenic law on January 17, 2003, the legislators were off the hook.

When the representatives and senators evade responsibility by leaving the tough choices in the formulation of the laws to agencies, we lose a key part of our right as citizens to hold the legislators we elect accountable for the laws. Reflecting a view held by many scholars, Bernard W. Bell wrote, "widespread delegation of lawmaking power to unelected officials surely undermines democracy." Similarly, the editorial board of the *New York Times* has deplored "abrogation of responsibility by Congress" in the Line Item Veto Act and Congress allowing law to be made by "administrative fiat" under the Clean Air Act. The editorial board of the *Washington Post* told Congress to stop fobbing off the hard choices on environmental law. The same editorial board, in arguing that "ever since [Congress] passed the USA Patriot Act after the events of Sept. 11, 2001, Congress has stood by in an alarming silence while a fabric of new law governing the balance between liberty and security has been woven by the other two branches of government," pointed out that "it is a matter of grade-school civics that in American democracy laws are made by the legislative branch." Some academics, however, argue that delegation really does not undermine democracy because agencies are accountable to Congress and Congress is accountable to voters.[13] I shared this viewpoint when I was an environmental advocate. The bureaucrats do feel closely watched by Congress, and the legislators do feel impelled to respond to constituents' complaints. I now see, however, that I was thinking from the perspective of an insider who participates in generating the laws in Washington rather than that of a citizen whose only power comes from a vote at the next election. Such citizens can complain to their legislators all they want, but as a general rule they still have no effective means to hold anyone accountable at the polls for the laws made by the EPA.

The arsenic law is the exception that proves the rule. After President Bush took a beating on arsenic, the House of Representatives voted 218 to 189 against delaying the arsenic law, and the Senate joined in with a vote of 97 to 1. Legislators thus did take responsibility for the arsenic law, but this truly was an exception.

It is feasible for legislators to take responsibility for any law made by the EPA or other agencies. The Congressional Review Act (which the Republican leadership backed in 1996 partly as a riposte to the Congressional Responsibility Act) created a streamlined legislative process in which legislators *gave themselves the option of voting on laws made by agencies*. In contrast, the Congressional Responsibility Act, like the Constitution itself, would have *forced them to vote on all laws*. In the seven years that have elapsed since the passage of the Congressional Review Act, the Senate has invoked it to vote on agency laws only three times, and the House has invoked it only once.[14] Legislators took responsibility for the arsenic law because only one in twenty voters lives in areas that exceed the 10-ppb standard and therefore might face higher water or tax bills. Voting for the new limit let them strike a pose in favor of environmental protection at minimal political cost.

Legislators have many ways of responding, or at least seeming to respond, to constituents' complaints about the EPA's laws without taking responsibility for anything that would anger a significant number of voters back home. They write letters to the EPA, make speeches, hold hearings, or add riders to appropriations bills restricting the EPA's activities for the coming year. They also regularly write into the committee reports that accompany bills appropriating money for the EPA numerous "requirements" and directives that the EPA report quarterly on its progress in carrying them out.[15] These requirements lack the force of statute because legislators have not voted on them, but the EPA must take them seriously because they come from those who hold the purse strings.

Letters, speeches, and other techniques allow legislators to pick their issues and frame them in ways that will sell back home—concretely if their constituents are of one mind and abstractly if they are divided. In contrast, when legislators have to vote on real laws on the floor of Congress, the hard choices are thrust upon them and they must come down on one side or the other. Their votes, moreover, are recorded in the *Congressional Record,* easily accessible to challengers in the next election. Voters thus usually cannot pin responsibility for the laws on the legislators whom they elect, and they do not elect the EPA administrator, who does take personal responsibility for the laws.

Voters do elect the president who appoints the EPA administrator, but that gives them little control over environmental laws. The Framers did not structure the office of the president to stop lawmaking without representation, and the office of the president is even more unsuited to that task today. The two-term limit on the presidency put into the Constitution in 1951 means that many presidents can act with the certain knowledge that they will never again have to take responsibility at the polls. President Clinton was evidently not thinking much about public opinion when his EPA administrator promulgated the arsenic law; three days later he issued the infamous pardons scorned by friend and foe alike.

Even a president who intends to run for reelection has far less reason than does a legislator to be concerned about the voters' reaction to environmental laws made during the previous term. The president is judged on a much broader range of issues than are legislators (examples in President George W. Bush's case include his handling of September 11th and Iraq). If a law made by an EPA administrator becomes too much of a political liability, the president can disown it or get the administrator to take the blame. EPA administrator Whitman confessed that the arsenic matter was her "mistake entirely."[16] In contrast, legislators are stuck with the votes they cast. Presidents would actually be more accountable for environmental laws if Congress enacted them because then the president would have to take responsibility directly by either signing or vetoing the bill.

Although the courts require agencies to articulate the reasons behind their laws and review that reasoning, this activity does not, as I have argued elsewhere, produce better laws than would lawmaking by elected legislators. As Professor Joseph Sax wrote, "I know of no solid evidence to support the belief that requiring articulation, detailed findings or reasoned opinions enhances the integrity or propriety of administrative decisions. I think the emphasis on the redemptive quality of procedural reform is about nine parts myth and one part coconut oil."[17]

Although the citizens of Los Lunas cannot complain that the national legislators failed to take responsibility in the end for the arsenic law, they can complain that the national legislators should have left the question to the states. States have the power to limit arsenic in the water that comes from their taps, even if the water originates out of state. Although one might disagree with their decisions, they are not putting other states at risk. Leaving the regulation of chemical pollutants in drinking water to states or localities would do no harm to outsiders. There is no threat of contagion that could leap across state lines. Drinking water does not cause interstate pollution. Municipalities do not race to the bottom in drinking water. The water that residents provide for themselves is generally safe for visitors. In the case of arsenic, the EPA's conclusion that 50 ppb of arsenic will add 21 to 29 cancer deaths to the 550,000 cancer deaths that occur in the nation annually was based on drinking two liters of such water every day for seventy years.[18] Transients drinking water with 50 ppb arsenic are probably at much greater risk from being killed by a toppling vending machine while buying a soft drink.

Under my proposal, Congress would have been required to leave the arsenic law to states and localities, and the decision there should have been made by legislators.

The arsenic law shows why the foundational principle of a limited national government serves vital purposes in the modern world. The Framers wanted a limited national government in part because they thought that voters could more easily understand, control, and participate in governments that were closer to home.[19]

The citizens of Los Lunas, New Mexico, had a clearer grasp of the local arsenic issue than did citizens elsewhere. Newspapers in New Mexico framed the issue in terms of whether it made sense to require the citizens of the state to pay for removing the arsenic that nature had put in their drinking water. Newspapers elsewhere sometimes framed the issue in terms of whether the Bush administration had been paid off by corporations to shield them from cleaning up the arsenic they put in drinking water.[20] The citizens of Los Lunas had a better understanding of the stakes and a far more direct interest in them.

Even if the citizens of Los Lunas had accepted the EPA's analysis of the cancer risk, they might readily have concluded, if left to their own devices, that taking the arsenic out of the drinking water would actually make their town more dangerous. As a New Mexico newspaper pointed out, a new water-treatment plant requires heavy construction and heavy truck traffic.[21] The odds of a child being run over by a truck on its way to the new waterworks or a worker dying in a construction accident are small, but so are the odds of getting cancer from drinking water with 12–19 ppb of arsenic.

Moreover, according to Betty Behrend, Los Lunas's utilities and public works director, "The community need[ed] other things worse." She mentioned removing old septic systems that threaten water quality. Other municipalities might have spent the money to provide more school crossing guards or better ambulance equipment. No government, including the federal government, exhausts the possibilities for reducing risk. The village of Los Lunas surely would not have been considered rash if it had decided that the money would be better spent on improving the schools or avoiding a rise in water rates. According to Behrend, the rise in water rates likely to come from complying with the arsenic law meant that some homes were "going to go off the system back to their own [high arsenic] shallow wells. I think it's going to work in reverse." The author of an Op-Ed piece published in the *Washington Post* after the House and Senate had voted argued that the arsenic law would harm public health in many communities.[22]

Moreover, as Professor Marci Hamilton put it, "the smaller the polity in geography and in population, the easier it is for the people (1) to monitor what their government is doing, (2) to criticize or praise, and therefore (3) to affect public policy."[23]

Some of us want not only to affect public policy as voters but also to participate in its formulation. The desire to participate seems to be especially strong when the issue is environmental, as several studies have shown.[24] When Congress moves lawmaking from city halls and state houses to Washington, D.C., citizens find it much harder to participate. In smaller municipalities, getting involved takes no more than talking with friends and neighbors and, perhaps, a drive that can be measured in minutes to a meeting. Except in the largest municipalities and states, a local neighborhood association can get the extended, personal attention of its representative in the local or state legislature precisely because a little coterie of disgruntled neighbors can be a force to be reckoned with in the next election.

When, however, the EPA makes the laws, amateurs would do better to save their time rather than get involved. The participation that usually matters most is that by professionals, which means hiring lawyers, scientists, and lobbyists.

Ordinary people such as the citizens of Los Lunas can, of course, join a national organization that advocates for environmental quality, free enterprise, or some other cause. Members of such organizations pay dues and receive publications and pleas to send canned emails to the president or to members of Congress that boil down to "Get the carcinogens out of my faucet" or "EPA lies."

What the citizens of Los Lunas cannot do is join with neighbors to resolve the environmental problems in their own backyards. Even if they all agree on what should be done about arsenic in drinking water, they cannot deviate from the law decreed by the EPA—that is, unless Congress passes a special statute allowing them to do so and the chances of that are nil. That we know from the experience of some thirty citizens who regularly met at the Quincy, California, library to solve a long-deadlocked dispute about logging in their area. The group included local environmentalists, logging company executives, biologists, union representatives, and local government officials—but it managed to come up with a plan that got diverse support at the local level, including that of an Audubon Society chapter and a locally prominent environmental attorney. The U.S. Forest Service, however, was loathe to go along. The Quincy group asked Congress to enact a special statute requiring the Forest Service to implement the plan. The bill passed the House 429 to 1, which sent national environmental groups into action to defeat the bill in the Senate. The author of a column titled "Quincy Library Affair" in the *Washington Post* commented that "many local groups regard national organizations as more interested in protecting their turf than in achieving solutions that advance conservation." Senator Dianne Feinstein finally managed to get the bill passed despite opposition from fellow California senator Barbara Boxer. The Quincy bill squeaked through Congress because national environmental groups were slow to react, but according to Steve Evans, conservation director for Friends of the River in Sacramento, California, the next locally developed plan "that goes to Congress will be under full attack right out of the gate."[25]

The arsenic story shows that legislators in Congress leave the lawmaking to the EPA in order to protect themselves from accountability to us rather than to protect us from pollution. It also shows that they granted the EPA power over local environmental issues in order to increase their opportunities to claim credit rather than to increase our safety.

In short, legislators in Congress have cheated on the ground rules of our government of the people. When they cheat, we the people lose our rights as citizens and more, as the following chapters will show.

CHAPTER EIGHTEEN

The Boon of Liberty

Senator Muskie recognized in 1970 the importance of leaving states free to deal with air pollution in ways "most responsive to the nature of their air pollution problem and most responsive to their needs." Economic theory teaches that local knowledge is essential to efficiency. Experience teaches the same lesson. Witness the disaster of central planning in the Soviet Union. President Clinton and Vice President Gore promised to "reinvent government" in the belief that those closest to a problem can solve it better.[1]

Yet Congress often requires the EPA to impose a uniform standard on the entire nation, as in the case of the drinking-water standards, although the costs and benefits of such standards vary with the locale. The EPA estimated that the annual per-household cost of complying with the 10 ppb arsenic standard would average $327 for drinking-water systems that served fewer than a hundred households and only $0.86 for those serving more than a million households.[2] The benefits would depend on whether the arsenic level is slightly above 10 ppb, as in Los Lunas, or almost 50 ppb. Even when the EPA has leeway to take account of local conditions, it knows them less well than do those directly affected.

Congress has given the EPA too big a mandate to be discharged with intelligence. Because of the number of things it must regulate, the EPA necessarily deals with each environmental concern separately. The water office is, for example, split into four suboffices, which are further split into eight divisions, which are still further split into assorted branches, staffs, and task forces, each with specialized tasks. Such specialization means that in trying to solve one environmental problem the agency can exacerbate another. For example, by setting water pollution standards in terms of the concentration of pollutants in the discharge water, it gives factories an incentive to waste water because they can discharge larger absolute quantities of pollutants by diluting them with more water. For another example, air pollution regulation can increase the amount of pollutants disposed on land or in water. Ecology began with the understanding that everything is connected to everything else, but we have an environmental agency too large to see the connections.

Former EPA administrator William Ruckelshaus has argued that we would have smarter regulation if each source were controlled by a single team of regulators rather than by many teams, each with its own specialty. The Netherlands and New Zealand have adopted such integrated approaches, and Australia has done so for environmental problems of national significance.[3] The United States is, however, too large a country for such an integrated approach to work on the panoply of local as well as national environmental issues that Congress has put in the EPA's charge. The problem is, once again, Congress; it has set a national agency over state and local agencies that have the local knowledge needed to intelligently regulate local pollution.

We should also tap polluters' local knowledge. The EPA has, to its credit, carried out a study that proved this point. The study was of Amoco's Yorktown, Virginia, refinery. Regulators had set limits on the amount of pollution that could come out of each of its many smokestacks, pipes, and vents and, further, prescribed the methods to be used to achieve those limits. The researchers asked the refinery managers whether, if freed from these highly particular instructions, they could achieve similar environmental results more economically. The result, closely vetted by the EPA and state regulators and a team of peer reviewers assembled by Resources for the Future, was that the source could achieve "about 97 percent of the release reductions that regulatory and statutory programs require . . . for about 25 percent of today's costs for these programs. . . . These savings could be achieved if a facility-wide release reduction target existed [rather than separate limits for each smokestack, pipe, and vent], if statutes and regulations did not prescribe the methods to use, and if facility operators could determine the best approach to reach that target."[4]

The moral of this study is not that government should let those regulated do what they please, but rather that it should stick to controlling total emissions from a source and leave the rest to its operator. One way to do this is called "cap-and-trade." It is described by Resources for the Future president Paul Portney:

> each pollution source is given an initial emission limitation. It can elect to meet this limit any way it sees fit: rather than being required to install specific types of control technology, the source can reduce its pollution through energy conservation, product or process reformulation . . . , end-of-pipe pollution control, or any other means. Importantly, and not surprisingly, each source will elect to reduce its pollution using the least expensive approach available to it.
>
> More surprisingly, a source has one additional option under the cap-and-trade: it can elect to discharge *more* than it is required so long as it buys at least equivalent emissions reductions from one or more of the other sources of that pollutant. . . . Those sources that will elect to make significant emission reductions under this system are precisely those that can do so inexpensively. . . . Moreover, all sources have a continuing incentive to reduce their pollution—the more a source's emissions fall short of its limitations, the more emissions permits it will have to sell to other sources.[5]

Over the past quarter-century, academics have conducted many studies on whether such flexibility would reduce the cost of reducing pollution. The general opinion is that savings in the direct costs of pollution control could be massive.[6] Cap-and-trade and other market-based approaches cut costs by something like three-quarters.

Not only free market enthusiasts but also prominent liberal scholars have vigorously supported such flexible approaches, yet the rigid "command and control" approach predominates in air pollution control and has close to a monopoly in most other areas of pollution control.[7]

The EPA talks flexibility but generally practices rigidity. As recounted in chapter 14, its talk encouraged state commissioners to seek leeway to try flexible methods, but they were rebuffed in the end. The EPA has advertised programs that promise that it will give businesses and communities flexibility in how they meet environmental requirements if they can show they will use the flexibility to improve performance beyond existing standards, yet it does not make these programs widely available. According to a report from the National Academy of Public Administration, the paperwork required to qualify is so cumbersome that few businesses or communities find the programs worthwhile. The report concluded that EPA staffers were fundamentally hostile to giving up control. According to Commissioner Peder Larson of the Minnesota Pollution Control Board, corporations generally get involved "only because the chief executive officer is personally interested, not because there is any payoff for their bottom line." The EPA has implemented some schemes for emissions trading, but this was initially done under duress. Congress, with the support of the Environmental Defense Fund, built trading into the law controlling acid-rain emissions from power plants.[8]

EPA staffers have, according to scholar Robert Stavins, resisted

---

Hot Spots

With cap-and-trade, government controls the quantity of pollution that is emitted but not precisely where it is emitted. Environmentalists worry that this could result in emissions' concentrating in one area, thus producing a pollution "hot spot." Such hot spots are, according to a report by the National Research Council, possible but unlikely and have not been a regular result of previous cap-and-trade programs. The report recommends wider use of cap-and-trade, noting that there are ways of modifying such programs "to guard against even the possibility of" hot spots where they are a concern.[9]

---

market-based approaches in the past because their expertise is in command-and-control regulation and they do not want to cede power to those they regulate. There is a an exception. Congress's creation of the acid-rain program led to the establishment of a small staff within the EPA that did develop expertise in trading and this staff favors the broader use of trading. Yet, on the whole, the EPA remains a command-and-control agency. That control has grown more centralized because Congress has tightened the EPA's control over the states.[10]

Congress incorporated trading into the acid-rain program because legislators were responsible for the costs and so did what they could to get them down. In general, however, they avoid responsibility for the costs by leaving the lawmaking to the EPA. If legislators made the laws themselves, they would insist on more cost-saving flexibility. Leaving more environmental problems to state and local legislators would also encourage finding the least burdensome way of achieving environmental goals—if for no other reason, state and local legislators want to avoid imposing unnecessarily expensive regulations that would drive employers into competing jurisdictions.

For some environmentalists, the unnecessary burdens that the EPA places on companies such as Amoco are a matter of indifference; some even find them welcome—a fit way to spank the polluting plutocrats in the board room. Let us see, however, who actually gets spanked. Suppose for the sake of discussion that EPA-style pollution control adds $40 to the cost of making and delivering a refrigerator and that more flexibility would save $15. Imposing $15 of unnecessary costs is a bizarre way to punish environmental damage. The money is not paid to the government as a penalty or a tax but rather is spent on using resources, all of which are scarce and many of which are nonrenewable. That compounds the environmental damage. Besides, another consequence of hiking the cost of reducing pollution is that we will reduce it less.

The refrigerator makers pay out this wasted $15 for pollution reduction at their own factories or those of their suppliers, but all of us pay in the end. Economics 101 teaches that much of the waste will be passed along to consumers in the form of higher prices, *if* the unnecessary costs are spread more or less evenly among the firms. The rest of the waste will fall chiefly on the firms' employees, suppliers, and members of the general public who own stock directly or indirectly through mutual funds and pension plans. Government loses, too, as costs rise and the revenues from income taxes go down.[11] Very little of the $15 loss falls on the top corporate managers who are the ones who deserve punishment according to the environmental demonology. With profits down a little bit per refrigerator, there will be a slightly smaller pot available for their salaries and stock options, but more important in determining their compensation is how the corporation performed relative to its competitors and all competitors are similarly affected.

Pollution-control costs that fall more heavily on some competitors are a different matter. An order requiring one refrigerator manufacturer, say GE, to clean up toxic wastes such as PCBs in the Hudson falls on it alone and will come largely out of its bottom line. Similarly, a law requiring that air or water pollution be controlled in a way that imposes peculiarly heavy costs on one firm, but not its competitors, will also cut significantly into the bottom line. Corporate managers fight hard to avoid such laws, but not laws that inflict costs evenly among corporations, even if they believe science shows that the costs are unnecessary to protect the environment. GE's managers assiduously fought dredging the Hudson but not the EPA's banning future use of PCBs by all firms, even though they believed the EPA had the science wrong in both cases.

Managers of many large corporations prefer that the environmental laws be made by the EPA rather than the states individually, as the Environmental Law Institute points out.[12] One reason is that the EPA is more likely to spread the costs evenly. The wasted pollution control costs are not a problem to them personally.

How much does this waste cost us? The EPA estimated in 1990 that pollution control then cost $115 billion per year, or approximately $1,850 per family per year. The numbers are probably larger now, but the EPA has stopped compiling data on the total cost of pollution control.[13] Suppose that the EPA were to estimate the present cost per family at $2,000. Most people would agree that a healthy environment is worth that much but would surely prefer to get it for less. The studies on flexible methods of environmental protection suggest that they could ideally cut the cost significantly. A cut of three-quarters would bring savings of $1,500 per family per year. Flexible methods would not work ideally, and shifting the making of environmental law from the EPA to the legislators in Congress and their state and local counterparts would lead only part of the way to those flexible methods, but a chunk of a wasted $1,500 would nonetheless be meaningful.

This savings is only a small part of the gain that we as a society would realize. Here is why: the EPA's estimate of the cost of pollution control includes only the expenses involved in installing and operating pollution-control equipment. These *direct* costs, however, produce far greater *indirect* costs. One reason is that the direct costs raise prices and consume resources capital that would otherwise be invested to make the economy more productive. The ripple effects over the long haul are large and negative. Economists Michael Hazilla and Raymond Kopp showed in a much-cited paper that although the EPA estimated that the direct cost of implementing the Clean Air Act and the Clean Water Act in 1990 was $78.6 billion, taking the indirect effects into account raised the total cost to $203 billion, or 6 percent of production in the U.S. Several other studies also published in peer-reviewed journals show that pollution control has significantly slowed growth in productivity and that the negative consequences accumulate. Other indirect costs result from the expense of pollution controls exacerbating the distortions that taxes cause in labor and capital markets. According to a committee of economists that the EPA appointed to its Science Advisory Board, these "tax-interactions can cause social costs to exceed direct costs by at least 25 percent, and in some cases by 100 percent or more." The committee went on to point out that the EPA's effort to minimize the tax-interaction effect "lacks balance" and "gives readers [an] erroneous impression."[14]

These ripple effects *do not* mean that environmental protection is a bad deal for society. Environmental protection produces large direct benefits and also indirect benefits. What the ripple effects *do* mean is that the waste of direct costs of pollution control inherent in the EPA's inflexible command-and-control approach gets amplified through the various indirect costs. This waste lowers the incomes we receive and raises the prices and taxes we pay. We do not know the size of the impact, but we do know it is large. Thus, although environmental protection is a good deal for society, it could be a much better deal.[15]

It is worth pausing to review the route that has led us to get a worse deal than we should have gotten. It starts with legislators in Congress bending the ground rules of our republic to claim credit and shift blame. The upshot is a system that denies flexibility to states, localities, and sources. What is wrongly denied is not the license to harm others but the right to choose the least onerous way to avoid doing so. This denial of flexibility restricts our ability to pursue happiness. In sum, because legislators shirk responsibility, we lose liberty.

CHAPTER NINETEEN

The Appeal of Law

"A deep chesty bawl echoes from rimrock to rimrock, rolls down the mountain, and fades into the far blackness of the night."[1] Thus begins one of Aldo Leopold's gems. The essay harks back to his time as a young Forest Service officer in the southwestern United States. Out in the wild, he and his colleagues spotted a wolf and her gamboling cubs. "In those days we had never heard of passing up a chance to kill a wolf." They fired. "We reached the old wolf in time to watch a fierce green fire dying in her eyes. I realized then, and have known ever since, that there was something new to me in those eyes—something known only to her and to the mountain. I was young then, and full of trigger-itch; I thought that because fewer wolves meant more deer, that no wolves would mean hunters' paradise. But after seeing the green fire die, I sensed that neither the wolf nor the mountain agreed with such a view."[2]

The essay, "Thinking Like a Mountain," shows how the pursuit of a hunters' paradise led to a hunters' hell. Hunters killed off the wolves, and the deer multiplied, stripped the mountains of foliage, and starved. The essay's message—"understand nature"—seems commonplace today but was new in 1947, when the essay was written, and new to me in 1970, when I first read it.[3]

The essay got crowded out of my mind by the clutter of law practice and teaching but came back with a jolt on a visit to the Yale Law School twenty years later. In 1989 the alma mater gathered to her bosom graduates who had helped launch modern environmental law. We were awarded medals and invited to give talks. Some spoke of where environmental law was today, and others of the path it had traveled, but John Bonine spoke of what had started us on the way. "Thinking Like a Mountain" was his refrain. To conclude his talk, he pushed a button on a little box and suddenly the howl of a wolf bawled forth from powerful speakers and echoed through the classrooms where long ago we had heard modulated discourses on contracts and torts.

Most of us had gone to law school without any thought of becoming environmental lawyers. "Environmental law" had yet to enter the legal lexicon, let alone to be included in the list of courses offered in New Haven. We had been called to the law in general, not to environmental law in particular. It turned out, however, that together the call of the law and the call of the wild held an attraction greater than either did alone.

David Sive understood why. Sive graduated from the Columbia Law School in 1948 and went to work in a corporate law firm in Manhattan. Out of personal interest, he took on a few cases to defend the environment. His success had generated an environmental practice long before my peers and I had graduated from law school. When the field of environmental law gained recognition around 1970, David was its senior statesman. He was a founding trustee of the NRDC and one of its wisest counselors.

Back in the 1970s he was often asked to explain this new field. Usually implicit in the requests, especially when they came from persons of means, was the question, "Is this environmental law of yours going to disrupt my way of life?" I heard David answer so many times that I can almost hear him now. In a quiet, measured voice, he would define first "environment" and then "law." His point was that the environment is society's home and the law is society's official way of stopping harmful conduct. "Environmental law" was not something that would be done to society but rather what society, acting through its government, would do to protect its home from harm. Environmental law would be safe because law is safe.

Sive was drawing upon the comforting tradition of the rule of law. The source of the comfort is a collective memory of what common law aspired to be—rules proscribing conduct that society deems unjust. That is, as Oliver Wendell Holmes put it, "the first requirement of a sound body of law."[4]

The common-law system was structured to serve this noble aspiration. Judges were to have no stake in the outcomes of cases. They were required to ground their decisions in precedent, whose ultimate source was custom. They were to announce the law in specific controversies. They were to demand that the plaintiff explain why the court must act and hear the defendant on the difficulties posed. The law was rooted in society's vision of justice rather than that of the judge. It was crafted case by case rather than in sweeping generalizations that would apply to people not present and situations not yet imagined and would inevitably cause unanticipated difficulties.[5]

Common-law judges, of course, sometimes fell short of these ideals. Yet the common law's mistakes could be corrected by laws made in the legislature. That was acceptable in the rule-of-law tradition because a law made by elected legislators also reflects the values of society.[6]

The "law" in environmental law was critical to the field's climb to respectability, but environmental law today is not the rule of law. The statutes with which Congress empowered the EPA in the early 1970s told the agency to disregard society's customs, and indeed to change them. The goals were protection from unhealthy air pollution by the end of the 1970s and complete elimination of water pollution by 1985.[7] Thirty years later, we have yet to achieve these ideals. The EPA is nothing like either a common-law court charged with enforcing society's binding customs or a court charged with enforcing the laws of a legislature accountable to society. It does not resemble the agencies that Congress created in the era before 1970 to make laws in "the public interest" or other formulas based on society's values. The EPA's mandate was to force society to change its values, not to enforce those values.

The disjuncture between the type of environmental law that was launched in 1970 and the law that came before it went unnoticed in 1970 because the new environmental law was, as I have already noted, thought to follow in the footsteps of civil rights law. In retrospect, however, it is clear that modern environmental law is not justified by civil rights law. While both movements had idealistic goals for changing society, the civil rights movement ultimately fit squarely within the legal tradition. The environmental movement does not. After the Supreme Court, in *Brown v. Board of Education,* declared school segregation unconstitutional and the southern states shamefully balked, Congress passed real laws—real rules of conduct written into the statutes themselves—forbidding government from discriminating. Society at the national level had told one of its noncomplying segments to cut it out. Congress had the power to impose the national will on state and local governments because the Fourteenth Amendment to the U.S. Constitution authorized Congress to make laws to enforce constitutional rights. In contrast, in the environmental area, Congress left most of the lawmaking to the EPA and never seriously considered which environmental issues were the proper business of the federal government.[8]

Society did need to change how it dealt with the environment, but Aldo Leopold would have started with persuasion. Society had already been changing and making laws to match. Pollution had been slowly coming under control, as we now know, from the beginning of the twentieth century. The spirit of 1970, however, demanded faster change. As our protest chants went:

> What do we want?
> [insert the ideal of the day]
> When do we want it?
> Now!

An ideal such as perfectly healthy air by a deadline becomes real only when enforceable laws require people to reduce pollution to the required extent. It turned out that no one in public office was willing to back the EPA by taking the kinds of actions needed to achieve that ideal.

Yet Congress had made achieving such ideals the right of every citizen. It is no good saying there is time enough for Congress to face the hard choices after the ideal is a legal right. Once government grants a right, such as to healthy air, those who hold it dear feel entitled to it and will fight even harder to keep it than they would have fought to get it in the first place. By turning ideals into rights, Congress evades the Constitution's procedural checks on making rash laws, but those checks come fully into play if one wants to revise rash laws made by the EPA. And once Congress legislates a new ideal, a coterie of interest groups grows up to defend it.

The upshot is that the EPA as Congress has instituted it necessarily perverts the rule of law. Whereas the rule of law seeks to proscribe conduct that society deems unjust, the EPA's laws are based on whatever expediently serves its statutorily mandated goals. Whereas common-law judges have no stake in how they define the law, the EPA does have a stake because the stricter the environmental goals, the greater its power. Whereas common-law judges are forced to consider practical consequences because they make the law case by case in the context of concrete facts presented by those directly affected, the EPA makes laws applicable to society at large.[9] Should the EPA hesitate to pursue its statutorily mandated goals, a citizen can haul it into court and get an order forcing it to proceed.

In areas other than environmental law, Congress and agencies also announce laws that apply generally rather than case by case, but with the EPA there is a difference. When Congress makes law, legislators must consider the consequences for the public or suffer personal consequences themselves because they are responsible. When agencies before the EPA made laws, they were told to consider practicalities. The EPA was told to give short shrift to practicalities.[10]

Congress is also disingenuous. Legislators would react with a vengeance if the EPA failed to take practicality into account, but it must do so secretly or at least on the sly because Congress has decreed that it is wrong, or at least dubious, to compromise environmental ideals. Thus miseducated, a majority of the public opposes compromise in protecting health from pollution.[11] The public would not have such a naïve perspective if Congress regularly and openly engaged in such compromise. The legislators would then have to explain to the voters why this was the best way to achieve agreed-upon environmental ideals.

Making it a secret that practicality counts turns public discussions of environmental issues into stale cartoons that insult everyone's intelligence. In the case of arsenic, environmentalists charged President Bush with killing the EPA law in return for campaign contributions from the mining and smelting industries. His defenders countered that the environmentalists were lying—that he had not killed the arsenic law but had ordered its reconsideration, along with all agency laws issued in the last days of his predecessor's administration, just as President Clinton had done when he took office, and that a great fuss was being made about a few months of reconsideration while no fuss was made about the Clinton administration's having let the arsenic regulation linger for eight years. Because it is officially suspect to talk in the open about striking a pragmatic balance between risk and cost, public discussion thus focuses on questions of motive: Was President Bush bought by industry? Are his opponents using the arsenic question to posture? In the end, the debate, as Cass Sunstein describes it, turned on questions of motive and the simplistic perception that arsenic is a poison.[12] Sunstein laments that there was so little focus on the various factors that ought to go into a pragmatic compromise.

When debate comes to focus on motive, it gets nasty. Environmental politics are generally nasty. As one professor of environmental law put it, "Since almost immediately after [Congress started passing the modern environmental statutes] in the early 1970s, two extreme and opposing philosophies—one devoted to protecting the economy and the other to protecting the environment—have waged a war of annihilation that has left in its wake the mish-mash of laws, regulations, judicial opinions, and countless administrative decisions and policies that we today call environmental law. Any notion that the remnant heap of rules represents a reasoned 'middle ground' of political deliberation is utterly naive." The problem, he concludes, is that public discussion of environmental issues "is framed by two opposing philosophies [with] a vacuum in the middle and, frankly, I am sick of it."[13] Me too.

Such polarization and nastiness are to be expected with abortion, a topic on which public opinion is sharply divided. But public opinion on the environment is not. The overwhelming majority of voters say they support environmental protection and, if probed about specific situations, concede that practicality must play a part. Differences, of course, remain about the weight to give practicality, yet environmental politics feels like a religious war. The question is: Why does the environmental debate lack a strong middle that overshadows the zealots on either extreme?[14]

The problem of zealous or selfish interests trying to hijack public policy was anticipated by the Framers of the Constitution. Their solution was to have the law made by a *congress* of all the interests in society.[15] In Congress, the lawmakers would look to the interests of the middle as well as those of the extremes. Speaking for the whole of society, Congress could bring peace.

Legislators today do not want to do this job. It requires them to take heat. So they refer the zealous and selfish factions to the EPA. The EPA, however, cannot produce a durable peace. It is not a credible umpire because it is alternately (depending on who is in office) accused of being aligned with one side or the other and is always accused of self-aggrandizement.

The issue in Congress then becomes the terms—such as the extent to which considerations of cost might temper the drive to protect health—on which to refer the hard choices to the EPA. It is at this abstract level that polarizing rhetoric can grow most poisonous. In contrast, in dealing with concrete choices in local contexts, it is harder to posture. While national politicians fought bitterly on environmental issues in 2003, voters in sixteen states passed 64 of 77 local and state measures to raise money for parks and open space. Since 1999, voters have approved 643 such measures at a total cost of $22.9 billion. The conservative Republican who led the drive for one such measure in the Denver area explained its approval: "This is the kind of thing that we could find common ground on, because this issue is in our neighborhoods."[16]

The proposals in this book would help to give environmental law the virtues of common law. Laws would tend to be in accord with the values of society because they would be made by legislators who would be held accountable at the polls. Having to take responsibility for environmental laws, members of Congress would lose their stake in growing the power of the national government. Their interventions would likely take the form of specific fixes such as the law they enacted to limit emissions from new cars. Further congressional interventions would likely be limited to specific industries or even a specific industry in a specific region.[17] Such lawmaking would tend to replicate additional virtues of the common law. It would be evolutionary rather than cataclysmic, based on real rather than imagined facts, and cost sensitive rather than feigning to be cost ignorant. Indeed, with more latitude at the state level, states might find that some of the work of environmental law could best be done by the common law itself.[18]

It is time to put the law back into environmental law.

CHAPTER TWENTY

The Joy of Doing

When we left Dan Wilson and Susan Knapp back in chapter 1, it was summer 1998, and they were worried that well-intentioned laws from the FDA and the EPA would drive them out of their orchard. Their experience with the FDA made me see EPA regulation in a new light, but I am getting ahead of the story.

The FDA had gotten involved two years earlier, after *E. coli* contamination in bottled fruit juice had sickened many people and killed an infant. The juice was produced by Odwalla, a large West Coast company, but the FDA began to consider regulating all producers of fruit juices, down to small apple-cider makers like Dan and Susan.

E. coli can get into cider because deer and mice are among the bacterium's carriers, and they have a taste for apples. One response is to pasteurize the juice, which also brings the commercial benefit of a longer shelf life. Odwalla had, however, taken pride in not pasteurizing; it advertised its products as tasting better because they were organic and only minimally processed.[1] After the *E. coli* incident, it installed equipment that pasteurizes by heating and then recooling the juice in such a flash that the taste is not much affected.

The Apple Processors Association, which is dominated by large companies, urged the FDA to require that all juice be pasteurized. That would have been ruinous for many small cider producers. Flash-pasteurizers then cost upwards of $70,000. Budget pasteurizers cost $25,000, but they were prone to cooking the taste out of cider and required extra employees to operate. Higher costs and cider that tasted like canned apple juice spelled bankruptcy for Dan and Susan. Not so for the members of the Apple Processors Association. They already pasteurized, and they stood to pick up market share from small producers driven out of business.

In 1997 the FDA proposed issuing a law requiring that juice be put through a sanitizing process that in one step would cut *E. coli* levels by a factor of at least a hundred thousand. That meant pasteurization. While pondering this proposal, the FDA actually promulgated another law that the Apple Processors Association wanted: any unpasteurized juice must carry a label with the warning "This product has not been pasteurized and, therefore, may contain harmful bacteria which can cause serious illness in children, the elderly, and persons with weakened immune systems."[2] This was in summer 1998, three days before Dan and Susan's wedding.

During that fall's cider season, Dan and Susan heard from many customers at the cider barn that they would no longer buy cider if it were pasteurized. They liked the fresh taste of unpasteurized cider and were unconcerned about *E. coli*, since they and their forebears had been drinking cider from this orchard for more than a century without apparent incident. (So, too, do Europeans like the taste of real Brie, Camembert, and other young cheeses made from unpasteurized milk. They accept the small risk from *E. coli* and other pathogens that has prompted the FDA to allow only inferior, pasteurized substitutes into the United States.[3]) Other customers, who bought the cider at a few supermarkets in a nearby city, did not know the orchard and its family. These stores stopped carrying Dan and Susan's cider.

Going with other orchard owners to a training session conducted by Cornell University's Cooperative Extension the following winter, Dan was in a somber mood, but he met someone who gave him hope. Phillip Hartman, a fifty-two-year-old engineer, was displaying the prototype of a machine that he claimed would sanitize cider without hurting the taste yet could be sold for $12,000 and required no extra employees to operate. That was his promise, but he also made clear that he could not yet deliver on it. He had no approval from the FDA and did not even have a company to build the machines. His full-time job was as an engineer with a company in the computer industry. A colleague at work with a friend in the same predicament as Dan and Susan had asked Phil to brainstorm over lunch about using ultraviolet light to sanitize cider. Ultraviolet is sometimes used to sanitize water, but the cloudiness of cider prevents the light from penetrating deeply. That is where Hartman came in. His engineering specialty is creating the thin films on computer wafer board. Hartman and his colleague hit upon a way to make the cider run by the light source in a film so thin—30/1,000 of an inch—that the ultraviolet could sanitize every last drop.[4]

By fall 1997, Hartman had an ultraviolet device ready for bench testing but needed a biologist to confirm that it really killed the *E. coli*. Dr. Randy Worobo, who had just joined the faculty of Cornell University's Agricultural Experimental Station, agreed to help. Scientists in Worobo's position get many requests for help, most of which they must turn down, but he did test the device and found that it cut the bacteria by a factor of a hundred thousand. Hartman then built this device into the prototype that he brought to the training session.[5]

Although Hartman still had many hurdles to overcome, the orchard owners got the sense that, as Dan put it, "this guy would do everything he could to make things right." The opinion that counted most was that of Russell French, a distributor of orchard equipment.

Hartman had to have a distributor because he could not both manufacture and sell. French agreed to do the selling. He was running a risk. If the machines failed to work or if the FDA refused to sanction them, he would alienate his customers and might even face lawsuits from them or, worse still, from people who got sick from drinking cider. Hartman quit his job and set up a company that would make cider-sanitizing machines.[6]

Dan and Susan placed one of the first orders, thus linking their future to Hartman's ability to deliver machines that worked and satisfied the FDA. Their machine arrived in time for the 1999 cider season, but some of the early machines had glitches. Hartman would get phone calls from orchard owners desperate because a balky machine stood between a barn full of perishable apples and customers with cash. Hartman would respond by getting into his van and driving through the night from his home in western New York to orchards as far away as Vermont, Virginia, and Michigan. Driving was the only option. A paraplegic, he cannot negotiate an airport with his wheelchair, tools, and spare parts.

Fixing the glitches proved to be easier than winning regulatory approval. One hurdle was the FDA's law requiring that cider be pasteurized or labeled as dangerous. Because Hartman's machines did not literally pasteurize, the cider they processed arguably had to carry the warning label even though the machines achieved the one-hundred-thousand-fold reduction in E. coli required by the FDA's other law, which it ultimately promulgated.[7] Professor Worobo supplied data to back up Hartman's claims and offered to test and certify each ultraviolet device at no charge. Nonetheless, the makers of pasteurizers told cider producers that Hartman's machine was not approved by the FDA, which temporized, not making a final decision until 2001. Meanwhile, many cider producers, fearful of spending $12,000 on a machine that might not be approved, bought pasteurizers or went out of business.

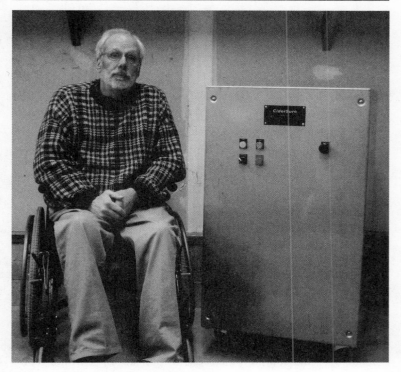

8. Philip Hartman and his cider machine, 2003.

New York regulators told the state's cider producers that they should consider themselves in compliance if they used Hartman's UV machine. According to the state's chief food-safety regulator, Joseph Corby, "We told the cider producers, 'we license you and we approve Hartman's machine. The FDA has no reasonable basis to withhold its approval and, if it does, there will be a battle.' As a result, we got a lot of nasty calls from pasteurizer manufacturers."[8] According to Worobo, "Usually, the FDA acts first and the state agencies follow, but some state regulators stuck their necks out this time because lots of local businesses were in trouble. These little businesses were beneath the notice of the FDA."

Joe Corby's solicitude for New York cider makers saved dozens of them from being driven out of business. From 1997 to 2000, the period in which the FDA laws were driving producers out of business elsewhere, the number of cider producers in New York increased. In contrast, in Vermont, just a few miles away from Dan and Susan's orchard, fully 60 percent of the cider producers ceased operation during the same period. Overall, in the states like New York that supported sanitizing by ultraviolet, the number of producers declined by a scant 1 percent while in the states that took a hands-off position, leaving matters to the FDA, the number of producers declined by 38 percent.[9]

Hartman ran into a less obvious but more ominous regulatory hitch. The FDA had long had a law that limited the exposure of food to ultraviolet light, not because it had any evidence that the light was dangerous, but because it lacked definitive evidence that the light was safe. This law included an exception for a company whose machine used higher levels of ultraviolet than did Hartman's, but the exception did not cover his. FDA officials told him that if he were to emulate the other company's successful application, he would get his exception. He did as he was told, but a year later the FDA wrote to tell him that his application could not be considered without more information. It also warned that, until he got an exception, it would shut down any cider maker found to be using his machine. His customers, now friends, would be out of business.[10]

Hartman decided he needed a lawyer and found one who had once worked for the FDA. The lawyer asked for a $10,000 retainer, which Hartman took from his savings. The lawyer filed a new application. Eventually called to a meeting at FDA headquarters, a hopeful Hartman drove to Washington, D.C., only to have an official read him a prepared statement that his new application was faulty. He was told, however, that Naked Juice, then like Odwalla a major West Coast brand, had filed its own application to use ultraviolet light on fruit juice. (Naked Juice is now owned by Chiquita Brands and Odwalla by Coca Cola.) FDA officials advised Hartman not to reapply again because that would delay the Naked Juice application, whose approval would cover him as well.

The FDA did approve the Naked Juice application on November 29, 2000, but in a form that failed to cover Hartman's original machines. The Naked Juice machine ran a thick but turbulent stream of cider by a much higher dose of ultraviolet. The amendment to the FDA law permitted the use of an unlimited amount of ultraviolet on juice provided there was a turbulent flow.[11] This proviso was bizarre. It had nothing to do with protecting the public from any danger from ultraviolet—the point of the FDA's law on ultraviolet—but it excluded Hartman's machines, even though they used a lower dose of ultraviolet because they relied on a thin rather than a turbulent flow to comply with the FDA law on *E. coli*.

Fortunately for the cider makers who bought Hartman's original machines, he had a way of retrofitting them to meet the FDA proviso and drove hither and yon to install it. He remained bothered, however, by the FDA's action. The agency had put him through the regulatory wringer on the theory that ultraviolet might be dangerous but in the end put no limit on ultraviolet exposure. It required a particular technique (turbulent flow) rather than a good outcome (safe cider), thereby limiting the ways in which he might use his expertise in thin-film technology to produce a still better machine. The FDA's procedural rules did, however, give him recourse: to file a formal objection. That he did with Worobo's help.[12] It was lucid and well documented. The FDA never responded.

Hartman makes his machines with the help of his niece and three other young part-time employees in rented space in someone else's factory. His office is in his home. The 120 machines he has sold have nearly saturated the market. He does not know what he is going to do next, but when he quit his job to start this business he knew his income would be lower and less secure. Is he glad that he did it? "Oh hell yes. I have enjoyed myself immensely. I enjoy the cider makers. I enjoy the traveling. I enjoy the young people."

For Randy Worobo, too, it is all about enjoyment. In helping Hartman, he ran risks. Not only did he divert time from more conventional academic work, but he also made enemies who could have been dangerous to an untenured professor. As he recalls, "On Good Friday in 1999 two salesmen from a pasteurizing machine company came into my office and screamed and hollered at me for four hours. They said they didn't like competing with Cornell." Why did he do it? "Phil Hartman is a brilliant engineer, and I enjoy working with him. I also feel compassion for the cider makers. I am from a farming background myself. I know what it was like when my parents got screwed. Someone from another background wouldn't have had the compassion." He enjoyed the work and also enjoyed helping Phil Hartman and the farmers do what they enjoy.

I had never thought about environmental law from the perspective of those regulated until I witnessed the apple-cider odyssey. As an environmental activist, my focus had been on getting the government to protect health. Complaints from business about the difficulties involved in compliance mattered to me chiefly as obstacles to my goal. The actual costs often turned out to be less than business predicted. Refiners, for example, predicted that reducing lead in gasoline would raise gas prices much more than it actually did. I thought businesses habitually lied about the costs, which was enough for me to stop taking their complaints seriously.

Complying with the FDA's requirements turned out to be much less difficult than Dan and Susan had predicted, but not because they had lied. I had thought that businesses lied because I had assumed that calculating compliance costs involved little more than adding up the expenses involved in buying and operating readily available pollution-control equipment. But, as I learned from Dan and Susan as well as a half dozen friends from the environmental movement who now work for industry, compliance often requires inventing new equipment; changing processes, which can have consequences that are difficult to foresee; and guessing what regulators will demand in practice. The cost of eliminating a given quantity of pollution is sometimes less than business predicts but is about as often more than the EPA predicts.[13]

Dan and Susan wanted health protected, but in a way that gave them the best life. Before the *E. coli* outbreak, they had culled the fruit in the orchard to get rid of any that was nibbled or damaged, culled it again at the cider barn, and washed it before putting it in the press. Parents do no more in feeding apples they pick to their own children. The FDA itself now finds such techniques an acceptable alternative to pasteurization for orange juice.[14] But apples are different from oranges, and Dan and Susan are very glad to have purchased Hartman's machine. It gives them peace of mind. But the FDA could have protected the public to the same degree—with less harm to those regulated—had it not suggested for a long while that the reduction in *E. coli* had to be achieved through pasteurization, not required that the reduction be done in one step, or not specified how to achieve that one-step reduction with ultraviolet. By seeing regulation from Dan and Susan's perspective, my focus shifted from *whether government protects us* to *whether it protects us while doing the least harm possible, including not killing the joy of doing.*

Many people want to pursue such joy by running a small business. A majority (56 percent) of Americans dream of starting their own business and another 10 percent have already done so. Among their reasons, "doing something you love" far outweighs "being your own boss" or "get[ting] rich."[15]

The EPA, as constituted by Congress, sometimes unnecessarily kills joy. One reason is that the agency unnecessarily limits the flexibility of state and local governments and pollution sources, and that ends up harming all of us, as chapter 18 showed. But there are other reasons too and they are illustrated by Dan and Susan's experience with the EPA under the Food Quality Protection Act.

The act commands the EPA to issue laws ensuring that pesticide residues in food are limited to safe levels. Safe food is, of course, essential, but as the reader knows by now, there is no clear answer to the question "How safe is safe enough?" when it comes to chemicals that in extreme doses cause cancer in laboratory animals. To get the statute passed, high officials at the EPA and the White House told farm organizations that the act would codify existing agency practice and the organizations reciprocated by supporting it. For example, a coalition of farm organizations wrote a letter to Senator Lugar stating, "While we had concerns initially with some provisions in the bill, the diligent work by the Committee and assurances from EPA and USDA that the new higher standard of protection will be interpreted with common sense and reason have reassured us that this is meaningful change." Not long after the statute was passed, the EPA staff implementing it went off in a different direction, threatening a quick ban of many pesticides on which farmers relied. That was why the leaders of the American Farm Bureau Federation were so upset at their meeting in 1998, as recounted in chapter 1. As William O'Connor, majority staff director of the House Agriculture Committee, later commented, "The act went from reform to nightmare very quickly. I would never again write a bill that depends so much on implementation."[16]

The EPA has so far issued no law that leaves Dan and Susan without the means to control some critical pest, but it is considering banning some chemicals for which they now have no substitutes. Feeling threatened, Dan wanted to find out what the EPA was thinking. He spent hours on the EPA's Web site trying to fathom his future but came away more confused than enlightened. He then called the EPA's telephone help line, but found that the employees who answered could not help. "I got the impression that their computer screens showed the same materials as mine and they knew less than I did."

Dan and Susan have of course thought of going organic, but that is plainly impossible for them. "We have many friends who are organic farmers," Dan reports, "but they grow annual crops that can be rotated. Apple trees are banks of diseases that compound over time unless stopped. Doing so organically is easier in the drier climates out west or in a tiny orchard, but our orchard is here and we have diseases such as scab that makes the fruit unmarketable and can even defoliate a tree. To deal with it organically would take fourteen sprayings a season to achieve only 60 to 70 percent control. Without synthetic sprays, thinning the fruit would have to be done by hand, and that would be some job on eighty acres." His conclusion: "I would spend twice as much time and fuel spraying to get a crop reduced in quantity and perhaps in quality too." To make up the cost and time, Dan and Susan would have to charge more, but theirs has been a U-pick orchard catering to local customers since 1905. These customers would not pay the premium. "Our customers are not far removed from the farm and don't have a knee jerk reaction to pesticides." Lois Swirsky Gold would approve. Meanwhile, he and Cornell are jointly experimenting with protocols using newer, softer chemicals on several test blocks in his orchard. "I am trying to learn enough to survive when the crunch comes from EPA."

Reflecting on the experience, Dan wrote: "I guess if I could characterize my outlook to the whole process, it would be variations on the theme of resignation. I am frustrated sometimes by what seems to be the EPA's monumental lack of understanding about the complexities that are inherent in running a little farm like ours. But I can't find the muster to add much energy to this fight. I can't do everything else I need to do in a day with the weight of concern about the EPA on my shoulders. In some ways, this controversy makes my relationship with the farm easier; if I am out of control of my farm destiny, then I should be investing my energy more in family, friends and a future that might grow away from this place. My love moves elsewhere and the farm becomes in my mind just a business."

Dan's point, that the EPA does not understand the complexities of running his little farm, is critical. All farming, like all politics, is local. Apple farmers in northeastern New York face different challenges from corn farmers in New York or apple farmers in Oregon. Dan and Susan's orchard is even different from apple orchards in nearby towns. Each has its own pests, many pesticides are pest specific, and in spraying, timing is all. To apply the right chemicals at the right time, Dan must sometimes ride his tractor from before dawn until midnight. The EPA staffers in Washington fail to understand the complexities of Dan's farming problems not because they do not care, but because one agency regulating so many diverse actors simply cannot comprehend them all.

Nor can small businesses readily understand what the EPA expects of them. Even specialists have trouble understanding it. Donald Elliott wrote in 1998 that "a decade ago I used to argue with my tax colleagues [on the Yale Law School faculty] about whether tax law or environmental law was more complicated. They gave up long ago." Writing of the time when he, as EPA general counsel, was being briefed by four of the attorneys on his staff about "new proposals implementing section 304(l) of the Clean Water Act," he recalls, "As an academic . . . , I quite naturally asked if what they were telling me about section 304(l) fit together with what I had heard the day before about section 304(m). There was a momentary hesitation followed by an uneasy silence in the room as they looked from one to another. Finally, one of them said, we're the section 304(l) team; if you want to know about section 304(m) you'll have to call in another lawyer in the office." A recent *New York Times* editorial rightly called the Clean Air Act a "regulatory maze."[17]

Environmental law is this complex because of Congress. Congress gives instructions to the EPA on how it should make its laws and more instructions on how it should instruct the states on how they should make and administer their laws. All this is very important but is still just the foreplay before the making of the actual laws—the rules of conduct. None of the foreplay would be necessary if all of the environmental laws came from legislatures. If most of these laws came from the state or local level, most sources would be faced with a set of laws that is far smaller and far less abstract than the national environmental battle plan.

This complexity makes it practically impossible to be in full compliance with environmental laws. As an EPA publication pointed out, "A regulated hazardous waste handler must do hundreds of things correctly to fully comply with the regulations, yet doing only one thing wrong makes the handler a violator." And almost every violator is potentially a criminal. As an environmental-law treatise acknowledges, "It is virtually impossible for a major company (or government facility) to be in complete compliance with all regulatory requirements. [And yet] virtually every instance of noncompliance can be readily translated into a [criminal] violation." When asked to explain why there is so much noncompliance with environmental laws, more than half of the environmental attorneys surveyed identified the following factors as "important" or "very important": "sheer number of regulations" (90 percent), "complexity of regulations" (80 percent), "too many different and conflicting requirements" (75 percent), "keeping track of changes in regulations" (74 percent), "size of business operation" (72 percent), "ambiguity of regulations" (71 percent), and "agencies relying on informal guidance" (53 percent).

Only 38 percent identified "costs of compliance." A Resources for the Future study found that "The existing pollution control system has become so disjointed and cumbersome that no one can understand or make sense of it. A few law firms may benefit, but the situation undermines both compliance and public support."[18]

The upshot is that even the well intentioned can get severely punished. Take the case of Precision Plating of Akron, Ohio, a chrome-plating company with two employees. "In 1997, it installed pollution control equipment at a cost of $50,000. However, the company relied on the installer to inform it of the regulatory requirements, and failed to obtain the proper inspections and permits. . . . EPA fined the company $108,000 (later reduced to $30,000) for the paperwork delinquency, even though no actual pollution had occurred. Precision paid the fine by tapping cash reserves set aside to pay for additional pollution control equipment." Former NRDC colleagues who now work on compliance for corporations tell me that the EPA often metes out heavy fines for technical violations. The statutes allow the EPA to seek in court "a civil penalty of not more than $25,000 *per day for each violation*." Alternatively, the EPA itself may assess "a civil administrative penalty of up to $25,000 per day of violation," provided that the total penalty does not exceed $200,000. Civil penalties can be assessed even though the violation was innocent and did no harm, as in the case of Precision Plating.[19]

Innocent or not, violators get hit because state and federal environmental enforcers are under pressure to rack up high numbers of prosecutions and penalties in order to avoid budget cuts. The term within the EPA for this pressure is "bean counting." To ensure his office got credit for all the beans racked up that year, one EPA regional counsel sent his staff an email entitled "REMEMBER THAT IT AIN'T A BEAN 'TILL IT'S BEEN COUNTED!" Professor Shelley Metzenbaum, a former Clinton-era EPA official (and daughter of the liberal former senator) urges enforcers to refocus their attention—from bean counting to improving environmental quality.[20]

Precision Plating could have been criminally prosecuted. To secure a felony conviction under environmental statutes, the federal government must show that the accused acted "knowingly," but the EPA has successfully fought for an interpretation under which prosecutors need show only that the accused knew he was operating a plant emitting a pollutant rather than that he knew he was doing so illegally. That is why nearly every violation can conceivably be punished criminally. Most are not. According to an experienced defense lawyer, "Most agencies treat innocuous [violations] as civil administrative matters, as they should. Nevertheless, the apparent corporate indifference to the ongoing problems, a perception that the discharger is attempting to cover up the violations, or even a perceived disrespect for environmental values (often meaning a lack of respect for environmental investigators), can change that reasonable agency attitude. The monumental difference between paying a fine in the context of civil litigation and going to jail is the consequence of subjective perceptions of government employees." The upshot, according to a prominent environmental advocate, is that people get "incarcerated in the absence of violation of certain traditional norms of moral culpability."[21]

The difficulty of understanding the EPA's environmental laws and coping with the enforcement actions that follow falls much more heavily on farmers and small firms such as Precision Plating than on giant firms. The giants have in-house environmental staffs and outside lawyers, often hired away from the EPA and national environmental organizations. Even firms of medium size cannot afford such legal overhead, but a firm operating one large plant must decode almost as much regulatory complexity as a large corporation running fifty. It is difficult enough to raise the money to begin or expand a smallish business without the delay and uncertainty in securing permits and the risk of unwittingly stepping on regulatory land mines. As Phil Hartman's experience with the FDA illustrates, a regulatory problem that would have been a minor irritation to a big firm can topple a start-up.

Smaller firms are also at a disadvantage in meeting the EPA's paperwork requirements. To get a sense of the scope of the work involved in securing permits and filing reports, consider EPA administrator Carol Browner's announcement in 1995 that the agency had made changes in paperwork requirements in that year that would save businesses and state and local governments fifteen million hours of unnecessary paperwork annually and would make further changes the next year that would save an additional eight million hours annually.[22] Rooting out twenty-three million hours wasted on paperwork every year is commendable. Because most such paperwork is done by engineers, lawyers, and other professionals, its cost is large. Browner said nothing about why the EPA had imposed these superfluous requirements in the first place or about how many millions of hours of paperwork would still be required. Paperwork is the inevitable result of a chain of command, and a chain of command that stretches back to Washington is going to require much more paper than would a shorter one.

Smaller firms are put at a competitive disadvantage in still another way by environmental policy being made in Washington rather than closer to home. Smaller firms and farmers cannot, of course, afford to have their own representatives in Washington. At best, they can join trade associations that try to represent their interests, but such associations are usually outclassed by the lobbying operations run by the largest firms and by national environmental organizations. The largest firms use their sophisticated lobbyists to seek laws that put competitors at a disadvantage. For instance, big refiners pushed for a law requiring the elimination of all lead from gasoline in the early 1980s. They did this in order to give themselves an edge over small refiners. As many scholars have documented, firms use environmental law to restrict the entry of competitors and subject them to higher costs as well as to increase the public's demand for their product and restrict its supply. No wonder that, when the EPA announces new regulatory initiatives, the stock prices of established firms sometimes go up.[23]

A final way that the EPA puts smaller firms at a competitive disadvantage is by imposing tougher requirements on new plants. This slows the rate at which newer, more efficient plants replace older, highly polluting ones. The blame here, as in so much else, belongs to Congress. It reasons that it is cheaper for new plants to install pollution controls at the start than for old plants to retrofit, so new plants should meet higher standards. But this cost differential could be taken into account without stacking the deck against new plants. The same limits could be imposed on all plants, but plants could be allowed to buy and sell emission rights. Among the supporters of such an approach is Byron Swift of the Environmental Law Institute, who calls for establishing "uniform standards [for] old and new plants," permitting trading of emission rights, and allowing "business flexibility to choose different compliance approaches." The owners of older plants would object, of course, that buying emission rights from a squeaky-clean new plant would cut into profits, perhaps even making their plants unprofitable. Quite right, but now we know what we are talking about: protecting entrenched companies from competition. In those limited instances where the EPA or Congress has allowed the buying and selling of pollution rights, they have required that new plants not only meet tougher standards than old plants but also buy pollution rights from them, thus doubly disadvantaging new plants.[24]

Protectionist legislation is not the exclusive province of the federal government. State and local legislatures engage in it, too. Yet the danger is greater at the national level. An old plant might get its home state to protect it, but not other states that seek to attract new businesses. The Clean Air Act, however, mandated tougher standards for new plants throughout the nation precisely in order to suppress interstate competition. The primary support came from rust-belt legislators who wanted to make it difficult for local firms to relocate. Close analysis of their voting behavior shows they cared more about protecting their constituents from economic loss than protecting them from pollution.[25]

This chapter has discussed a series of ways that the EPA puts smaller firms at a disadvantage: a legal system that they cannot understand or predict, punishments that seem to come out of the blue, paperwork that they do not have the staff to handle, and tougher regulatory requirements, especially on new plants. The impacts are real. A study that scholars did for the Small Business Association found that the annual cost *per employee* of complying with environmental laws is $717 for firms with more than five hundred employees and $3,328 for firms with fewer than twenty employees.[26]

Based on his empirical research, Peter Pashigian found that "compliance with environmental laws . . . has placed a greater burden on small than on large plants. Small plants have found it more difficult to compete and survive with larger plants under environmental regulation. . . . The evidence suggest that environmental regulation not only terminated but reversed the erosion of the larger plants' market share due to the entry and success of small plants."[27] The burdens on smaller firms would be lighter if the law were made by legislators and mostly at the state or local level.

Why should those of us who do not run small firms care about the burdens of complying with environmental law that are superfluous to achieving environmental quality? Many major corporations and their chief executives, attorneys, and lobbyists do not care. The chief executives are shielded from smaller competitors but can pass the legal, paperwork, and lobbying expenses along to the public, just as they pass along the costs of pollution-control equipment. Their environmental attorneys and lobbyists worked hard to gain specialized knowledge in the ways of the EPA. So long as it makes environmental laws, they can command premium salaries.[28]

But the average citizen loses. In discouraging smaller firms, the EPA attacks the growth buds of our economy. When they lose, we lose with them. These losses come on top of the waste embedded in the EPA's inflexibility, which is embedded in the direct $2,000 or so per family cost of buying and operating pollution-control equipment. That direct cost does not include the costs of legal work, paperwork, and economic growth forgone.[29] For example, when a new plant goes unbuilt, there is no direct pollution-control cost, but society nonetheless loses the benefits of a more efficient, productive capital structure. The result again is lower incomes and higher prices and taxes.

On another plane altogether, the EPA's heavy hand takes joy away from people who want to run their own businesses. The EPA is a killjoy to Dan Wilson and Susan Knapp and the operators of other small farms and businesses. Others are driven into working for big businesses, which are equipped to deal with the regulatory complexity. But it is not just in smaller businesses that the joy of doing is lost. Consider Bruce Adler, who did administrative work in the NRDC's Washington office in the early 1970s, got a law degree, and went on to the EPA and then to General Electric. Here is how he reacted to my statement that big corporations do not care about the EPA's heavy hand: "Umm . . . just not true. Everything we do in large corporations is dedicated to finding ways to do things faster, cheaper, and smarter. We cannot just turn that culture off and say, 'It's OK, we'll pass these costs on,' especially when we see the requirements as roadblocks to producing a product that is better or less expensive for the customer."

How would my proposals change things for Dan and Susan? Assuming principles like I propose for the EPA applied also to the FDA, it would not regulate cider that was locally distributed. The laws on such locally distributed produce would come from state or local legislatures.

Pesticides are, in contrast, nationally distributed and Congress has reasonably decided that the federal government should vet them for safety before they can be distributed. Whether to permit manufacturers to distribute them, however, necessarily encompasses control of how farmers apply them. As the toxicological wisdom goes, the poison is in the dose and the dose depends on the manner of application. While my proposals would not reduce federal power, they would require Congress to take more responsibility. Its Food Quality Protection Act told the EPA to permit no pesticide unless there is "reasonable certainty of no harm."[30] The term "reasonable" is, of course, elastic, and the EPA used that elasticity to change its criteria for approving pesticides after the statute was passed. Congress needs to take responsibility for the hard choices.

CHAPTER TWENTY-ONE

Conclusion
Spaceship Earth without a Captain

> Of all tyrannies a tyranny sincerely exercised for the good of its victims
> may be the most oppressive. It may be better to live under robber barons
> than under omnipotent moral busybodies. The robber baron's cruelty may
> sometimes sleep, his cupidity may at some point be satiated; but those who
> torment us for our own good will torment us without end for they do so
> with the approval of their own conscience. They may be more likely to go
> to Heaven yet at the same time likelier to make a Hell of earth. This very
> kindness stings with intolerable insult. To be "cured" against one's will and
> cured of states which we may not regard as disease is to be put on a level of
> those who have not yet reached the age of reason or those who never will; to
> be classed with infants, imbeciles, and domestic animals.
>
> —C. S. LEWIS, "The Humanitarian Theory of Punishment"

The managers of the Kaiser's forests decided in the late 1700s that the
scientific way to produce saleable lumber was to replace the natural
chaos with trees of the same species and age planted in rows. With
trees lined up like soldiers on a parade ground, the managers could
see everything worth seeing and control everything worth controlling, or so they thought.

This "scientific forestry," as it was called, spread through Europe
and to the United States. Within Germany itself, the scientific approach spread from the forestry department to other departments.
Department heads were expected to hand down rigorously specified
procedures for underlings to follow. German scientific administra-

tion inspired imitators throughout Europe and in the United States, where the national class pressed for putting power in the hands of expert national agencies.

Scientific forestry had won over the German leaders by increasing the take from timber sales. Although it yielded more in cash for them to spend, it yielded less of what the peasants used—dead branches for their hearths, wild mushrooms for their pots, rare herbs for their folk medicines, and all the other gifts that experience had taught them to take from ancient woods. For the leaders, the virtue of the supposedly scientific method was that it kept its focus on the main thing—revenue. The rest meant little to them. Yet, it came out in time—the long time it took two rotations of trees to grow—that scientific forestry's monoculture methods were slowly destroying the little things in the soil that were essential to producing the big thing they did care about. By then, however, scientific administration had become the vogue in many fields of government in many countries.

James C. Scott, a professor of political science and anthropology at Yale, thinks the failure of monoculture forestry typifies a surprisingly broad array of other modern failures, including Stalinist collective farms, the compulsory "modernization" of villages in some developing countries, and the corporatist control of markets that J. P. Morgan and John Rockefeller sought through national agencies. The similarity is that in all of these cases, elite leaders imposed binding plans based on the false assumption that they could comprehend nature, and human nature, in their full complexity. Their plans attempted to reduce reality to the simplified terms in which they saw the world. In his book *Seeing Like a State* Scott argues that the results are equally pernicious whether elite planners seek to engineer nature or human society. For example, Le Corbusier and his followers built new cities and massive public-housing projects that failed because they overlooked the local networks that glue neighborhoods together, as Jane Jacobs pointed out in *The Death and Life of Great American Cities.*[1]

Too often, Scott argues, elite planners systemically overrate what they know and underrate the importance of the local knowledge and know-how of the people whose lives they want to direct. Scott has no quarrel with science, bureaucracies, or planning as such. His quarrel is with those bureaucratic planners who co-opt the legitimacy of science to say that they know better. He calls theirs the "high-modernist ideology."[2]

In 1970 Congress cast the EPA in the high-modernist mold. There is no wonder in this. High modernism was then the fashion in Washington, D.C. It seemed to be the only solution for the pollution problem as it was perceived. Science was required to understand the pollution that imperiled Spaceship Earth and devise a solution. The solution had to come from Washington, D.C., rather than state capitals and city halls because pollution has no respect for boundaries. Besides, these lower levels of government had failed, or so Congress said.

Congress and the president thus set up the EPA administrator to captain the American compartment of Spaceship Earth. Now, thirty-four years later, under the aegis of a single administrator, the EPA's system of plans, protocols, and permits controls millions of activities—industrial, commercial, agricultural, governmental, and residential. It is high modernism in action.

Yet the EPA failed to work as promised. It did not even come close to producing healthy air by the end of the 1970s. The problem was not any shortage of dedication or intelligence in the EPA staff but that the premises upon which Congress and the president had built the EPA were either false from the start or became false in time.

One such premise was that pollution laws had to be imposed from some entity insulated from the political foibles of legislative politics and state and local government. Yet in retrospect we know that these supposedly flawed institutions made the hard choices that produced the most dramatic reductions in air pollution. The EPA failed to react promptly to lead in gasoline and many other threats because, when faced with intense controversy, it often curls up like a frightened caterpillar. On new cars, acid rain, and toxic air pollutants, the key choices came from Congress. Today voters strongly support pollution control and that support gets well-organized expression.

Another premise was that the EPA would base its pollution-control laws on science. It turns out, however, that science cannot tell the EPA what laws to issue. As lead in gasoline again illustrates, the science is full of uncertainties and, in any event, does not answer the questions of priority that are an inevitable part of making laws. The EPA's decisions thus reflect politics as well as science. Indeed, no EPA administrator has been a hard scientist, and most have been lawyers. Yet because its legitimacy is premised on its speaking in the name of science, it carries on a "science charade," in which it covers its political tracks by exaggerating the certainty of science. The result, as Lois Swirsky Gold's work reveals, is distorted policy and a misinformed public. The EPA's handling of PCBs in the Hudson River is a case in point. The choice is not whether environmental laws will be based on science or politics, but whether the lawyers and other politicians who make the laws will be accountable to voters.

While empowering the EPA in 1970 was understandable, and was indeed a decision I cheered at the time, experience has shown that we can now control pollution without the phony scientism, awkward centralization, and unwarranted elitism of high-modernist ideology. To do so, our elected representatives need to take seriously two central principles of our republic: (1) that government should be as close to home as possible and (2) that laws should be made by elected legislators.

To bring environmental governance as close to home as possible, but no closer, Congress should leave pollution control to state gov-

ernments unless the states would inflict significant harm on outsiders, as when, for example, (a) pollution sources do much of their
harm out of state and states fail to control them adequately, (b)
pollution sources harm our great national parks or other federal
properties with special pollution-control needs and states fail to
control the pollution adequately, or (c) state-by-state regulation
would place significant barriers in the way of interstate travel or
trade. State governments should similarly leave the making of most
pollution-control laws to local governments unless the latter lack
institutional competence. Under these guidelines, the federal government could participate in international solutions to international
pollution problems.

As to the laws being made by elected legislators, legislators at
every level should take responsibility for the environmental benefits
they promise and the costs they impose by making the laws themselves. For example, when Congress decides that a federal law is
needed, the federal legislators should enact it themselves, rather than
assigning that task to the officials of a federal administrative agency
or a lower level of government.

As a result, the EPA would be limited to (a) gathering information on pollution, its effects, and options for its control; (b) making
this information public; (c) proposing laws to Congress on pollution problems appropriate to federal control, along with assessments
of their advantages and disadvantages; and (d) enforcing the laws
made by Congress. State and local pollution-control agencies should
(a) consider the EPA's information along with their own, (b) provide
their legislatures with proposed laws and assessments of their advantages and disadvantages, and (c) enforce their laws. The result would
be a *revolutionary* change in how we make environmental law, both
in transferring power back to state and local governments and in
pinning responsibility for the laws on the "lawmakers" who are
accountable at the polls.

A Revolutionary Change

The radical scope of the change required is illustrated by the consequences for the regulation of air pollution. To control pollution sources that do much of their harm out of state and are inadequately controlled by states, Congress could continue its laws to limit acid-rain emissions from power plants and gases that harm stratospheric ozone. It should also enact a "golden rule" of interstate pollution. To the extent this golden rule of interstate cooperation fails to abate remaining problems, and in order to control pollution sources that harm our great national parks and are inadequately controlled by states, Congress should adopt laws tailored to the regions and sources that cause the problems. To supplant state-by-state regulation that would put significant barriers in the way of interstate travel or trade in goods, Congress could, if it judged necessary, regulate emissions from new vehicles or fuels.

Congress has already made some of these laws itself. For example, the 1990 Clean Air Act provides the basic law for regulating emissions from acid-rain-producing power plants and new cars, light trucks, and buses. But Congress authorized the EPA to strengthen the laws for these vehicles and make new ones for other sorts of vehicles.[3] Such laws and their amendments should go through Congress.

Much of the rest of the Clean Air Act would have to go. In particular, the EPA could no longer issue air quality standards (at least not in a form that bound anyone), require states to adopt plans to implement these standards or prevent deterioration of air quality, control sources through permits, or regulate hazardous pollutants. The objectives behind these programs are laudable but would generally be objectives for states and localities to pursue. Congress should step in to control only that small minority of sources that should not be left to the states. States and localities do, of course, already have laws seeking to achieve these objectives. The difference would be that states and their subdivisions could change their laws in light of experience and the wishes of their voters rather than marching strictly under federal orders.

There would be similar radical changes in other areas of federal environmental law. The federal government would exit entirely from some areas of regulation, such as drinking-water safety. It would exit almost entirely from many other areas, such as the cleaning up of abandoned hazardous waste sites, the regulation of underground storage tanks, and the storage and disposal of hazardous waste. In these areas of regulation, it would be the very rare source that would do much of its harm out of state and could not be controlled adequately by state officials. A golden rule of interstate pollution and interstate cooperation might well allow courts to deal with most of the remaining problems of interstate pollution under these programs. Transportation of hazardous waste is another matter. Wastes from one state can be illegally dumped in another. The federal government should have a system tailored to stop such dumping. Water pollution would be handled analogously to air pollution.

Such a radical change seems implausible, at least at first blush. The EPA system suits the best-organized interests in Washington, D.C. It minimizes responsibility for legislators in Congress, empowers the president, and is congenial to the leaders of national environmental groups and many large corporations.

Yet before 1970 the creation of anything like the EPA we have today seemed implausible because the powerhouses in Washington were thought likely to line up against it. What brought this change was that a significant fraction of voters came to believe that action was needed. Should a significant fraction of voters come to understand that there is a better way to deal with pollution, change would again be possible. Polling data shows that most people believe that Washington, D.C., has taken too much power over environmental policy from states and localities. The *New York Times* and the *Washington Post*, as chapter 17 observed, call for Congress to stop fobbing the hard choices off on the executive, at least on some issues. While many people believe in government's staying as close as possible to home and legislators' having to take responsibility for laws, this belief is far from universal. It is stronger the farther one gets from places like Washington, D.C., or New York. It is more apt to be found in farmers, small-business people, and physicians than in lawyers and policy analysts.[4] I have written this book in the hope of convincing people that we all are harmed by the gross deviation from these principles in controlling pollution.

Even with a shift in public opinion, a significant change in environmental law requires overcoming the inertia built into our legislative process. That inertia is reinforced by the many interest groups that have come to depend on the EPA as it is. What broke the logjam in 1970 was Earth Day and a competition for the environmental mantle among presidential aspirants. The future could bring other kinds of logjam breakers. Our environmental statutes are so detailed that they cannot go for long without revision. Indeed, President Bush, the NAS, and the *New York Times* all want to revise the Clean Air Act. Such a revision must itself overcome legislative inertia and so would be vulnerable to a demand by a significant number of legislators that Congress take responsibility for environmental laws —in particular, that any new pollution-control statute require that *all* new federal environmental laws be enacted by Congress.[5]

There is precedent for Congress's recognizing that it needs to take responsibility for the hard choices in environmental law. Bureaucratic paralysis on new cars led Congress to make law in 1970. Bureaucratic paralysis on acid rain and hazardous air pollutants led Congress to take responsibility on these subjects in 1990. The demand would be that Congress now take responsibility for federal environmental law systematically and as a matter of principle.

It is difficult to predict how such a legislative clash would play out. One possibility is a compromise in which legislative responsibility for pollution law would come piecemeal. Another possibility is that a Democratic president would come out for reform. A Democratic president would have credibility in asserting that legislative responsibility would improve environmental regulation law, while a Republican president would be accused of subverting it. Whether a Democratic president would support reform is another question, but politicians often gain politically by acting contrary to stereotype. It took a Republican president, Richard Nixon, to establish the EPA, pass the Clean Air Act of 1970, and recognize China. A Democratic president who pushed Congress to accept responsibility for environmental laws would rightly receive respect for transforming the pollution issue from a partisan club to a bipartisan search for balance.

Once federal legislators had that responsibility, regulating local environmental matters would lose much of its charm for them.

Those in Washington, D.C., who are likely to line up against the demand for democracy might in the end find reasons to go along. The legislators have an interest in avoiding responsibility for the laws, but those now in office could take credit for upholding democracy in the present, but leave the votes on the more controversial laws until later. The president has an interest in being able to change environmental laws by the fiat of an appointee, but could avoid the unfair blame that comes when Congress orders that appointee to make laws to achieve irreconcilable objectives. Large corporations have an interest in maintaining EPA regulation as a buffer against new competitors and action by legislators at all levels of government and in the one-stop shopping afforded by the federal government, but could benefit from the more vibrant economy that would come with the end of the centralized planning that Congress requires the EPA to impose.

Finally, national environmental groups have an interest in maintaining the EPA's power because it is the vehicle through which they presently exercise their own power. Yet the environmental cause would, on balance, do well in federal, state, and local legislatures, as discussed in chapters 14 and 16. Indeed, aggressive legislative action worries many large corporations. The real problem for national environmental groups is institutional rather than environmental. They, like some large corporations, want the one-stop shopping afforded by central control. Yet they could adapt and even be strengthened, as has been the ACLU, by sharing power and money with state and local counterparts, as discussed in chapter 14. The payoffs would be gains for the environment and an increase in the civility of environmental public debate, as discussed in chapter 19.

Although the environmental movement could adapt to a more decentralized and accountable process for making environmental laws, there would still be a line of resistance that went like this: "Let legislatures at every level pass any environmental protection laws they wish, but keep EPA-made laws as a floor beneath which environmental quality cannot fall. We should not subject nature to peril when all we have to gain is more greedy consumption."

The choice we have, however, is not between nature and greed. The high-modernist method of protecting nature is itself an affront to nature. Jane Jacobs, having shown the baneful effects of modernist methods of city planning, has now turned her attention to modernist methods of environmental protection. She believes strongly in environmental protection, but argues that tightly centralized methods of achieving it are self-defeating because "human beings exist wholly within nature as part of natural order in every respect." She cautions against policy makers who believe that "reason, knowledge, and determination make it possible for human beings to circumvent and outdo the natural order."[6] Their hubris hurts us all. We lose democracy and home rule, as the arsenic example showed. We lose the flexibility to find the least onerous ways of not harming others— that is, liberty. We lose justice because environmental law as applied has lost its connection to society's sense of right and wrong. We lose the "joy of doing," as illustrated by the regulatory sagas of Dan Wilson and Susan Knapp. In sum, nature deserves reverence, but so do many other values squashed by the high-modernist methods of protecting it.

There is also no shame in caring about the economic losses caused by high-modernist environmental protection. A recently published book, *You Can't Eat GNP*,[7] argues that seeming increases in GNP from saving pollution-control costs are an arid abstraction and really no savings at all when they come at the expense of spoiling the earth. I agree. But there are savings in eliminating our unnecessarily undemocratic, centralized, inflexible, unjust, and joy-killing way of protecting the environment and you *can* eat them. The savings would, moreover, strengthen the case for more environmental protection.

The argument for keeping the EPA administrator as captain is that humans are by nature too selfish and shortsighted to take care of themselves, future generations, and the earth. The high-modernist idea that ordinary people will fail to see the big picture and so must be put under the tutelage of masterminds was the basis for the argument, prevalent in elite circles before World War II, that authoritarian regimes would beat democracies in battle. George Orwell rightly replied, "One has to belong to the intelligentsia to believe things like that: no ordinary man could be such a fool." History is full of environmental disasters, but to ascribe them to lack of concern is often anachronistic. Historians who are careful to avoid imputing to our ancestors our environmental knowledge and worldly wealth observe that "human beings have been interested in the quality of the environment for almost as long as there are written records available. Men and women have long deemed it their responsibility to tend to the environment and the world about them." For example, "medieval people were driven to create an environment as clean and healthy as their technology, priorities and civilization permitted."[8] It is no anomaly that much of the environmental progress during the twentieth century came from the bottom up rather than the top down.

We should not even try to avoid relying on ordinary people in the urgent business of safeguarding the earth, argued Aldo Leopold. Having called the German way of planting trees "cubistic forestry," Leopold would have instantly grasped what Scott means by "seeing like a state." Leopold argued that the state alone could not handle the biggest environmental issue of his day—the loss of diversity in flora and fauna—because government lacked the capacity to manage all the land where the diversity was being lost. "[G]overnment, no matter how good, can only do certain things. . . . [W]hen we lay conservation in the lap of government, it will always do the things it can, even though they are not the things that most need doing. . . . Therefore government neglects the superior things that need doing, and does the inferior things that it can do. It then imputes to these things an importance and an efficacy they do not merit, thus distorting the growth of public intelligence." He wanted "conservation . . . to grow from the bottom up, instead of from the top down, as is now the case."[9]

Leopold sought to put responsibility for environmental policy on the same foundation on which the Framers of the Constitution (many of whom were devoted naturalists) sought to place all the laws and policies of the United States—on the people. The Framers aimed to base our laws on popular support by requiring that they be made by elected legislators, and usually by legislators far closer to home than Washington, D.C. Such laws would not be deductions from rational cogitation, but rather would emerge from the wilderness of passions and ambitions that is the political process. They would reflect human nature and therefore not square perfectly with anyone's preconceptions. No one could guarantee that they would be good enough. To that concern Aldo Leopold provided the answer: "We all strive for safety, prosperity, comfort, long life, and dullness. The deer strives with his supple legs, the cowman with trap and poison, the statesman with pen, the most of us with machines, votes, and dollars. . . . A measure of success in this is all well enough, and perhaps is a requisite to objective thinking, but too much safety seems to yield only danger in the long run. Perhaps this is behind Thoreau's dictum: In wildness is the salvation of the world. Perhaps this is the hidden meaning in the howl of the wolf, long known among mountains, but seldom perceived among men."[10]

Congress built an environmental protection system that promises us more safety than the EPA has delivered or can ever hope to deliver. The legislators designed the system so that they could claim maximum credit and take minimum responsibility. If we could make them rebuild the system to suit our needs rather than their ambitions, we would have a better world.

Notes

Chapter 1. Introduction

1. 63 *Federal Register* 37,030 (1998). For cider regulation, see chapter 20.

2. Pub. L. No. 104-170, 110 Stat. 1489 (1996) (codified as amended at 7 U.S.C. § 136 et seq.). The act is discussed in chapter 20.

3. See David Schoenbrod, *Power without Responsibility: How Congress Abuses the People through Delegation* (New Haven: Yale University Press, 1993), at ch. 10 (hereafter cited as *Power without Responsibility*).

4. See, e.g., *Friends of the Earth v. Carey,* 552 F.2d 25 (2d Cir. 1977), application denied, *Beame v. Friends of the Earth,* 434 U.S. 1310, 1311–12 (1977), certiorari denied, *Beame v. Friends of the Earth,* 434 U.S. 902 (1977).

5. *The Oxford English Dictionary,* vol. 8 (2nd ed.; Oxford: Clarendon, 1989), at 711–16.

6. Rachel Carson, *Silent Spring* (Boston: Houghton Mifflin, 1962) (hereinafter cited as *Silent Spring*). *Clean Air Act of 1963,* Pub. L. No. 88-206, 77 Stat. 392 (1963). For state legislation, see Mary Graham, *The Morning after Earth Day: Practical Environmental Politics* (Washington, D.C.: Brookings Institution Press, 1999), 44.

7. For Earth Day advertisement, see *New York Times,* Jan. 18, 1970. For establishing the EPA, see Reorganization Plan No. 3 of 1970, 84 Stat. 2086, 35 *Federal Register* 15,623 (1970).

8. See 116 *Congressional Record* 32,901 (1970) (remarks of Sen. Muskie) ("State and local governments have not responded adequately to this challenge.").

9. See, e.g., Bruce A. Ackerman & William T. Hassler, *Clean Coal/Dirty Air* (New Haven: Yale University Press, 1981); Stephen Breyer, *Breaking the Vicious Circle: Toward Effective Risk Regulation* (Cambridge, Mass.: Harvard

University Press, 1993) (hereinafter cited as *Breaking the Vicious Circle*); E. Donald Elliott, "Environmental TQM: Anatomy of a Pollution Control Program That Works!" 92 *Michigan Law Review* 1840 (1994) (hereinafter cited as Elliott, "Environmental TQM"); E. Donald Elliott & Gail Charnley, "Toward Bigger Bubbles," 13 *Forum for Applied Research and Public Policy* 48 (1998); Bruce A. Ackerman & Richard B. Stewart, Comment, "Reforming Environmental Law," 37 *Stanford Law Review* 1333 (1985); Cass R. Sunstein, *Risk and Reason: Safety, Law, and the Environment* (New York: Cambridge University Press, 2002) (hereinafter cited as Sunstein, *Risk and Reason*).

10. The Gingrich bill was the *Risk Assessment and Cost Benefit Analysis Act of 1995*, HR 1022, 104th Cong., 1st sess., § 202(a)(2) (1995). For my arguments against it, see David Schoenbrod, "Rule of Law: On Environmental Law, Congress Keeps Passing the Buck," *Wall Street Journal*, March 29, 1995, at A13.

11. Thomas L. Friedman, "In Oversight We Trust," *New York Times*, July 28, 2002, at § 4, p. 13.

12. Arsen J. Darnay, *Statistical Record of the Environment* (Detroit: Gale Research, 1992), at 844 (hereinafter cited as Darnay, *Statistical Record*). The poll is a result of a household survey of 1,154 consumers. It asked whether they thought the public, the government, and industry were concerned enough about the environment.

Chapter 2. Coming to the Environmental Movement

1. President Kennedy's team was referred to as "the best and the brightest" by David Halberstam in *The Best and the Brightest* (New York: Random House, 1972).

2. 347 U.S. 483 (1954).

3. *Silent Spring*, at ch. 1.

4. For 1968 presidential campaign, see Stephen F. Hayward, *The Age of Reagan, 1964–1980: The Fall of the Old Liberal Order* (Rocklin, Calif.: Prima, 2001), at 249. Gladwin Hill, "Slick off California Coast Revives Oil Deal Disputes," *New York Times*, Feb. 2, 1969, at A1. For 1970 public opinion, see S. Robert Lichter & Stanley Rothman, *Environmental Cancer—A Political Disease?* (New Haven: Yale University Press, 1999), at 9 (hereinafter cited as Lichter & Rothman).

5. For Hatcher, see "The Rise of Anti-Ecology," *Time*, Aug. 3, 1970, at 42. For Whitney Young Jr. quote, see Christopher H. Foreman Jr., *The Promise and Peril of Environmental Justice* (Washington, D.C.: Brookings Institution Press, 1998), at 15. For ecology quote, see Editorial, "The Ecology Craze," *The New Republic*, March 7, 1969, at 8–9.

6. See, e.g., "New City Unit Moving against Landlords Who Allow Poisonous Paint in Their Buildings," *New York Times*, March 18, 1970, at 31.

Chapter 3. Congress Does Its Thing

1. *The Clean Air Act Amendments of 1970*, Pub. L. No. 91-604, 84 Stat. 1676 (1970) (hereinafter cited as 1970 Act); for "Mr. Environment," see Philip Shabecoff, "Environmentalists Fear Major Loss in Muskie Departure from Senate," *New York Times*, May 9, 1980, at 17; for Muskie's presidential hopes, see, e.g., E. Donald Elliott et al., "Toward a Theory of Statutory Evolution: The Federalization of Environmental Law," 1 *Journal of Law, Economics & Organization* 313, 327–38 (1985) (hereinafter cited as Elliott, "Toward a Theory").

2. For pollution, see 116 *Congressional Record* 42, 381–82 (1970) (remarks of Senator Muskie). For Lindsay, see Deirdre Carmody, "City's Air Cleaner Than in 1960's but Pollution Level Is Unknown," *New York Times*, May 26, 1981, at A1 (noting Lindsay's frequent use of this line). For deaths due to pollution, see Arnold W. Reitze Jr., "A Century of Air Pollution Control Law: What's Worked; What's Failed; What Might Work," 21 *Environmental Lawyer* 1549, 1585–88 (1991); *Silent Spring*, at ch. 14.

3. John C. Esposito, *Vanishing Air: The Ralph Nader Study Group Report on Air Pollution* (New York: Grossman, 1970) (with an introduction by Nader), at 293, vii–ix.

4. See, e.g., Robert C. Fellmeth, *The Interstate Commerce Omission: The Public Interest and the ICC* (New York: Grossman, 1970).

5. For slowing down states, see Elliott, "Toward a Theory," at 330–33. For the 1967 statute, "hardly a credible regulatory scheme," see William Rodgers, *Hornbook on Environmental Law* (St. Paul, Minn.: West, 1977), at 211.

6. For manufacturers' expense to comply, see Senate Report No. 91-1196, at 36 (1970) (hereinafter cited as 1970 Senate Report) and House Report No. 1146, 91st Cong., 2nd sess. 3 and 116 *Congressional Record* 42, 381–82 (1970). For tough state emission limits, see David Schoenbrod, "Goals Statutes or Rules Statutes: The Case of The Clean Air Act," 30 *UCLA Law Review* 740, 745 (1983) (hereinafter cited as Schoenbrod, "Goals Statutes")

7. Elliott, "Toward a Theory," at 330–33.

8. 116 *Congressional Record* 42, 381 (1970).

9. 1970 Act, §§ 108(a), 109(a) (corresponding versions at 42 U.S.C. §§ 7408(a), 7409(a)).

10. 1970 Act, § 109(b)(1) (corresponding version at 42 U.S.C. § 7409(b)(1)). The act also called for secondary national ambient air quality standards to protect welfare, which includes environmental values. 1970 Act, § 109(b)(2) (corresponding version at 42 U.S.C. § 7409(b)(2)).

11. For three key pollutants, see 1970 Act, § 202(b)(1) (corresponding version at 42 U.S.C. § 7521(b)(1)). For "extent feasible" language, see 1970 Act, § 111 (corresponding version at 42 U.S.C. § 7411). For state implementation plans, see 1970 Act, § 110(a) (corresponding version at 42 U.S.C. § 7410(a)). For state failures, see 1970 Act, § 110(c) (corresponding version at 42 U.S.C. § 7410(c)).

12. For extra time to meet standards, see 1970 Act, § 110(e),(f) (corresponding version at 42 U.S.C. § 7410(e),(f)). For Muskie quote, see 116 *Congressional Record* 42,381 (1970).

13. For hazardous pollutants, see 1970 Act, §§ 111(d), 112 (corresponding versions at 42 U.S.C. §§ 7411(d), 7412). For Muskie quote, see 1970 Senate Report, at 20.

14. For conference bill passage, see 116 *Congressional Record* 42,395 (Senate), 42,524 (House). On the new-car emission fight, Sen. Gurney's amendment lost: for 22, against 57; and Sen. Dole's amendment lost: for 32, against 43; see 116 *Congressional Record* 33,088–89 (1970). For Muskie's guarantee and extra time for automakers, see 116 *Congressional Record* 32,904 (1970) (remarks of Senator Muskie).

15. Kenneth E. Boulding, "Earth as a Space Ship," May 10, 1965, Kenneth E. Boulding Papers, University of Colorado at Boulder Libraries, Archives Box #38. Available at csf.colorado.edu/authors/Boulding.Kenneth/spaceship-earth .html.

16. For David Sive's suggestion, see Ross Sandler & David Schoenbrod, *Democracy by Decree: What Happens When Courts Run Government* (New Haven: Yale University Press, 2003), at 27 (hereinafter cited as *Democracy by Decree*). For citizens' suits, see 1970 Act § 304 (corresponding version at 42 U.S.C. § 7604).

Chapter 4. Leaving the Lead In

1. For lead in house paint, see 59 *Federal Register* 54,984, 54,985 (1994). For lead in gasoline, see EPA, "EPA Takes Final Step in Phaseout of Leaded Gasoline" (press release; Jan. 29, 1996), available at www.epa.gov/history/topics/ lead/02.htm. For lead and voters, see Gregg Easterbrook, *A Moment on the Earth: The Coming of Age of Environmental Optimism* (Washington, D.C.: Penguin, 1996), at 182 (hereinafter cited as *A Moment on the Earth*).

2. For Muskie and lead, see 1970 Senate Report, at 9. The 1970 Act's timetable allowed the administrator thirty days to list pollutants such as lead, twelve months to propose an air quality standard, ninety days to promulgate the standard, nine months to receive state plans, and four months to approve the plans if, inter alia, they would meet the air quality standard in three years. See 1970 Act §§ 108(a)(1), 108(a)(2), 109(a), 110(a)(1), 110(a)(2)(A)(i). The act permitted additional delay for reasons of technological infeasibility, but it was feasible to reduce the lead content of gasoline. See 1970 Act §§ 108(e), (f).

3. EPA, Office of Air Quality Criteria Development, *Airborne Lead* (draft, Jan. 7, 1971). On the omission of lead from list of pollutants, see 36 *Federal Register* 1502 (1971).

4. On NAS panel and lead, see Robert Gillette, "Lead in the Air: Industry Weight on Academy Panel Challenged," 174 *Science* 800, 801 (1971).

5. For the EPA proposal to reduce lead in gas, see 37 *Federal Register* 3882 (1972). For protecting fetuses and young children, see EPA, *EPA's Position on the Health Implications of Airborne Lead* (Nov. 28, 1973), at IV-5 to 15, VII-5. For industry objections, see David Schoenbrod, "Why Regulation of Lead Has Failed," in *Low Level Lead Exposure: The Clinical Implications of Current Research* (ed. Herbert L. Needleman; New York: Raven Press, 1980), at 261.

6. In *NRDC v. EPA*, No. 72–2233, 1973 (U.S. App. D.C. Oct. 28, 1973), the EPA was ordered to make its final decision on whether to promulgate across-the-board controls on lead additives within thirty days. For White House battle, see John Quarles, *Cleaning Up America: An Insider's View of the Environmental Protection Agency* (Boston: Houghton Mifflin, 1976), at 123–42 (hereinafter cited as Quarles, *Cleaning Up*). For the EPA law reducing lead, see 38 *Federal Register* 1254 (1973).

7. *NRDC v. Train*, 545 F.2d 320, 328 (2d Cir. 1976), affirming *NRDC v. Train*, 411 F.Supp. 864 (S.D.N.Y. 1976).

8. For adding lead to list of pollutants, see 41 *Federal Register* 42,675 (1976). For time comparison, see 1970 Act, § 108(a)(1). See *Ethyl Corp. v. EPA*, 541 F.2d 1 (D.C. Cir. 1976) (en banc).

9. See, e.g., Herbert L. Needleman et al., "Deficits in Psychologic and Classroom Performance of Children with Elevated Lead Levels," 300 *New England Journal of Medicine* 689, 689–95 (1979). For urban lead pollution, see EPA, *Air Quality Criteria for Lead*, draft no. 1 (1976).

10. For Carter quote, see Cover Story, "Man of the Year: I'm Jimmy Carter, and...," Time, Jan. 3, 1977, at 21. For air quality standard, see 43 *Federal Register* 46,246 (1978). For protecting health, see *Lead Industries Ass'n v. EPA*, 647 F.2d 1130 (D.C. Cir. 1980). For Carter, see Executive Order No. 12,044, 43 *Federal Register* 12,661 (1978). For EPA cost-benefit analysis of lead, see 43 *Federal Register* 46,246 (1978). For Eagleton's demand, see Joint Appendix, at 2717–21, *Lead Industries Ass'n v. EPA*, 647 F.2d 1130 (D.C. Cir. 1980).

11. 15 Weekly Comp. of Pres. Doc. 1235 (July 15, 1979).

12. See *Power without Responsibility*, at 155–58.

13. For emission reduction, see 1970 Act, § 202(b)(1)(A) (corresponding version at 42 U.S.C. § 7521(b)(1)(A)). For pollution-control devices, see 1970 Act, §§ 211(c)(1)(B), 211(c)(2)(B) (corresponding version at 42 U.S.C. §§ 7545(c)(1)(B), (c)(2)(B)).

14. Calculations are based on *Lead and Gasoline Usage Summary: 1967–1991*, provided by the Fuels and Energy Division, EPA. For reduction in lead in gasoline, see EPA, *Benefits and Costs of the Clean Air Act: Final Report to Congress on the Benefits and Costs of the Clean Air Act, 1970–1990* (Oct. 1997), at App. G-33 (hereinafter cited as *Benefits and Costs 1970–1990*).

15. 50 *Federal Register* 9386, 9397 (1985). Congress removed the rest of the lead itself. See *The 1990 Clean Air Act Amendments*, Pub. L. No. 101-549, 104 Stat. 2399 (1990) (hereinafter cited as 1990 Act). For section of 1990 Act that pro-

hibited lead in gasoline see § 211(n) (corresponding version at 42 U.S.C. § 7545(n)).

16. *Benefits and Costs 1970–1990*, at App. G-34. EPA's estimates are exaggerated, according to Sergio Piomelli, the physician who invented the blood-lead test and was a hero in building the case against lead in gasoline, but the benefits of getting rid of lead in gasoline, and the harm that would have been done by leaving it in, are still massive.

17. President Bill Clinton, 1996 WL 23253 (Jan. 23, 1996), at 9.

18. Schoenbrod, "Regulation," at 263.

19. See 1970 Act § 211(c)(4)(A)(i), (ii).

Chapter 5. Failure and Success in Cleaning the Air

1. For five pollutants, see 1970 Senate Report, at 10; 1970 Act, § 109(a)(1)(A) (corresponding version at 42 U.S.C. § 7409(a)(1)(A)). For nitrogen dioxide, see 36 *Federal Register* 1515 (1971). For air quality standards, see 36 *Federal Register* 22,384 (1971); 37 *Federal Register* 9577 (1972).

2. 1970 Act, § 111(a)(1) (corresponding version at 42 U.S.C. § 7411(a)(1)).

3. For forcing technology, see, e.g., *Train v. NRDC*, 421 U.S. 60, 91 (1975). On the failure of technology forcing, see Schoenbrod, "Goals Statutes," 30 *UCLA Law Review* at 766, 792. On feasibility of agency cuts, see, e.g., *Portland Cement Assoc. v. Ruckelshaus*, 486 F.2d 375 (D.C. Cir. 1973), certiorari denied, 417 U.S. 921 (1974). On new and old plant emissions, see Richard B. Stewart, "Regulation, Innovation and Administrative Law: A Conceptual Framework," 69 *California Law Review* 1256 (1981).

4. 116 *Congressional Record* 42,386 (1970).

5. For Los Angeles, see 38 *Federal Register* 2194, 2195 (1973). For ignoring car pollutants, see *NRDC v. EPA*, 475 F.2d 968 (D.C. Cir. 1973).

6. 1970 Senate Report, at 3. The only challenge involved the non–health related "secondary" standards for sulfur oxides. See *Kennecot Copper Corp. V. EPA*, 462 F.2d 846 (D.C. Cir. 1972).

7. For impossible state emission cuts, see *Union Elec. Co. v. EPA*, 427 U.S. 246, 265 (1976). "No plan is infeasible since offending sources always have the option of shutting down if they cannot otherwise comply with standard of law." 427 U.S. at 265, n. 14.

8. The act allowed the state to ease the emissions cuts required of Union Electric by amending its implementation plan, but that could happen only if there were some other way of achieving the air quality standards by the deadline. 1970 Act, § 110(a)(3). Such an amendment would take at least a year.

9. For punishing businesses, see 1970 Act, § 113(c)–(f) (corresponding version at 42 U.S.C. § 7413(c)–(f)). For potential lawsuits, see 1970 Act, § 304(a) (corresponding version at 42 U.S.C. § 7604(a)).

10. *NRDC v. EPA*, 475 F.2d 968 (D.C. Cir. 1973). Of the many states required

to submit plans to control transportation, only two submitted plans that the EPA could approve. See John Quarles, "The Transportation Control Plans— Federal Regulation's Collision with Reality," 2 *Harvard Environmental Law Review* 241, 244–45 (1977).

11. Transportation Control Plan for the Metropolitan New York Area. See, e.g., *Friends of the Earth v. EPA,* 499 F.2d 1118 (2d Cir. 1974).

12. For Sandler and Schoenbrod litigation, see *Friends of the Earth v. Carey,* 401 F.Supp. 1386 (S.D.N.Y. 1975), decision affirmed in part and reversed in part by, *Friends of the Earth v. Carey,* 535 F.2d 165 (2d Cir. 1976), on remand to, *Friends of the Earth v. Carey,* 422 F.Supp. 638 (S.D.N.Y. 1976), decision vacated by, *Friends of the Earth v. Carey,* 552 F.2d 25 (2d Cir. 1977), on remand to, *Friends of the Earth v. Carey,* 76 F.R.D. 33 (S.D.N.Y. 1977), application denied by, *Beame v. Friends of the Earth,* 434 U.S. 1310 (1977), certiorari denied, *Beame v. Friends of the Earth,* 434 U.S. 902 (1977). For Beame quote, see Steven Marcus & George Arzt, "City Fights U.S. on Parking Ban," N.Y. Post, June 15, 1977, at 1.

13. *Democracy by Decree,* at 29–31.

14. For Holtzman protest, see Nathaniel Sheppard Jr., "New Yorkers in Congress Will Fight River Tolls," *New York Times,* Feb. 28, 1977, at 31. For Bingham, see "Letter to the Editor from Congressman Bingham," *New York Times,* March 8, 1977, at 30.

15. For EPA delays, see, e.g., *City of Riverside v. Ruckelshaus,* 4 Env't Rep. Cas. (BNA) 1728 (C.D. Cal. 1972). For Muskie quote, see 116 *Congressional Record* 42,381 (1970). For violations of standards, see National Commission on Air Quality, *To Breathe Clean Air* (1981), at 15 (describing failures by 1975) (hereinafter cited as National Commission).

16. See 41 *Federal Register* 55,524–26 (1976).

17. See EPA, *National Air Quality, Monitoring and Emission Trends Report* (1978), at 5–11. See also EPA, *Air Quality Criteria for Lead* (1977), at 1–3.

18. For deadlines, see *1977 Clean Air Act Amendments,* Pub. L. No. 95-95, § 129 (adding §§ 172(a)(1), (2) to Clean Air Act), 91 Stat. 685, 746–47 (1977) (hereinafter cited as 1977 Act). For unpopular measures, see 1977 Act, § 110(c)(5)(A).

19. For state sanctions, see 1977 Act § 176 (requiring EPA, the Department of Transportation, and other instrumentalities of the federal government to withhold support). For the EPA instructing states, see 1977 Act, part D.

20. See National Commission, at 17.

21. National Commission, at 16–17. Congress provides in the Internal Revenue Code that "Any person who . . . Willfully makes and subscribes any return, statement, or other document, which contains or is verified by a written declaration that it is made under the penalties of perjury, and which he does not believe to be true and correct as to every material matter; or . . . Willfully aids or assists in, or procures, counsels, or advises the preparation or presentation under, or in connection with any matter arising under, the internal revenue laws, of a return, affidavit, claim, or other document, which is fraudulent or is

false as to any material matter, whether or not such falsity or fraud is with the knowledge or consent of the person authorized or required to present such return, affidavit, claim, or document . . . shall be guilty of a felony." 26 U.S.C. § 7206(1), (2).

22. See 133 *Congressional Record* S 17798 (daily ed. 1987) (statement of Senator Mitchell).

23. For Los Angeles's ozone standard, see 1990 Act, §§ 181(a), 182(e) (corresponding versions at 42 U.S.C. §§ 7511(a), 7511a(e)). Los Angeles is labeled an "Extreme Area" under the 1990 Act. For state deadlines, see 42 U.S.C. §§ 7501–15.

24. The standards will be achieved or nearly achieved despite substantial increases in population (39 percent), GDP (161 percent), energy consumption (42 percent), and miles traveled by vehicles (149 percent) between 1970 and 2001. See EPA, *Latest Findings on National Air Quality: Status and Trends Report* (2001), at 4.

25. From 1970 to 2001, emissions of lead (Pb) in the air decreased by 98 percent, and emissions of the other principal air pollutants decreased by approximately 20 percent. See EPA, *Latest Findings*, at 1–2. For EPA estimates, see *Benefits and Costs 1970–1990*, at App. G-34. For EPA's estimates of costs and benefits, see Office of Management and Budget, Office of Information and Regulatory Affairs, *Informing Regulatory Decisions: 2003 Report to Congress on the Costs and Benefits of Federal Regulations and Unfunded Mandates on State, Local, and Tribal Entities* (2003), at 7 (hereinafter cited as OMB Report). The report revealed that the EPA's analysis claimed that the benefits of its recently issued major rules greatly exceeded their costs. The OMB report made it crystal clear that it was reporting the EPA's analysis rather than generating its own. OMB Report, at 5. Nonetheless, the *New York Times* devoted an editorial to the proposition that environmental protection must be a good deal because George W. Bush's OMB said so. See Editorial Desk, "Rules That Work," Oct. 1, 2003, at A22.

26. For limits on new-car emissions, see *Benefits and Costs 1970–1990*, at 13–17. While environmentalists complain that Congress postponed the original 1975 deadline for achieving the 90 percent target, that deadline was picked without any meaningful assessment of whether the automakers could comply. For a generally favorable review of Congress's performance on emission limits on new cars, see Christopher H. Schroeder, "Regulating Automobile Pollution: An Environmental Success Story for Democracy?" 20 *St. Louis University Public Law Review* 21, 30, 34–39 (2001). The EPA slants its calculation of compliance with the law in the automakers' favor, which makes them—and it—look better. See, e.g., Robert A. Weissman, Matthew A. Low & Norman D. Shutler, "Regulation of Motor Vehicles," in 2 *Law of Environmental Protection* § 11.07 (ed. Sheldon M. Novick, New York: C. Boardman, 1998).

27. See *Benefits and Costs 1970–1990*.

28. See *Benefits and Costs 1970–1990*.

29. For states' emission reductions, see Douglas M. Costle, EPA administrator, "Remarks at the Meeting of the Air Pollution Control Association in Montreal" (June 23, 1980), at 2 (on file with author). He was speaking of reductions achieved from 1964 to 1972 but acknowledged that those came from state actions in the 1960s. For states' accomplishments, see L. B. Lave & G. S. Omenn, *Clearing the Air: Reforming the Clean Air Act* (Washington, D.C.: Brookings Institution Press, 1981), at 1.

30. Indur Goklany, *Clearing the Air: The Real Story of the War on Air Pollution* (Washington, D.C.: Cato Institute, 1999), at 111–14, 132–33 (hereinafter cited as *Clearing the Air*). See also, e.g., Joel A. Tarr, *The Search for the Ultimate Sink* (Akron, Ohio: University of Akron Press, 1996), at ch. 8.

31. For the recurring pattern, see *Clearing the Air*, at 87–98. In 1950 Dr. A. J. Haagen-Smit, a biochemist at CalTech, reported to the California Assembly that automobiles were a major contributor to smog. See Thomas O. McGarity, "Regulating Commuters to Clear the Air: Some Difficulties in Implementing a National Program at the Local Level," 27 *Pacific Law Journal* 1521, 1535–36 (1996). For state solutions, see *Clearing the Air*, at 24, 26–31.

32. The EPA has recharacterized some of the pollutants on the list. For particularly hazardous pollutants, see 1970 Act § 112 (corresponding version at 42 U.S.C. § 7412). For the EPA's dilemma, see Senate Report No. 101–228, 101st Cong., 1st sess., at 128 (1989) ("EPA has not been willing to write standards so stringent because they would shut down major segments of American industry."). For idealistic statutory goals preventing the taking of sensible steps, see Daniel A. Farber, *Eco-Pragmatism: Making Sensible Environmental Decisions in an Uncertain World* (Chicago: University of Chicago Press, 1999), at 73 (hereinafter cited as *Eco-Pragmatism*); *Breaking the Vicious Circle*. For the comparison of EPA and state regulation, see Senate Report No. 101–228, at 3 (1989). See also John P. Dwyer, "The Pathology of Symbolic Legislation," 17 *Ecology Law Quarterly* 233, 261 (1990). For 189 pollutants, see 1990 Act.

33. Pub. L. No. 99–499, 100 Stat. 1729 (1986). E. Donald Elliott, writing only a few years after the TRI program began, concluded that "the recent reductions in the release of toxic chemicals to the environment, accomplished 'voluntarily' under public pressure stimulated by the TRI inventory, are probably many times larger than the reductions achieved over twenty years of traditional standard-setting regulation of air toxics." Elliott, "Environmental TQM," 92 *Michigan Law Review* at 1851. For community power, see EPA, *What Is the Toxic Release Inventory (TRI) Program,* available at www.epa.gov/tri/whatis.htm (last visited March 14, 2004). For resulting cuts in emissions, see Michael S. Baram et al., *Managing Chemical Risks: Corporate Response to SARA Title III* (rev. ed.; Boca Raton, Fla.: Lewis, 1992), at 10–11, 40–43; email from Michael S. Baram to the author, Feb. 2, 2004; 65 *Federal Register* 24,834, 24,838 (2000) ("Nationally, reported TRI emissions have fallen 43 percent since 1988, a time in which

industrial production has risen 28 percent. Although other factors contributed to the decline in emissions, negative press coverage appears to have led some facilities to reduce their TRI emissions.").

34. 1990 Act, § 401 (corresponding version at 42 U.S.C. § 7651).

35. The big breakthrough on water pollution came when Congress required municipalities to treat sewage. As with the emission limits on new cars, Congress took direct responsibility—in the case of sewage treatment, it did so not only by requiring cleanup but also by paying for much of it through federal grants. See, e.g., *Clean Water Act of 1972*, Pub. L. No. 92-500, 86 Stat. 816 (1972). Another important driver of water quality improvement was the permit program, which worked in fact much like the new source-performance-standard program under the Clean Air Act. See Clean Water Act of 1972, 33 U.S.C. § 1341. For Crandall quote, see Peter Brimelow & Leslie Spencer, "You Can Get There from Here," *Forbes*, July 6, 1992, at 60.

Chapter 6. Growing Power

1. When faced with this difficulty, the EPA issued implementation plans that required the states to do this work. When the states objected and their complaints were put on the docket of the Supreme Court, the EPA backed down. See *EPA v. Brown*, 431 U.S. 99 (1977). For Ruckelshaus, see, e.g., John Quarles, *Cleaning Up*, at 117–18.

2. Since 1970 "we have learned that any lack of enthusiasm or negativism or sign of weakness on the part of the national program directors is magnified tenfold at the local level. . . . There is built into this new law the very necessary provisions which will force communities to make choices, the result of which will be protection of public health." 123 *Congressional Record* 26,842 (1977) (remarks of Senator Muskie); see also National Commission, at 4 ("The structure of the Clean Air Act is sound."). On punishing states that miss deadlines, see 1977 Act, § 176(a).

3. Marc K. Landy, Marc J. Roberts & Stephen R. Thomas, *The Environmental Protection Agency: Asking the Wrong Questions* (New York: Oxford University Press, 1990), at 41 (hereinafter cited as Landy, *Environmental Protection Agency*).

4. "What Causes Cancer," *Newsweek*, Jan. 26, 1976, at 62. For Love Canal emergency, see, e.g., Adeline Gordon Levine, *Love Canal: Science, Politics, and People* (Lexington, Mass.: Lexington Books, 1982), at 27–29; Landy, *Environmental Protection Agency*, at 135.

5. Landy, *Environmental Protection Agency*, at 142.

6. New York State Department of Health, *Love Canal Follow-Up Health Study* (2001), available at www.health.state.ny.us/nysdoh/lcanal/cancinci.htm. The overall cancer rate of former Love Canal residents included in the study was no greater than that of upstate New Yorkers as a whole and was lower than that

of Niagra County residents as a whole. For toxic waste cleanup, see EPA, *Unfinished Business: A Comparative Assessment of Environmental Problems* (February 1987), at xix, 77–78.

7. See Philip Shabecoff, "Environmental Agency Chief Says Critics Are Politically Motivated," *New York Times,* April 24, 1982, at § 1, p. 10. See also Philip Shabecoff, "Mrs. Gorsuch as a Crusading Tiger? Critics Wonder Why," *New York Times,* Dec. 26, 1982, at § 4, p. 14. President Reagan said that Mr. Ruckelshaus had been guaranteed "the broad, flexible mandate that he deserves." Mr. Ruckelshaus said that he expected to have a "free hand" in picking his deputies. See Steven R. Weisman, "President Names Ruckelshaus Head of Troubled EPA," *New York Times,* March 22, 1983, at A1.

8. For public opinion, see Darnay, *Statistical Record,* at 844. For public anxiety, see R. Shep Melnick, "Pollution Deadlines and the Coalition for Failure," *The Public Interest* (Spring 1984).

9. For an example of a sanction that seemed to hurt only business, EPA could require that new sources buy more pollution rights from existing sources, thus not only reducing pollution but also making it more expensive to build new factories. See, e.g., 42 U.S.C. § 7509(b)(2). For federal control of state air programs, see 1970 Act, § 110(a); 1977 Act, § 110(a), 171–79; 1990 Act, § 110(a), 171–93. Page counts are based on approximately 420 words per page; there are 875 words per page in the U.S. Code.

10. For fees, see 1990 Act, § 502(b)(3) (corresponding version at 42 U.S.C. § 7661a(b)(3)). If the state did not collect the fee, then the federal government would. See 42 U.S.C. § 7661a(b)(3)(C)(i). Sources in the state would thus have to pay the fee in any event. The act gave each state the choice of whether the money would go to it or to the EPA. This was an offer the states could not refuse. The 1977 Act, §§ 110, 171–79, required permits only for major new or modified sources. For state fees' covering EPA costs, see 42 U.S.C. § 7661a(b)(3)(A).

11. In 1997, the EPA predicted that only 45 counties would be in violation of the current particulate matter air standard and only nine "areas" (usually comprising multiple counties) to be in violation of the current air quality standard for ozone. EPA, *Regulatory Impact Analyses for the Particulate Matter and Ozone National Ambient Air Quality Standards and Proposed Regional Haze Rule* (July 17, 1997), at 4–58. With the new standards, the counties in violation of the particulate matter standard would increase to 102 and the areas in violation of the ozone standard would increase to 19. The violations would increase not only in number, but also in intensity. An earlier, more specific EPA analysis found that most of the violations of the old ozone standard would have been "marginal." EPA, *Regulatory Impact Analysis for Proposed Ozone National Ambient Air Quality Standard* (draft, Dec. 1996), at VI-6. In 2004, EPA identified approximately 500 counties that would need to take action in response to the stronger ozone standards. Jennifer 8. Lee, "Clear Skies No More for Millions as Pollution Rule Expands," *New York Times,* April 13, 2004, at A22.

For power over states that EPA gets from violations, see, e.g., 42 U.S.C. §§ 7501–15. In addition, the violations also increase the agency's power over emissions from new cars and light-duty trucks. See 42 U.S.C. §§ 7521(i)(2)(A), (i)(3)(B). For EPA's strengthening standards, see 62 *Federal Register* 38,652 (1997); 62 *Federal Register* 38,856 (1997). For the EPA's analysis of new standards, see Cary Goglianese & Gary E. Marchant, "Shifting Sands: The Limits of Science in Setting Standards," 152 University of *Pennsylvania Law Review* 1255, 1321–23 (2004) (hereinafter cited as "Shifting Sands"). Brenner's remark was related to me by E. Donald Elliott, who participated in the panel. Interview with the author, Jan. 14, 2003.

Chapter 7. The EPA Today

1. For Clean Air Act commands, see 42 U.S.C. §§ 7490(b)(2), 7470–79, 7651–51(o), 7671–71(q), 7491–92. The EPA lists most of the other statutes it administers at www.epa.gov/epahome/laws.htm and www.epa.gov/epahome/lawintro.htm.

2. See EPA, *Enforcement and Compliance Assurance: FY98 Accomplishments Report* (June 1999), at 10. See also James V. DeLong, *Out of Bounds, Out of Control: Regulatory Enforcement at the EPA* (Washington, D.C.: Cato Institute, 2002), at 3.

3. For growth of the Clean Air Act, see 42 U.S.C. § 1857 et seq. (Supp. 1965) and 42 U.S.C. § 1857 et seq. (1970). Page counts based on approximately 420 words per page; there are 875 words per page in the U.S. Code.

4. For EPA regulations, see 40 C.F.R. §§ 50, 55, 61, 63, 65, 76, 77, 80, 82, 85–87, 89–92, 94. Page counts based on approximately 420 words per page; there are approximately 600 words per page in the Code of Federal Regulations. The page counts do not include the appendices of the respective sections. For particulate matter standard, see 40 C.F.R. §§ 50.6, 50.7. For the EPA's "concise general statement," see 62 *Federal Register* 38,652 (1997).

5. For court quotes, see *Appalachian Power Co. v. EPA*, 208 F.3d 1015, 1020 (D.C. Cir., 2000). For EPA guidance documents, see House Committee on Government Reform, *Non-Binding Legal Effect of Agency Guidance Documents*, House Report 106–1009, 106th Cong., 2nd sess. 34, at 466 (2000). The documents listed include guidelines, manuals, handbooks, and letters giving guidance. Although most of the documents are technically not binding, an attorney representing a client regulated by the EPA would be remiss to ignore relevant guidance to the extent it can be discovered.

6. For benefits to society and the environment, see 42 U.S.C. § 7503(a)(5). For quote, see Richard B. Stewart, "Controlling Environmental Risks through Economic Incentives," 13 *Columbia Journal of Environmental Law* 153, 154 (1988). See also Jonathan H. Adler, "Free and Green: A New Approach to Environmental Protection," 24 *Harvard Journal of Law and Public Policy* 653, 662 (2001).

7. Herman Wouk, *The Caine Mutiny* (New York: Doubleday, 1951), at 120.

8. Office of Management and Budget, Office of Information and Regulatory Affairs, *Informing Regulatory Decisions: 2003 Report to Congress on the Costs and Benefits of Federal Regulations and Unfunded Mandates on State, Local, and Tribal Entities* (2003), at 7.

9. For EPA and FDA budgets, see Susan Dudley & Melinda Warren, *Regulatory Spending Soars: An Analysis of the U.S. Budget for Fiscal Years 2003 and 2004* (Arlington, Va., and St. Louis, Mo.: Mercatus Center and Weidenbaum Center, July 2003), at 14–16, available at wc.wustl.edu/Reg_Budget_final.pdf. The comparison is for fiscal year 2004. I have excluded from the comparison the Coast Guard and Transportation Security Administrations of the Department of Homeland Security because their resources go primarily to policing rather than to lawmaking. For agency staff comparisons, see Dudley & Warren, *Regulatory Spending*, at 20–22. For paperwork violations, see 65 *Federal Register* 19,618 (2000). For a discussion of the complexity of the EPA's requirements, see chapter 20.

10. For an example of the EPA's leaving tasks incomplete, see John J. Fialka, "EPA Report Says Pollution-Control Effort Is Hurt by Bureaucracy, Lack of Funds," *Wall Street Journal,* March 12, 2002, at A28. Although the 1990 Clean Air Act mandated that all major sources have permits by 1997, more than a third still did not by 2002. For court review of EPA regulations, see Jonathan H. Adler, "Environmental Performance at the Bench: The EPA's Record in Federal Court," *Reason Public Policy Institute* (May 2000), which reports that the D.C. Circuit handed down decisions on sixty-nine EPA regulations from 1993 to 2000. The court reached the merits on sixty. In 62 percent of these (thirty-seven cases), the court struck down or remanded all or a substantial portion of the regulation. In contrast, Adler reports, "OSHA has a near-perfect record in setting workplace standards covering 'toxic materials' and 'hazardous physical agents.'" Another study of the EPA's record in all courts of appeal over a slightly longer period found that EPA's rules were "completely sustained in only 53% of the 111 rulemaking cases." Christopher H. Schroeder & Robert H. Glicksman, "Chevron, State Farm, and the EPA in the Courts of Appeals During the 1990s," 31 *Environmental Law Reporter* 10371, 10374 (2001). For courts' power to reject agency rules, see 5 U.S.C. § 706.

11. For meeting deadlines, see Richard J. Lazarus, "The Tragedy of Distrust in the Implementation of Federal Environmental Law," 54 *Law and Contemporary Problems* 311, 323–24 (1991) (hereinafter cited as Lazarus, "Tragedy of Distrust"). For environmental groups' suits, see 42 U.S.C. § 7604(d). For environmental priorities, see R. Shep Melnick, *Regulation and the Courts: The Case of the Clean Air Act* (Washington, D.C.: Brookings Institution Press, 1983).

12. William Ruckelshaus, quoted in Richard D. Morgenstern, "The Legal and Institutional Setting for Economic Analysis at EPA," in *Economic Analyses at EPA: Assessing Regulatory Impact* (ed. Richard D. Morgenstern; Washington,

D.C.: Resources for the Future, 1997), at 12. Richard B. Stewart, "Madison's Nightmare," 57 *University of Chicago Law Review* 335, 347 (1990).

Chapter 8. What's Science Got to Do with It?

1. This boils down to a simple formula: air quality standard = *the amount of lead children can tolerate in their blood without harm to health* minus *the amount of lead in children's blood that comes from sources other than air pollution* divided by *the ratio of lead in children's blood to the lead in air.*

2. For calculating children's lead levels, see 43 *Federal Register* 46,246, 46,252–54 (1978). Plugging these numbers into the formula produced the following result:

$$\text{Air quality standard} = \frac{(15\mu g/dL - 12\mu g/dL)}{(2\mu g/dL \div 1\mu g/m_3)} = 3/2\mu g/m_3 = 1.5\mu g/m_3$$

43 *Federal Register* 46,254 (1978). For the current standard, see 40 C.F.R. § 50.12 (2003).

3. For interpretations of studies, see EPA, *Air Quality Criteria for Lead* (1977). For uncertainty in setting standards, see National Academy of Sciences, *Lead in the Human Environment* (Washington, D.C.: National Academies Press, 1980), at 214–15.

4. See Centers for Disease Control and Prevention, *Screening Young Children for Lead Poisoning: Guidance for State and Local Public Health Officials* (Nov. 1997), at 9. For non-air sources, see NAS, *Lead,* at 214–15. For drop in blood lead levels, see CDC, *Children's Blood Lead Levels in the United States,* available at www.cdc.gov/nceh/lead/research/kidsBLL.htm. The dramatic drop in median lead levels can also not be explained by taking lead out of certain food cans and water pipes, which were important measures but are unlikely to have had an impact sufficient to cause such a large and widespread drop in blood lead levels. That this drop correlates so in time with decreases in the lead content of gasoline further suggests it was the primary cause of the drop.

5. On my amateur speculations, see my preface to Herbert L. Needleman and Sergio Piomelli, *The Effects of Low Level Lead* Exposure (NRDC and the American Lung Assoc. April 25, 1978), at vi–vii. Sergio Piomelli, et al., "Blood Lead Concentration in a Remote Himalayan Region," 210 *Science* 1135 (1980).

6. National Academy of Sciences/National Research Council, Committee on the Institutional Means for Assessment of Risks to Public Health, *Risk Assessment in the Federal Government: Managing the Process* (Washington, D.C.: National Academies Press, 1983). Indeed, even assessing risks in the face of uncertainty requires policy judgments. "Shifting Sands," 152 *University of Pennsylvania Law Review* 1279–80. See, e.g., National Research Council, Assembly of Life Sciences, Institute of Medicine, Committee for a Study of Saccharin and Food Safety Policy, *Saccharin: Technical Assessment of Risks and Benefits,* Report No. 1

(Nov. 1978) (large range in predicted human health consequences of saccharin). See, e.g., Alvin M. Weinberg, "Science and Its Limits: The Regulator's Dilemma," in *Hazards: Technology and Fairness* (National Academy of Engineering; Washington, D.C.: National Academies Press, 1986), at 9.

7. Lorenz R. Rhomberg, "A Survey of Methods for Chemical Health Risk Assessment among Federal Regulatory Agencies," 3 *Human and Ecological Risk Assessment* 6, 1029–1196 (1997).

8. Tina Turner, "What's Love Got to Do with It" (Capitol 1984).

9. *Clean Air Act Amendments of 1977: Hearings before the Subcommittee on Environmental Pollution of the Senate Committee on Environment and Public Health,* 95th Cong., 1st sess., part 3, at 8 (1977).

10. Quoted in Mark R. Powell, *Science at EPA: Information in the Regulatory Process* (Washington, D.C.: Resources for the Future, 1999), at 91. The researcher got the law wrong, but only slightly. The EPA is supposed to set the standard to protect the most sensitive group, not the most sensitive individual. See 1970 Senate Report, at 10. This requires knowing when individuals leave off and groups begin, which is still a ludicrous exercise.

11. On cost considerations in setting air quality standards, see sources cited in "Shifting Sands," 152 University of *Pennsylvania Law Review,* at n. 369; Powell, *Science at EPA,* at 2–3.

12. E. Donald Elliott, "Strengthening Science's Voice at EPA," 66 *Law and Contemporary Problems* 45, 48 (2003).

13. For Elliott & Reilly, see Powell, *Science at EPA,* at 130. In 2002 Dr. Paul Gilman was appointed "agency science advisor" by Administrator Whitman. See EPA, "Whitman Appoints Gilman Science Advisor," available at www.epa.gov/ord/htm/sci-advi.htm.

14. "Agency scientists and bureaucrats engage in a 'science charade' by failing first to identify the major interstices left by science in the standard-setting process and second to reveal the policy choices they made to fill each trans-scientific gap." Wendy E. Wagner, "The Science Charade in Toxic Risk Regulation," 95 *Columbia Law Review* 1613, 1629 (1995). See, e.g., "Shifting Sands," at 1292–1301; Lazarus, "Tragedy of Distrust," 54 *Law and Contemporary Problems,* at 354; Melnick, *Regulation,* at 216. See also E. Donald Elliott et al., "Science, Agencies, and the Courts: Is Three a Crowd?" 31 *Environmental Law Reporter* 10125, 10126 (2001) ("In my experience at EPA—where I was in many meetings with the Administrator or Deputy Administrator when options were presented to them for decision—I cannot remember a single case in which there was a significant discussion of the underlying scientific emphasis.").

15. For Burford and EPA scientists, see Sheila Jasanoff, *The Fifth Branch: Science Advisers as Policymakers* (Cambridge, Mass.: Harvard University Press, 1990), at 89 (noting also that the EPA denied any connection between the dismissals and the scientists' views). For 1999 study quotes, see Powell, *Science at EPA,* at 118, 7.

16. On the pressure felt by scientists, see the broad range of reports cited in Office of Management and Budget, "Peer Review and Information Quality," 68 *Federal Register* 54,023 (2003). See also Jasanoff, *Fifth Branch*, at 91. Marchant reports that "the procedure evolved [by the EPA for appointing scientists to its advisory panels] was far removed indeed from the elite technocratic model recommended by the 1977 NAS study. In place of short rotations of top-flight research scientists, the EPA began using repeat assignments and informal interest balancing to acculturate scientists into the special subculture of regulatory science." Email to the author, Oct. 21, 2003.

Chapter 9. Lois Swirsky Gold, Chemicals, and Cancer

1. For background on TRIS, see *Springs Mills, Inc., v. Consumer Product Safety Commission*, 434 F. Supp. 416, 418–19 (D.C.S.C., 1977).

2. Lois Swirsky Gold, Bruce N. Ames & Thomas H. Slone, "Misconceptions about the Causes of Cancer," in *Human and Environmental Risk Assessment: Theory and Practice* (ed. D. Paustenbach; John Wiley & Sons, 2002), at 1415–60 (hereinafter cited as Gold, Ames & Slone) (all page citations are to the text as available on the Internet at potency.berkeley.edu/text/Paustenbach .pdf).

3. The chapter, cited in the previous note, can be read by lay people. A more complete version written especially for lay audiences is Lois Swirsky Gold, Thomas H. Slone, Neela B. Manley & Bruce N. Ames, *Misconceptions about the Causes of Cancer* (Vancouver: Fraser Institute, 2002) (hereinafter cited as *Misconceptions*). It is available at potency.berkeley.edu/text/Gold_Misconceptions .pdf.

4. Gold, Ames & Slone, at 2.

5. Gold, Ames & Slone, at 2.

6. Gold, Ames & Slone, at 2.

7. Gold, Ames & Slone, at 4.

8. Gold, Ames & Slone, at 5–6.

9. *Silent Spring*, at 219. Gold, Ames & Slone, at 9.

10. *Misconceptions*, at 29, 45. On many instances of increasing exposure to carcinogens, see Cross, "Paradoxical Perils," 53 *Washington & Lee Law Review* 851, 873–76 (1996) (hereinafter cited as Cross, "Paradoxical Perils").

11. Gold, Ames & Slone, at 6.

12. Lois Swirsky Gold, interview with the author, Aug. 11, 2003. For articles by Bruce Ames and Lois Swirsky Gold, see, e.g., Bruce N. Ames, Renae Magaw & Lois Swirsky Gold, "Ranking Possible Carcinogenic Hazards," 236 *Science* 271–80 (1987); Bruce N. Ames & Lois Swirsky Gold, "Chemical Carcinogenesis: Too Many Rodent Carcinogens," 87 *Proceedings of the National Academy of Sciences* 7772–76 (1990); Bruce N. Ames, M. Profet & Lois Swirsky Gold, "Dietary Pesti-

cides (99.99% All Natural)," 87 *Proceedings of the National Academy of Sciences* 7777–81 (1990); Bruce N. Ames, M. Profet & Lois Swirsky Gold, "Nature's Chemicals and Synthetic Chemicals: Comparative Toxicology," 87 *Proceedings of the National Academy of Sciences* 7782–86 (1990).

13. For cancer reports, see Robert N. Proctor, *Cancer Wars* (New York: Basic Books, 1995), at 54–74. For 1993 polls of cancer researchers, see Lichter & Rothman, at 110, 115, 122, 115.

14. *Breaking the Vicious Circle*, at 6. See also R. Doll & R. Peto, *The Causes of Cancer* (New York: Oxford University Press, 1981). For the EPA's overregulating, see *Breaking the Vicious Circle*, at 11–29, 39–50. Breyer noted that the EPA's regulation of wood-preserving chemicals cost $5.7 trillion per life saved.

15. For efforts to control workplace chemicals and other carcinogens, see Lois Swirsky Gold & Thomas H. Slone, "Aristolochic Acid, an Herbal Carcinogen, Sold on the Web after FDA Alert," 349 *New England Journal of Medicine* 1576 (Oct. 16, 2003); Lois Swirsky Gold et al., "Ranking the Potential Carcinogenic Hazards to Workers from Exposures to Chemicals That Are Tumorigenic in Rodents," 76 *Environmental Health Perspectives* 211–19 (1987); Lois Swirsky Gold, Georganne Backman Garfinkel & Thomas H. Slone, "Setting Priorities among Possible Carcinogenic Hazards in the Workplace," in *Chemical Risk Assessment and Occupational Health: Current Applications, Limitations, and Future Prospects* (ed. C. M. Smith et al.; Westport, Conn.: Auburn House, 1994). For quote, see Gold, Ames & Slone, at 20.

16. For NRC recommendations, see National Research Council, *Risk Assessment in the Federal Government: Managing the Process* (Washington, D.C.: National Academies Press, 1983), at 81. For NAS report, see National Academy of Sciences, *Science and Judgment in Risk Assessment* (Washington, D.C.: National Academies Press, 1994), at 91. The report approved continued reliance on default assumptions provided the assumptions are all identified, stated to be default positions from which departures can be made, and accompanied by explanations of the reasons for them and the criteria for departures. *Science and Judgment*, at 104–5. The report expressed the hope that further research would reduce the uncertainty that gives rise to the need to make assumptions in cancer risk assessment. *Science and Judgment*, at 86, 90. One hope for reducing such uncertainty in the long run is the emerging field of "toxicogenomics." See Gary E. Marchant, "Genomes and Toxic Substances: Part I—Toxicogenomics," 33 *Environmental Law Reporter* 10071 (2003). For draft guidelines, see EPA, "EPA Seeks to Update Guidelines for Cancer Risk Assessment," March 3, 2003, available at www.epa.gov/newsroom/headline_030303.htm.

17. For American Cancer Society reports, see Ted Gansler, "The Risk of Dying of Cancer," available at http://www.cancer.org/docroot/PED/content/PED_11_1_Myth_About_Increasing_Cancer_Risk.asp (downloaded July 19, 2004); Ted Gansler, "Air Pollution or Smoking: Which Is Greater Risk?" avail-

able at http://www.cancer.org/docroot/PED/content/PED_11_1_Pollution_ Versus_Tobacco.asp (downloaded June 30, 2003).

18. Lichter & Rothman, at 162.

19. Lichter & Rothman, at 173. Other well-documented works find that leading media outlets often report the allegations of environmental advocates as fact. See *A Moment on the Earth*; Gideon Kanner, "Lucas and the Press: How to Be Politically Correct on the Taking Issue," in *After Lucas: Land Use Regulation and Taking of Property without Compensation* (ed. David L. Callies; Chicago: ABA, 1993), at ch. 5; Gideon Kanner, "Redwoods, Junk Bonds, and Tools of Cosa Nostra: A Visit to the Dark Side of the Headwaters Controversy," 30 *Environmental Law Reporter* 10756 (2000). The best known is Bjorn Lomborg's *The Skeptical Environmentalist* (New York: Cambridge University Press, 2001). Some environmentalists who sharply criticize Professor Lomborg on other points acknowledge that he is nonetheless correct in asserting that the bad science from environmental organizations often gets reported as good science in the press. E.g., Michael Grubb, "Relying on Manna from Heaven?," 294 *Science* 1285, 1285 (2001).

20. For example, Keith Schneider, "What Price Cleanup?" *New York Times*, March 21, 1993, at § 1, p. 1 (first article of a series); Jane E. Brody, "In a World of Hazards, Worries Are Often Misplaced," *New York Times*, Aug. 20, 2002, at F11; Jane E. Brody, "Calming Parents' Fears about Environmental Hazards," *New York Times*, July 13, 2004, at F5.

21. Lois Swirsky Gold, interview with the author, Aug. 11, 2003. John O'Mahony, "STUDY PUTS CANCER SCARE IN AIR: 4 Boroughs on National Top 10 List for Pollution," *New York Post*, Oct. 12, 1999, at 6.

22. On public's misconceptions about pollution and smoking, see Ted Gansler, "Air Pollution or Smoking: Which Is Greater Risk?" American Cancer Society, available at http://www.cancer.org/docroot/PED/content/PED_11_1_ Pollution_Versus_Tobacco.asp (downloaded on June 30, 2003). There was a time it did. See EPA, *Unfinished Business: A Comparative Assessment of Environmental Problems* (Feb. 1987), at 28–34 (estimating numbers of cases coming from pollution and pesticides and other hazards such as occupational exposure).

23. Speech, Harvard University School of Public Health, Boston, Mass., Nov. 1, 1997, available at http://yosemite.epa.gov/administrator/speeches.nsf.

24. American Cancer Society, *Cancer Facts and Figures 2000* (2000), at 18.

25. "A few studies have identified potential associations [between chemicals and childhood cancer]. . . . However, other studies have not found these associations, and all such studies have been limited in their ability to adequately evaluate and quantify the exposure of interest. More research is needed to clarify the association, if any, that these factors [including the multitude of others previously discussed] may have with childhood cancer risk. If any of these factors is truly associated with cancer risk, the magnitude of the effect is expected to be small." ACS, *Cancer Facts and Figures 2000*, at 22–23.

Chapter 10. Angus Macbeth and the Hudson River

1. See, e.g., *Calvert Cliffs' Coordinating Committee v. Atomic Energy Commission*, 449 F.2d 1109 (D.C. Cir. 1971); *Hudson River Fishermen's Association v. Federal Power Commission*, 498 F.2d 827 (2d Cir. 1974).

2. U.S. Commission on Wartime Relocation and Internment of Civilians et al., *Personal Justice Denied* (Washington, D.C.: Government Printing Office, 1982). David Schoenbrod, Angus Macbeth, David I. Levine & David J. Jung, *Remedies: Public and Private* (St. Paul, Minn.: West Group 3d ed., 2002).

3. GE was not involved in the earlier litigation about the power plants. For PCBs in the Hudson, see Richard Severo, "State Says Some Striped Bass and Salmon Pose a Toxic Peril," *New York Times,* Aug. 8, 1975, at 1. EPA, "Whitman Decides to Dredge Hudson River" (press release; Aug. 1, 2001) (on file with the author). For Whitman quote, see EPA, *Hudson River PCB Site: Record of Decision* (2002), at 2. For scope of dredging operation, see EPA, "EPA & General Electric Reach Agreement on Design of Hudson River Cleanup" (press release; Aug. 14, 2003) (on file with the author).

4. A recent article in the *New York Times Magazine* notes, despite expressing great admiration for Rachel Carson, that in "her 297 pages, [she] never mentioned the fact that by the time she was writing, DDT was responsible for saving tens of millions of lives, perhaps hundreds of millions." Tina Rosenberg, "What the World Needs Now Is DDT," *New York Times Magazine,* April 11, 2004, at § 6, p. 38. On banning of PCBs, see *Toxic Substances Control Act,* Pub. L. No. 94–469, § 6(e), 90 Stat. 2003 (1976) (current version at 15 U.S.C. § 2605(e)); *Comprehensive Environmental Response, Compensation and Liability Act,* §§ 104, 106, 107 (current versions at 42 U.S.C. §§ 9604, 9606, 9607).

5. Dr. Thomas Mack of the University of Southern California's Norris Comprehensive Cancer Center, quoted in Jack Welch, "In the Crosshairs," *The American Spectator,* Jan./Feb. 2002, at 65–66.

6. See Robert Golden & Peter G. Shields, "A Weight-of-Evidence Review of the Human Studies of the Potential Cancer Effects of PCBs"; Alan S. Kaufman, "Statement," in *Comments of General Electric Company on the Feasibility Study and Proposed Plan for the Hudson River PCBs Superfund Site* (Dec. 2000), at app. Q-1, Q-5. These analyses were part of GE's presentation. The EPA did not dispute their analyses of the epidemiological data. The agency did, however, decide not to rely on the epidemiological studies in its quantitative analysis because the researchers could not know with precision the dose of PCBs absorbed by the workers, whether the workers were exposed to other chemicals, or whether there were other factors. See EPA, *Responsiveness Summary: Hudson River PCBs Site Record of Decision* (January 2002), at 3–2 to 3–5, 3–11 to 3–12. Because some such imprecision is unavoidable in retrospective epidemiological research, the EPA's position boils down to a rejection of all epidemiological studies that find no association between a chemical and adverse health affects.

After the EPA made its decision, a major study of women on Long Island found no association between exposure to PCBs and breast cancer. M. D. Gammon et al., "Environmental Toxins and Breast Cancer on Long Island II, Organochlorine Compound Levels in Blood," 11 *Cancer Epidemiology, Biomarkers & Prevention* 686 (2002), cited in *Misconceptions,* at 65.

Kaufman's work was published in Domenic V. Cicchetti, Alan S. Kaufman, and Sara S. Sparrow, "The Relationship Between Prenatal and Postnatal Exposure to Polychlorinated Biphenyls (PCBs) and Cognitive, Neuropsychological, and Behavioral Deficits: A Critical Appraisal," 41 *Psychology in the Schools* 589 (2004). The article argued that the studies claiming to find statistically significant correlations between PCB exposure and neurological deficits fail to meet scientific standards. One criticism, among many, was that these studies claim to find statistical significance without taking adequate account of making multiple comparisons between the exposed population and the unexposed population. The article appeared in a special issue of *Psychology in the Schools* entitled "PCBs and Developmental Outcomes: A Critical Debate." The issue also carried responses by some of the authors of the studies criticized. In these responses, the authors argue the criticisms of their work are invalid because Cicchetti, Kaufman, and Sparrow imposed unreasonably high requirements. They also argued that Cicchetti, Kaufman, and Sparrow were funded by General Electric. The targets of this ad hominem attack, all with the Yale Child Study Center, replied that their arrangement with General Electric was that the company would have no control of their research and they would be allowed to publish the results regardless of the conclusions reached. Cicchetti, Kaufman, and Sparrow, "PCB Research Results Derive From a False Belief System: You've Come the Wrong Way, Baby!" 41 *Psychology in the Schools* 715, 716 (2004). They also argued that the scientific standards that they demanded of the PCB studies are the scientific norm and that PCB toxicology should be no exception. The symposium also included a comment from Nancy Hebben of McLean Hospital, Harvard Medical School, who had no connection to General Electric or the studies criticized. She concluded that Cicchetti, Kaufman, and Sparrow "demonstrate that numerous flaws limit the reliability of the results and the subsequent conclusions that can be drawn" from the studies criticized and that the debate as a whole carries "a clear moral message: That good intentions and the desire to promote good public health do not necessarily lead to scientifically valid and sustainable data. Ultimately, the entire scientific community, clinicians, and the health of the public will be better served by research studies that observe fundamental principles of scientific method and study design." See "Commentary on Polychlorinated Biphenyls (PCBs), Toxins, and Neuropsychological Deficits: Good Science Is the Antidote," 41 *Psychology in the Schools* 681, 684 (2004). Even if the studies are invalid, exposure to PCBs at the levels found in the Hudson may still cause neurological deficits and that possibility warrants a degree of precaution, as the next chapter discusses.

7. EPA, "Phase 2 Report, Further Site Characterization and Analysis," in *Revised Human Health Risk Assessment, Hudson River PCBs Reassessment RI/FS,* volume 2F (Nov. 2000), at ES-10 (emphasis added).

8. For the EPA not defending its laws, see *American Forest & Paper Ass'n and General Electric Co. v. EPA,* No. 93–0694 RMU, Partial Settlement Agreement (D.C. Cir. 1995), which the EPA settled on terms requiring it to reassess its regulation and allowing states to deviate from its law in the meantime. See also *American Iron and Steel Institute v. EPA,* 115 F.3d 979 (D.C. Cir. 1997), in which the EPA abandoned its defense of its regulation at oral argument; *Central and South West Services, Inc. v. U.S. EPA,* 220 F.3d 683 (5th Cir. 2000), certiorari denied by *Utility Solid Waste Activities Group v. EPA,* 532 U.S. 1065 (2001), in which the regulation was remanded to the EPA with its acquiescence. These cases are discussed in Angus Macbeth, James F. Warchall & Lesley C. Foxhall, "Cartoon Science: The Struggle between Politics and Science at the Environmental Protection Agency," *National Legal Center for the Public Interest,* May 2002, at 7–12. For attempting to avoid judicial review, see *GE v. EPA,* 290 F.3d 377 (D.C. Cir. 2002).

9. EPA, "Phase 2 Report," at ES-2.

10. Carol M. Browner, oral statement before the Committee on Environmental Conservation, New York State Assembly (July 9, 1998) (on file with the author). For risk assessment of dredging, see EPA, "EPA Proposes Comprehensive Plan to Clean Up Hudson River PCBs" (press release; Dec. 6, 2000) (on file with author). For Whitman, see EPA, "EPA Signs Final Cleanup Plan for Hudson River; Makes Public Involvement a Top Priority" (press release; Feb. 1, 2002) (on file with the author).

11. The prohibition is at 42 U.S.C. § 9613(h). GE filed a suit in which it argued that this prohibition is unconstitutional as a denial of due process. A federal district court ruled that the prohibition bars GE from bringing this constitutional claim, but an appellate court ruled that the lower court must hear the company's constitutional argument. See *GE v. EPA,* 360 F.3d 188 (D.C. Cir. 2004). For deference to agencies, see, e.g., *Baltimore Gas & Elec. Co. v. NRDC,* 462 U.S. 87 (1983). For penalties, see 42 U.S.C. § 9607(c)(3).

12. New York State Department of Environmental Conservation, *New York Statewide Angler Survey 1996, Report 2: Angler Preferences, Satisfaction, and Opinion on Management Issues* (April 1998), at 8.

13. On scope of excavation, see Kirk Johnson, "Dredging the Upper Hudson River, Without Slinging the Mud," *New York Times,* April 21, 2002, at § 1, p. 33. For local opposition, see a Zogby International poll of 809 voters in fourteen counties along the Hudson River that found that 59 percent favored GE's cleanup strategy, 27 percent opposed it, and 14 percent were not sure. Available at www.albany.edu/ihe/pro3.htm. For attempt to enjoin dredging, see *Farmers against Irresponsible Remediation ex rel. Hanehan v. EPA,* 165 F. Supp. 2d 253 (N.D.N.Y. 2001) (enforcing 42 U.S.C. § 9613(h)).

14. Lisa Guide, a deputy assistant secretary for policy in the U.S. Department of the Interior under President Bill Clinton, quoted in Katherine Q. Seelye, "As Whitman Deliberated Plan, the Pressures Mounted," *New York Times*, Aug. 2, 2001, at B6.

15. An assistant searched the *New York Times* database on LexisNexis for all articles that contained the words "PCB," "Hudson River," and "General Electric"; 293 articles appeared. The first one was dated Aug. 8, 1975. He used only items published from Aug. 8, 1975, through Aug. 1, 2001, the day Christine Whitman announced that the EPA would dredge the Hudson River. This eliminated 39 items, thus bringing the number down to 254 articles. Of these 254, 19 were letters to the editor, 2 were corrections of previous articles, and 12 mentioned PCBs incidentally. This left 221 articles, editorials, and other items. Of these, 150 linked PCBs to some serious disease; 145 of them mentioned cancer. For mentions of inconclusive science, see, e.g., "GE Disputes Federal Finding That PCB's Are Flowing Down the Hudson," *New York Times*, Aug. 20, 1998, at B5. The article on Kimbrough study is John H. Cushman Jr., "Study Finds Little Risks from PCB's," *New York Times*, March 10, 1999, at A14 (emphasis added). On the water's safety, the *New York Times* did report in 1986, fifteen years before the decision to dredge, that "the Hudson is a source of drinking water for many upstate communities—as well as for New York City on occasion—and is used by thousands of people each year for swimming and fishing. State officials, however, have warned against eating many species of fish from sections of the river contaminated by PCB's, or polychlorinated biphenyls, which are believed to cause cancer, and has banned all commercial fishing of striped bass." This statement was preceded by the suggestion that state officials were lax in safeguarding the river. See Elizabeth Kolbert, "Toxic Pollutants Linger as Threat to the Hudson," *New York Times*, April 28, 1986, at B2. From this article, a careful reader would have gleaned that the river water was drunk but would have wondered whether it was safe to do so. On the article reporting the drinking water as risky, see Robert Worth, "PCB Worries Are Spreading from Hudson to Its Shores," *New York Times*, April 17, 2001, at B1 ("It is hard to say what kind of health risks PCB's pose on land. The federal environmental agency has focused on the river because it has determined that eating fish or drinking water contaminated with the chemical poses a cancer risk, said Douglas Tomchuk, a project manager for the agency's Hudson River PCB site."). For more balanced accounts, see, e.g., Gina Kolata, "Farmed Salmon Have More Contaminants Than Wild Ones, Study Finds," *New York Times*, Jan. 9, 2004, at A12; Keith Schneider, "Efforts Revive River but Not Mohawk Life," *New York Times*, June 6, 1994, at B8; Keith Schneider, "Progress, Not Victory, on Great Lakes Pollution," *New York Times*, May, 7, 1994, at § 1, p. 1.

16. The state tried twice and lost both times. *In the Matter of Washington County Cease, Inc. v. Persico*, 64 N.Y.2d 923 (1985); *New York State Superfund*

Coalition, Inc., v. New York State Department of Environmental Conservation, 536 N.Y.S.2d 886 (3rd Dept. 1989). For state officials' request, see Langdon Marsh to William Muszynhski, July 26, 1989 (on file with author).

Chapter 11. Precaution and Policy

1. *Ethyl Corp. v. EPA,* 541 F.2d 1, 25 (D.C. Cir. 1976) (en banc). For a survey of precaution in federal environmental law, see Gail Charnley & E. Donald Elliott, "Risk versus Precaution: Environmental Law and Public Health Protection," 32 *Environmental Law Reporter* 10363 (2002).

2. Agency for Toxic Substances and Disease Registry, *Case Studies in Environmental Medicine: Polychlorinated Biphenyl (PCB) Toxicity,* available at www .atsdr.cdc.gov/HEC/CSEM/pcb/physiologic_effects.html (downloaded Oct. 1, 2003), raises concerns about reproductive, developmental, and other effects. For EPA's precautionary approach to such concerns and the validity of the studies upon which they are based, see note 6 to the previous chapter. These studies warrant further follow-up on the effects suspected and greater precaution in the meantime, just as Dr. Kimbrough's finding of tumors in PCB-dosed rodents warranted follow-up and precaution on the suspected cancer effects. Epidemiology generally cannot detect cancer risks of less than one in a thousand. See, e.g., *Eco-Pragmatism,* at 80, citing John Graham et al., *In Search of Safety: Chemicals and Cancer Risk* (Cambridge, Mass.: Harvard University Press, 1988), at 181. If, however, the epidemiology is on occupational groups exposed to high doses, it would act as a sentinel against smaller risks in a population exposed to much lower doses. Comparing the doses in the case of PCBs is complicated when considering the consumption of fish, in which the chemicals bioaccumulate.

3. Former EPA staff member, quoted by E. Donald Elliott in an interview with the author, Jan. 14, 2003.

4. For asbestos removal, see *Asbestos Hazard Emergency Response Act,* Pub. L. No. 99–519, 100 Stat. 2970 (1986) (codified as amended at 15 U.S.C. § 2641 et seq.). B. T. Mossman et al., "Asbestos: Scientific Development and Implications for Public Policy," 247 *Science* 294, 299 (1990).

5. Such rigidity is criticized in Cass R. Sunstein, "Beyond the Precautionary Principle," 151 *University of Pennsylvania Law Review* 1003, 1007 (2003) (discussing the Wingspread Declaration).

6. Cass R. Sunstein, "The Paralyzing Principle," 25 *Regulation Magazine* 32, 37 (2003). On the meaningless of the precautionary principle, see generally Cross, "Paradoxical Perils of the Precautionary Principle," 53 *Washington & Lee Law Review* at 873–76; Indur M. Goklany, *The Precautionary Principle: A Critical Appraisal of Environmental Risk Assessment* (Washington, D.C.: Cato Institute, 2001). For a spirited defense of the precautionary principle in its weaker form, see David A. Dana, "A Behavioral Economic Defense of the Precautionary

Principle," 97 *Northwestern U. Law Review* 1315 (2003). For dangers from dredging, see National Academy of Sciences, *A Risk Management Strategy for PCB-Contaminated Sediments* (Washington, D.C.: National Academies Press, 2001), 23–51. For discussion of studies suggesting clean up does more to shorten lives, see Cross, "Paradoxical Perils," 53 *Washington & Lee Law Review* at 900–902.

Jane E. Brody, "In a World of Hazards, Worries Are Often Misplaced," *New York Times*, Aug. 20, 2002, at F11. For Sunstein on health effects of lost income, see "The Paralyzing Principle," at 34. See also studies cited in the Office of Management and Budget, Office of Information and Regulatory Affairs, *Informing Regulatory Decisions: 2003 Report to Congress on the Costs and Benefits of Federal Regulations and Unfunded Mandates on State, Local, and Tribal Entities* (September 2003), at 62.

7. For sealing mine shafts, see Joel Brinkley, "Death Toll Rises But Money in Mine Fund Goes Unspent," *New York Times*, Sept. 26, 2002, at A20. "These tax revenues have collected in a government trust fund that now holds $1.54 billion. But the federal government refuses to spend most of the money, holding it back to help offset the budget deficit, raising continuing complaints from state officials as more people die.... The Interior Department keeps a detailed inventory of dangerous abandoned mine sites. It estimates that all of them could be repaired for $2.96 billion. Using the $1.54 billion in the abandoned mine fund and new receipts, the government could in theory accrue enough money to clear up all those problems in five or six years." A search of the databases of the *New York Times, Washington Post,* and *Los Angeles Times* from Jan. 1987 to Oct. 1, 2003, found forty articles mentioning the Surface Mining Control & Reclamation Act of 1977. None indicated that any advocacy organization had spoken up to avert this danger.

8. *Isaiah* 6:3 (King James).

9. See Robert H. Nelson, "Unoriginal Sin: The Judeo-Christian Roots of Ecotheology," *Policy Review* (Summer 1990), at 52. See also the responses to this article in *Policy Review* (Fall 1990), at 89.

10. *Genesis* 3:6 (King James).

11. For preference for PCBs, see R. F. Boykin, M. Kazarians & R. A. Freeman, "Comparative Fire Risk Study of PCB Transformers," 6 *Risk Analysis* 477–88 (1986). The officer found that the PCBs got in the river through "both corporate abuse and regulatory failure." See Richard Severo, "State Finds G.E. a PCB Polluter," *New York Times*, Feb. 10, 1976, at 1.

12. For Sierra Club, see letter from Carl Pope, Aug. 19, 1997 (on file with author). For Riverkeeper, see Andrew C. Revkin, "Savvy That Matched a River's Needs," *New York Times*, April 16, 2000, at 14WC1.

13. *Genesis* 1:28 (King James). See also Lynn White Jr., "The Historical Roots of Our Ecologic Crisis," 155 *Science* 1203–7 (1967).

Chapter 12. Coming Down to Earth

1. Aldo Leopold, *Sand County Almanac* (New York: Oxford University Press, 1949) (hereinafter cited as Leopold, *Sand County Almanac*). William K. Stevens, "Celebrating an Ecologist's Eloquence and Vision," *New York Times,* Oct. 19, 1999, at F4. See also Leopold, *The River of the Mother of God and Other Essays by Aldo Leopold* (ed. Susan L. Flader & J. Baird Callicott; Madison: The University of Wisconsin Press, 1991), at ix (hereinafter cited as *The River*) (in which the editors call Leopold's work "the philosophical touchstone of the modern environmental movement").

2. It was actually Sauk County, which had sandy soil. The book, which was published posthumously, was given its title by one of his sons.

3. *The River,* at 300.

4. For reports of opposition to dredging, see Andrew C. Revkin, "Invisible Stain—A Special Report: In War over PCB's in Hudson, the EPA Nears Its Rubicon," *New York Times,* June 5, 2000, at A1 (Revkin quotes Cara Lee, environmental director for Scenic Hudson, as saying, "This is the largest PCB contamination site in the country, and yet people who live here seem to have blinders on."); Kirk Johnson, "On Hudson, Cleanup Idea Stirs Emotions," *New York Times,* Dec. 2, 2000, at A1 (in which a local resident is quoted as saying, "People are definitely confused."); Kirk Johnson, "G.E. Switches Its Web Site about PCB's," *New York Times,* Sept. 30, 2000, at B5 ("The dot-com site, run by General Electric for the last several years, is stocked with scientific reports and glossy pictures that are part of the company's multimillion-dollar campaign to convince people that dredging the Hudson to remove PCB's is neither necessary nor wise."); Kirk Johnson, "Gipper Meets 'Survivor' as G.E.'s Image Hardens; PCB Battle Tests a Venerable Tradition," *New York Times,* March 4, 2001, at § 1, p. 29 ("Local residents . . . are being bombarded with sound-bites [by G.E.] about E.P.A. high-handedness and river hydrology."); Kirk Johnson, "On Hudson, Cleanup Idea Stirs Emotions," *New York Times,* Dec. 2, 2000, at A1 (on "the disdain that many people here feel for big government"); Kirk Johnson, "At Hearing, Hudson Cleanup Suddenly Becomes Personal," *New York Times,* Dec. 13, 2000, at B5 ("Some of the residents who came out tonight to oppose dredging were, they said, really opposing other things, like big government and people from New York City."). For *Times*'s reporters, see chapter 10.

5. None of the *Times*'s twenty-three articles discussing local opposition describe it as environmental. For EPA's rationale, see Carol M. Browner, speech to the Committee on Environmental Conservation, New York State Assembly, July 9, 1998, available at www.epa.gov/region02/news/speeches/980709.htm.

6. See Editorial Desk, "Dogged by a Clean Air Tail," *New York Times,* July 3, 1980, at A18. The *Times* was correct.

7. R. A. Chudd, Ross Sandler & David Schoenbrod, *A New Direction in*

Transit: A Report to Mayor Edward I. Koch from Robert F. Wagner, Jr., Chairman, City Planning Commission (City of New York, 1978).

Chapter 13. A Government of the People

1. Robert H. Wiebe, *Self-Rule: A Cultural History of American Democracy* (Chicago: The University of Chicago Press, 1995), at 28–40, 66–68.
2. Gordon S. Wood, *The Creation of the American Republic, 1776–1787* (New York: Norton, 1969), 472.
3. U.S. Constitution, Art. I. §§ 2, 3, 4, and Art. II. § 1. One of the chief issues about the presidency was whether it would be held by more than one person. The convention chose a unitary president and opted for election by a college of electors rather than by Congress or the people themselves partly in order to reduce the executive's responsiveness to popular opinion. James Madison, *Notes of Debates on the Federal Convention of 1787* (New York: W.W. Norton, 1987), at 45–47, 58–60, 306–9, 356–62; *The Federalist No. 68* (ed. Jacob E. Cooke; Middletown, Conn.: Wesleyan University Press, 1961), at 458.
4. U.S. Constitution Art. I, § 5, ¶3. For Parliament, see A. F. Pollard, *The Evolution of Parliament* (2nd ed.; New York: Russell & Russell, 1968), at 180. See also Norman Wilding & Philip Laundy, *An Encyclopedia of Parliament* (3rd ed.; New York: Frederick A. Praeger, 1968), at 209.
5. *The Oxford English Dictionary* (2nd ed., vol. 13, 1989), at 673. "Republic; republique; *res* thing, affair; *publicus* public; the state, the common weal; a state in which the supreme power rests in the people and their elected representatives or officers, as opposed to one governed by a king or similar ruler; a commonwealth."
6. For limiting the federal government, see U.S. Constitution Art. 1, § 8; Laurence Tribe, *American Constitutional Law,* vol. 1 (3rd ed.; New York: Foundation, 2000), at 795, 801–58. See also Marci Hamilton, "Federalism and the Public Good: The True Story Behind the Religious Land Use and Institutionalized Persons Act," 78 *Indiana Law Journal* 311, 320–22 (2003). For republican form of government, see U.S. Constitution Art. IV, § 4 (emphasis added). The Supreme Court has decided that this clause is not judicially enforceable, not that it is unimportant. *Baker v. Carr,* 369 U.S. 186, 208–11, 217–20 (1962).
7. For changes after the War of 1812, see Wiebe, *Self-Rule,* at 27–28, 72–77, 83–85. For lack of respect for aristocrats, see Wiebe, *Self-Rule,* at 42–47, 56–58, 61–63. Frances Trollope quoted in Victoria Glendinning, *Anthony Trollope* (New York: Alfred A. Knopf, 1993), 45.
8. For class structure, see Wiebe, *Self-Rule,* at 117–21. For the vote, see Wiebe, *Self-Rule,* at 91, 115–21, 124–26.
9. Wiebe, *Self-Rule,* at 64–68, 82–85.
10. Wiebe, *Self-Rule,* at 115–16, 138–48.
11. For national class, see Wiebe, *Self-Rule,* at 147–48. For new inventions,

see generally, Leonard C. Bruno, *Science and Technology Firsts* (ed. Donna Olendorf; Detroit: Gale Research, 1997), at 207–8, 322, 407, 213, 513, and 515, respectively.

12. For science, see Robert Wiebe, *The Search for Order, 1877–1920* (New York: Hill and Wang, 1967), at 111–13, 129, 144–51, 168–75. John B. Watson, quoted in Lynn Z. Bloom, *Doctor Spock: Biography of a Conservative Radical* (Indianapolis: Bobbs Merrill, 1972), at 121–22, 124. Watson also opined in his 1928 book, "Never hug and kiss [young children], never let them sit in your lap. If you must, kiss them once on the forehead when they say good night. Shake hands with them in the morning. Give them a pat on the head if they have made an extraordinary good job of a difficult task." John B. Watson, *Psychological Care of Infant and Child* (New York: Arno Press & The New York Times, 1972), at 81–82. Similarly, one prominent pediatrician advised parents to resist the impulse to feed babies who cry for food because deviating from strict schedules would cause "loose bowels." Luther Emmett Holt, *The Care and Feeding of Children* (2nd ed.; New York: D. Appleton, 1901), at 80–81.

13. Wiebe, *Self-Rule*, at 135–37.

14. Wiebe, *Self-Rule*, at 134–37, 143, 164–65, 173–80, 206–7, 217–22.

15. Interstate Commerce Act of 1887, Ch. 104, 24 Stat. 379 (1887), as amended at 49 U.S.C. § 10101 (1980). For Morgan and the ICC, see Ron Chernow, *The House of Morgan: An American Banking Dynasty and the Rise of Modern Finance* (New York: Touchstone, 1990), at 56–58, 176–78.

16. *National Industrial Recovery Act of 1933*, Ch. 90, 48 Stat. 195 (1933), amended by Ch. 246, 49 Stat. 375 (1935), repealed by Pub. L. No. 89-554, § 8(a), 80 Stat. 648 (1966). For Morgan and Rockefeller, see Chernow, *The House of Morgan*, at 56, 78, 83, 90. See also Wayne Gard, "Hot Oil from Texas," 35 *American Mercury* 71, 73 (1935).

17. There has been, in addition, the subsequent rise of what might be called the "international class." It is interesting to see major environmental and corporate leaders, each for quite different reasons, pushing for control of some environmental issues to be shifted to international institutions.

18. Robert C. Fellmeth, *The Interstate Commerce Omission: Public Interest and the ICC* (New York: Grossman, 1970), at 311–25. For termination of the ICC, see "Re-regulate? Not on Your Life; Triumphs on the Road, on the Phone, in the Air," *New York Times*, June 10, 1990, at § 4, p. 22; *Interstate Commerce Commission Termination Act of 1995*, Pub. L. No. 104–88, 109 Stat. 803 (1996); *Staggers Rail Act of 1980*, Pub. L. No. 96–448, 94 Stat. 1895 (1980); *Motor Carrier Act of 1980*, Pub. L. No. 96–296, 94 Stat. 793 (1980).

19. *Whitman v. American Trucking Associations*, 531 U.S. 457, 472 (2001), quoting *Loving v. United States*, 517 U.S. 748, 771 (1996).

20. *Loving v. United States*, 517 U.S. 748, 757–58 (1996).

21. For enumerated powers, see *United States v. Lopez*, 514 U.S. 549, 552 (1995). For balance of power, see *Gregory v. Ashcroft*, 501 U.S. 452, 458 (1991).

22. *Whitman v. American Trucking,* 531 U.S. 457, 471–76 (2001); *Lopez,* 514 U.S. at 551–54, 563. See generally, David Schoenbrod, "Politics and the Principle That Elected Legislators Should Make the Laws," 26 *Harvard Journal of Law and Public Policy* 239, 242–43 (2003).

Chapter 14. Home Rule

Epigraph: Speech to the Environmental Law Institute's annual award dinner, Washington, D.C., Oct. 26, 1999.

1. T-shirt, "The states are not branches of the federal government," 1997 ECOS spring meeting, Carefree, Arizona (on hanger with the author); David Schoenbrod, "State Regulators Have Had Enough of the EPA," *Wall Street Journal,* May 8, 1997, at A22.

2. See Bill Clinton & Al Gore, *Reinventing Environmental Regulation* (Washington, D.C.: Government Printing Office, 1995). The phrase "reinventing government" was coined by David Osborne and Ted Gaebler in their book *Reinventing Government: How the Entrepreneurial Spirit Is Transforming the Public Sector* (New York: Plume, 1993). For Browner, see "Joint EPA/State Agreement to Pursue Regulatory Innovation" (Feb. 12, 1997) (on file with author).

3. See John H. Cushman Jr., "EPA Withdraws Plan to Empower States," *New York Times,* March 2, 1997, at A22.

4. Fred Hansen, Deputy Administrator, EPA, to reinvention ombudspersons (Feb. 1997) (on file with author).

5. The Environmental Council of the States to Carol Browner, Administrator, and Fred Hansen, Deputy Administrator, EPA, Feb. 26, 1997 (on file with the author). The letter was signed by the president of the Environmental Council of the States, Georgia Commissioner Harold Reheis, and the environmental commissioners of New Jersey, New Hampshire, Illinois, Minnesota, and Arkansas.

6. *Train v. NRDC,* 421 U.S. 60, 64 (1975). For federal takeover, see 1970 Act, § 101(a)(1) (corresponding version at 42 U.S.C. § 7401(a)(1)).

7. For state plans, see 1970 Clean Air Act, § 101(a)(2)(A), (E) (corresponding version at 42 U.S.C. § 7410 (a)(2)(A), (D)). For interstate pollution, see David Schoenbrod, *Time for the Federal Environmental Aristocracy to Give Up Power* (Center for the Study of American Business), February 1998, at 3–4.

8. In "Goals Statutes or Rules Statutes: The Case of The Clean Air Act," 30 *UCLA Law Review* 740, 778 (1983), I noted the building of 175 stacks taller than 500 feet since 1970. Richard L. Revesz, "Federalism and Interstate Environmental Externalities," 144 *University of Pennsylvania Law Review* 2341, 2350–53 (1996). On environmental federalism generally, see Henry N. Butler & Jonathan R. Macey, *Using Federalism to Improve Environmental Policy* (Washington, D.C.: American Enterprise Institute Press, 1996).

9. For tall stacks, see 1977 Act, § 123(a). Senate Report No. 101-228, 101st Cong., 1st sess., at 553 (1989). For acid rain, see 1990 Act, § 401–16. For limiting interstate pollution, see, e.g., *Michigan v. EPA*, 213 F.3d 663 (D.C. Cir. 2000), cert. denied, *Appalachian Power Co. v. EPA*, 532 U.S. 903 (2001); *Appalachian Power Co. v. EPA*, 249 F.3d 1032 (D.C. Cir. 2001); *Appalachian Power Co. V. EPA*, 251 F.3d 1026 (D.C. Cir. 2001).

10. Senate Report No. 101–228, 101st Cong., 1st sess., at 553 (1989).

11. For toxic waste statutes, see *Resource Conservation and Recovery Act* (RCRA), Pub. L. No. 94–580, 90 Stat. 2795 (1976) (codified as amended at 42 U.S.C. § 6901 et seq.); *Comprehensive Environmental Response, Compensation, and Liability Act*, Pub. L. No. 96–510, 94 Stat. 2767 (1980) (codified as amended at 42 U.S.C. § 9601 et seq.). *Safe Drinking Water Act*, Pub. L. No. 93–523, 88 Stat. 1660 (1974) (codified as amended at 42 U.S.C. §§ 300f to 300j-26) (hereinafter cited as 1974 Drinking Water Act).

12. Indur Goklany argues that European nations have had considerable success at reducing pollution by negotiations rather than through impositions by a higher level of government. See *Clearing the Air*, at 142. See, e.g., Thomas W. Merrill, "Golden Rules for Transboundary Pollution," 46 *Duke Law Journal* 931 (1997) (hereinafter cited as Merrill, "Golden Rules").

13. For 1964 emission limit, see EPA, *Milestones in Auto Emissions Control*, available at www.epa.gov/otaq/12-miles.htm. For preempting, with the exception of California, state motor vehicle standards, see Air Quality Act of 1967, Pub. L. No. 90–148, 81 Stat. 485, 501 (1967). For state options today, see 42 U.S.C. § 7543. The law requiring the use of "reformulated" gasoline in states with pollution problems ought not to qualify. See 42 U.S.C. § 7545(k). Its supposed purpose is to help these states meet air quality standards, not remove barriers to trade. Its real purpose is to get votes from the farmers who grow the corn from which the ethanol in reformulated gasoline is made and to solicit campaign contributions from Archer Daniels Midland and other companies that turn the corn into ethanol.

14. The treaty establishing the European Community similarly provides that it may act "only if and in so far as the objectives of the proposed action cannot be sufficiently achieved by the Member States and can therefore, by reason of the scale or effects of the proposed action, be better achieved by the Community." Treaty Establishing the European Community (part 1 of 8), 1995 BDIEL AD LEXIS 96 (1995).

15. In such a situation, Justice Breyer concludes that the benefits would be "disproportionately local," while "the costs are widely dispersed." *Solid Waste Agency of Northern Cook County v. U.S. Army Corps of Engineers*, 531 U.S. 159, 195 (2001) See also Sam Kazman, "SWANCC Won't Put Environmentalism in the Tank," *Endangered Species & Wetland Report*, Feb. 2001, at 12. Whether Congress now deals with species preservation in a sensible way is quite a different question—one that is beyond the scope of this book. See Peter Huber, *Hard Green:*

Saving the Environmental from the Environmentalists: A Conservative Manifesto (New York: Basic Books, 2000), at 94.

16. This possibility of a milder alternative is discussed more extensively in chapter 18. Leavitt calls for "national standards and neighborhood solutions." See EPA, *Mike Leavitt on Environmental Stewardship: The Enlibra Principles,* available at www.epa.gov/adminweb/leavitt/enlibra.htm (downloaded Feb. 20, 2004).

17. On the connection between civil rights and environmental statutes, see *Democracy by Decree,* at 17–27.

18. Compare *Wickard v. Filburn,* 317 U.S. 111 (1942), with *United States v. Lopez,* 514 U.S. 549 (1995).

19. *Democracy by Decree.*

20. For slowing down states, see the discussion in chapter 5. For pesticides, see *Silent Spring,* at 87, 91, 156–72, 175.

21. For competition, see Wallace E. Oates, "A Reconsideration of Environmental Federalism," in *Recent Advances in Environmental Economics* (ed. John A. List & Aart de Zeeuw; Cheltenham, U.K.: Edward Elgar, 2002), at 1, 15 (discussing empirical studies, some of which find no effect, and other more recent studies finding substantial effects). As Jonathan Adler shows, proponents of the race-to-the-bottom theory assume that states competing for business will reduce environmental standards rather than search out ways to meet them more efficiently. Adler, "The Ducks Stops Here? The Environmental Challenge to Federalism," 9 *Supreme Court Economic Review* 205 (2001). I take issue with this assumption in chapter 18. For the race to the top, see Oates, "Reconsideration," at 12–15, 17 (summarizing studies). See also Adler, "Wetlands, Waterfowl, and the Menace of Mr. Wilson: Commerce Clause Jurisprudence and the Limits of Federal Wetlands Regulation," 29 *Environmental Law* 1 (1999) (finding that, before the federal regulation of wetlands, state regulation was precisely the opposite of what the race-to-the-bottom theory would have predicted).

22. Richard L. Revesz, "Rehabilitating Interstate Competition: Rethinking the Race to the Bottom Rationale for Federal Environmental Regulation," 67 *New York University Law Review* 1210, 1244 (1992). Revesz goes on in this article to argue that standard models of interstate competition show that competition in environmental standards increases public welfare. See 1211–12. For environmentalists' response, see, e.g., Kirsten H. Engel, "State Environmental Standard-Setting: Is There a 'Race' and Is It 'to the Bottom'?," 48 *Hastings Law Journal* 271 (1997); Daniel C. Esty, "Revitalizing Environmental Federalism," 95 *Michigan Law Review* 570 (1996); Joshua D. Sarnoff, "The Continuing Imperative (but Only from a National Perspective) for Federal Environmental Protection," 7 *Duke Environ. Law & Policy Forum* 225 (1997); Peter P. Swire, "The Race to Laxity and the Race to Undesirability: Explaining Failures in Competition among Jurisdictions in Environmental Law," 14 *Yale Journal on Regulation* 67 (1996). Revesz replied in "The Race to the Bottom and Federal Environmental

Regulation: A Response to Critics," 82 *Minnesota Law Review* 535 (1997). Oates, "Reconsideration," at 8 ("If there is a race to the bottom, we are left with a choice between two alternatives: suboptimal local decisions on environmental quality or inefficient uniform national standards. And which of these two alternatives leads to a higher level of social welfare is, in principle, unclear.").

23. For public support, see Willett M. Kempton, James S. Boster, and Jennifer A. Hartley, *Environmental Values in American Culture* (Cambridge: MIT Press, 1995), at 4–5 (reporting long-term trends); PollingReport.com, "Environment," http://pollingreport.com/enviro.htm (downloaded July 31, 2004) (reporting Gallup Poll of March 6–11, 2004, the responses to the question, "Do you think the U.S. government is doing too much, too little, or about the right amount in terms of protecting the environment?" as follows: "too much," 5%; "too little," 55%, "about right," 37%, "no opinion," 3%). For NRDC membership, see National Resources Defense Council, "About Us," available at www.nrdc.org/about/ default.asp (downloaded March 20, 2004). For budgets, see Hugo Gurdon, "The Grim Green Giant: The Environmentalist Establishment's Lobbying Behemoth," 16 *CEI Monthly Planet* 1, 3 (2003). For an example of working relationships, Citizens for Sensible Safeguards is a coalition of three hundred organizations, including environmental groups, major labor unions, consumer advocacy groups, and civil liberties organizations. Available at www.ombwatch.org/article/articlereview/208/1/69/ (downloaded Oct. 4, 2003). See also, e.g., Jill Abramson & Steven Greenhouse, "Labor Victory on Trade Bill Reveals Power," *New York Times,* Nov. 12, 1997, at A1 (labor's effort against the trade bill was joined by environmental groups, consumer safety groups, and civil rights organizations).

24. See chapter 18.

25. Lichter & Rothman, at 26.

26. There are of course many differences in the political structures of federal and state governments. Richard Revesz has investigated them and concluded that there is no systematic reason to suppose that the federal government is more sensitive to environmental concerns. See Revesz, "Federalism and Environmental Regulation: A Public Choice Analysis," 115 *Harvard Law Review* 553 (2001). For the law review issue, see "The Advent of Local Environmental Laws," 20 *Pace Environmental Law Review* 1 (2002). The quote is by one of the faculty sponsors of the law review issue, John R. Nolon, in his article "In Praise of Parochialism: The Advent of Local Environmental Law," 26 *Harvard Environmental Law Review* 365 (2002). For state and local governments, see DeWitt John, *Civic Environmentalism: Alternatives to Regulation in States and Communities* (Washington, D.C.: Aspen Institute and National Academy of Public Administration, 1994), at xiv ("States and localities stepped forward in the 1980s, when federal environmental policy was hampered by stagnant budgets and political gridlock."). Evan J. Ringquist, *Environmental Protection at the State Level: Politics and Progress in Controlling Pollution* (1993), at xiii.

J. Clarence Davies and Jan Mazurek, *Pollution Control in the United States: Evaluating the System* (Washington, D.C.: Resources for the Future, 1998), at 42 (hereinafter cited as Davies, *Pollution Control*). For bulk of enforcement actions, see Susan Bruninga, "Enforcement: Increases Seen in Civil Penalties, Jail Time for Breaking Environmental Laws, EPA Says," 31 *Environmental Reporter* (BNA) 113 (2000)

27. See *Clearing the Air*, at 118–19.

28. Carol M. Browner, remarks prepared for the release of the Toxics Release Inventory Data, Washington, D.C., May 20, 1997, available at yosemite.epa.gov/administrator/speeches.nsf/.

29. Arthur Schlesinger Jr., "Board of Contributors: In Defense of Government," *Wall Street Journal*, June 7, 1995, at A14.

30. An alternative to thinking of environmental quality as a national right or a matter of state policy is to think of it as a matter over which both federal and state governments can compete for the allegiance of citizens. James Madison hoped for such competition. See *The Federalist*, No. 46 (ed. Gary Willis; New York: Bantam Books, 1982), at 237. However, Madison's dream has turned into a nightmare because, as described in the text, the federal government has skewed the competition in its favor. See Richard B. Stewart, "Madison's Nightmare," 57 *University of Chicago Law Review* 335 (1990). *Unfunded Mandate Reform Act of 1995*, Pub. L. No. 104–4, 109 Stat. 48 (1995) (codified at 2 U.S.C. §1501 et seq.). "Remarks on Signing the Unfunded Mandate Reform Act of 1995," *Public Papers of the Presidents of the United States: William J. Clinton, 1995, Book I* (Washington, D.C.: Government Printing Office, 1996), at 382. For EPA's unfunded mandates, see *Democracy by Decree*, at 39–43.

31. For belief in federal government, see Richard B. Stewart, "Environmental Quality as a National Good in a Federal State," 1997 *University of Chicago Law Forum* 199, 210 (1997). For burning rivers, see Browner quote in Jonathan H. Adler, "Fables of the Cuyahoga: Reconstructing a History of Environmental Protection," 14 *Fordham Environmental Law Journal* 89, 90–91 (2002); John H. Adams, "Illogical Extremes," *OnEarth Magazine*, Winter 2004; and Robert F. Kennedy Jr., "Crimes against Nature," *Rolling Stone*, Dec. 11, 2003. This less dramatic account of the Cuyahoga fire is drawn from Adler, "Fables." For 1952 photo in 1969 coverage, see "The Cities: The Price of Optimism," *Time*, Aug. 1, 1969, at 41

32. For the Vieques case, see *Weinberger v. Romero-Barcelo*, 456 U.S. 305 (1982). See Dana Canedy, "Navy Leaves a Battered Island, and Puerto Ricans Cheer," *New York Times*, May 2, 2003, at A22.

33. TRB, "A Promise Kept," *The New Republic*, Sept. 1, 1997, at 6. For apportionment, see *Baker v. Carr*, 369 U.S. 186 (1962). *Voting Rights Act of 1965*, Pub. L. No. 89–110, 79 Stat. 439 (1965). In 1960, per capita income in the southeast was 27 percent below the national average, but by 2000 that disparity had been reduced by more than half, to 11 percent. See U.S. Department of

Commerce, Bureau of Economic Analysis, available at www.bea.gov/bea/regional/spi/drill.cfm. Alan Rosenthal, *The Decline of Representative Democracy: Process, Participation, and Power in State Legislatures* (Washington, D.C.: Congressional Quarterly, 1998), at 4. New York has the most dysfunctional legislative process in the nation, according to Jeremy M. Creelan and Laura M. Moulton, *New York State Legislative Process: An Evaluation and Blueprint for Reform* (New York: Brennan Center for Justice, 2004). In "Demanding the Right Size Government," *New York Times*, Oct. 4, 1999, at A27, Alan Ehrenhalt argues that state and local legislatures generally function better than the U.S. Congress.

34. Douglas M. Costle, "Brave New Chemical: The Future Regulatory History of Phlogiston," 33 *Administrative Law Review* 195 (1981). See also Thomas O'McGarity, "The Courts and the Ossification of Rulemaking: A Response to Professor Seidenfeld," 75 *Texas Law Review* 525 (1997); Davies, *Pollution Control*, at 28. For new air quality standard, see 62 *Federal Register* 38,652 (1997). Editorial, "Paralysis on Clean Air," *New York Times*, Jan. 4, 2004, at § 4, p. 6. Matthew L. Wald, "Environmentalists Head for the States," *New York Times*, Feb. 1, 2004, at § 4, p. 7.

35. *Breaking the Vicious Circle*, at 49; *Eco-Pragmatism*, at 73.

36. For example, National Research Council, *Air Quality Management in the United States* (Washington, D.C.: National Academies Press, 2004), at 229, 232–34, 247. Alice M. Rivlin, *Reviving the American Dream: The Economy, the States, and the Federal Government* (Washington: Brookings Institution Press, 1992), at 117.

37. Nadine Strossen, interview with the author, Dec. 2, 2003.

38. Marc K. Landy & Mary Hague, "The Coalition for Waste: Private Interests and Superfund," in *Environmental Politics: Public Costs, Private Rewards* (ed. Michael S. Greve & Fred L. Smith Jr.; New York: Praeger, 1992), at 76; Jonathan H. Adler, *Environmentalism at the Crossroads: Green Activism in America* (Washington, D.C.: Capital Research Center, 1995), at 109–10; Todd J. Zywicki, "Environmental Externalities and Political Externalities: The Political Economy of Environmental Regulation and Reform," 73 *Tulane Law Review* 845, 878 (1999) (hereinafter cited as Zywicki, "Environmental Externalities"). Email from Stasea-Noele, information@sierraclub.org, Dec. 5, 2003; emails from John Bianchi, Jbianchi@audubon.org, Dec. 2, 2003.

Chapter 15. Vicki Been and Environmental Justice

1. See Executive Order No. 12,898, 59 *Federal Register* 7,629 (1994).

2. For Browner, see David Schoenbrod, "Rule of Environmental 'Injustice' Is about Politics, Not Racism," *Wall Street Journal*, Feb. 23, 1994, at A21.

3. United Church of Christ, Commission for Racial Justice, *Toxic Waste and Race in the U.S.: A National Report on the Racial and Socioeconomic Charac-*

teristics of Communities with Hazardous Wastes Sites (New York: Public Access Data, 1987).

4. Vicki Been, "Locally Undesirable Land Uses in Minority Neighborhoods: Disproportionate Siting or Market Dynamics?" 103 *Yale Law Journal* 1383, 1386 (1994); Vicki Been & Francis Gupta, "Coming to the Nuisance or Going to the Barrios? A Longitudinal Analysis of Environmental Justice Claims," 24 *Ecology Law Quarterly* 1, 7 (1997). For census tracts, see Been & Gupta, "Coming to the Nuisance," at 10–13. For quote, see 9. For support for disproportionate impact, see 21–22, 27, 30, 9, 32.

5. Compare studies cited in U.S. Commission on Civil Rights, Office of the General Counsel, draft report for commissioners' review, "Not in My Backyard: Executive Order 12,898 and Title VI as Tools for Achieving Environmental Justice" (Sept. 2003), at ch. 2, with those cited in Brett M. Baden & Don L. Coursey, "The Locality of Waste Sites within the City of Chicago: A Demographic, Social, and Economic Analysis," 24 *Resources and Energy Economics* 53, 55–57 (2002). Christopher H. Foreman Jr., *The Promise and Peril of Environmental Justice* (Washington, D.C.: Brookings Institution Press, 1998), at 27. The CDC report is available at www.cdc.gov/exposurereport/.

6. Institute of Medicine, *Toward Environmental Justice: Research, Education, and Health Policy Needs* (Washington, D.C.: National Academies Press, 1999), at 16. The report argues that this uncertainty about causality should not stand in the way of its recommendations for research, education, and health policy. It should stand in the way of any decision to maintain federal control of pollution control that is based on the assumption that racial discrimination *causes* disproportionate exposure to pollution. The analysis behind the report's conclusion that there is disproportionate impact seems off key in a report conducted by an august scientific body. The report cites only sources supportive of this view, does not probe their validity, and ignores the work reaching contrary conclusions. See pp. 14–16. Nonetheless, I think this conclusion is correct for reasons I give in the text. Whether the disparity is significant relative to environmental risks in general or other health-related disparities felt by the poor and minorities, the report does not say.

7. For Chicago study, see Baden & Coursey, "Locality," at 72–90. For 2003 draft study, see "Not in My Backyard," at 1, 4.

8. David Schoenbrod, "Large Lot Zoning," 78 *Yale Law Journal* 1418 (1969). See also "Not in My Backyard," at 17–18.

9. M. Lavelle & M. Coyle, "Unequal Protection: The Racial Divide in Environmental Law," *National Law Journal*, Sept. 21, 1992, at S1. For approval of the *National Law Journal* report, see Mark Atlas, "Rush to Judgment: An Empirical Analysis of Environmental Equity in the U.S.: Environmental Protection Agency Enforcement Actions," 35 *Law and Society Review* 633, 635 (2001). For verification, see Christopher Boerner & Thomas Lambert, "Environmental In-

justice," 118 *The Public Interest* 61, 65 (1995). For criticism of the NLJ study, see Shreekant Gupta, George Van Houtven & Maureen L. Cropper, "Do Benefits and Costs Matter in Environmental Regulation? An Analysis of EPA Decisions under Superfund," in *Analyzing Superfund: Economics, Science, and Law* (ed. Richard L. Revesz & Richard B. Stewart; Washington, D.C.: Resources for the Future, 1995), at 83; John A. Hird, "Environmental Policy and Equity: The Case of Superfund," 12 *Journal of Policy Analysis & Management* 323, 337 (1993) (finding no relationship between the pace at which sites are cleaned up and the host county's socioeconomic characteristics); Evan J. Ringquist, "A Question of Justice: Equity in Environmental Litigation, 1974–1991," 60 *Journal of Politics* 1148 (1998) (penalties not smaller in minority areas); Atlas, "Rush to Judgment" (penalties if anything larger in minority areas). Atlas's "Rush to Judgment" criticized the statistical methods used by Ringquist, which provoked an exchange between them. See Evan J. Ringquist, "The Need for Sound Judgment in Analyzing U.S. Environmental Protection Agency Enforcement Actions," 35 *Law and Society Review* 683 (2001); Mark Atlas, "Safe and Sound Judgment," 35 *Law and Society Review* 699 (2001). Atlas and Ringquist agree, however, that the *National Law Journal*'s analysis is invalid. On the unreliability of the *National Law Journal* report, see Atlas, "Rush to Judgment," at 633.

10. See, e.g., *Alexander v. Sandoval*, 532 U.S. 275 (2001).

11. EPA, *Environmental Justice*, available at www.epa.gov/compliance/environmentaljustice/index.html.

12. For complaints, see "Not in My Backyard," at 35. See EPA, *Interim Guidance for Investigating Title VI Administrative Complaints Challenging Permits* (Feb. 4, 1998), available at www.epa.gov/civilrights/docs/interim.pdf. The EPA's guidance actually consists of two documents, "Revised Draft Guidance for Investigating Title VI Administrative Complaints Challenging Permits" and "Draft Title VI Guidance for EPA Assistance Recipients Administering Environmental Permitting Programs." See 65 *Federal Register* 39,650 (2000). For Commission on Civil Rights quote, see "Not in My Backyard," at 56 (reporting views of industry, local governments, and environmental justice advocates). For pending cases, see "Summary of Information on Title VI Complaints," available at www.epa.gov/civilrights/t6complnt.htm (downloaded Oct. 8, 2003).

13. "Not in My Backyard," at 8, 10.

14. Section of Individual Rights & Responsibilities, American Bar Association and Public Law Research Institute, Hastings College of Law, *Environmental Justice for All: A Fifty State Survey of Legislation, Policies, and Initiatives* (October 2003), at iii, available at www.abanet.org/irr/committees/environmental/statestudy.pdf. National Academy of Public Administration, *Models for Change: Efforts by Four States to Address Environment Justice* (June 2002), at 2.

15. See Kemba Johnson, "Green with Envy," *City Limits*, January 2000, at 16, 17.

16. "Not in My Backyard," at 42–44.

17. Email from Vicki Been, Professor of Law, New York University School of Law, to the author, Oct. 17, 2003.

18. Atlas, "Rush to Judgment," at 677.

Chapter 16. Legislative Responsibility

1. I elaborate on the distinction between lawmaking and law interpretation in chapter 12 of *Power without Responsibility*.

2. For cutting emissions from new cars, see the discussion in chapter 3. For hazardous air pollutants, see 1990 Act, § 112(d)(3)(A) (corresponding version at 42 U.S.C. § 7412 (d)(3)(A)). See Robert N. Stavins, Letter to the Editor, "Emissions Trading Will Lead to Less Pollution; What's Immoral?" *New York Times*, Dec. 17, 1997, at A30 ("a tradable permit system among electrical utilities [reduced] emissions . . . faster than anyone had predicted and saving up to $1 billion a year for electricity consumers").

3. The act requires nonattainment plan provisions to provide for the implementation of all "reasonably available control technology" ("RACT") in achieving the air quality standards. See 42 U.S.C. § 7502(c)(1). For more statutory language, see 42 U.S.C. § 7409(b)(1). For lack of inherent meaning, see the discussion in chapter 8.

4. Compare Justice Scalia's opinion for the majority in *Whitman v. American Trucking Assoc.*, 531 U.S. 457, 462 (2001), with the concurring opinion by Justice Stevens, 531 U.S. at 487 and with his own article, Antonin Scalia, "A Note on the Benzene Case," *Regulation*, July/Aug. 1980, at 25.

5. For scientific methods, see *Power without Responsibility*, at 31–35. For lack of time, see *Congressional Responsibility Act: Hearings on HR 2727 before the Subcommittee on Commercial and Administrative Law*, 104th Congress (1996) (testimony of Gregory S. Wetstone, Legislative Director, Natural Resources Defense Council).

6. The average of five is derived from the data on the number of major rules the EPA issued over the past five years in Clyde Wayne Crews Jr., *Ten Thousand Commandments: An Annual Snapshot of the Federal Regulatory State—2003 Edition* (Washington, D.C.: Cato Institute, 2003), at 3. In 2000, the EPA had 449 rules under consideration. Only 31 of those rules were rated as "economically significant," and the agency promulgated only 5 "major" rules that year too. See Unified Agenda of Federal Regulations, Regulatory Information Service Center (October 2000). Stephen Breyer, "The Legislative Veto after Chadha," 72 *Georgetown Law Journal* 785 (1984).

7. Sheryl Gay Stolberg with Matt Richtel, "Do-Not-Call Listing Remains Up in Air after Day of Twists," *New York Times*, Sept. 26, 2003, at A1 (reporting on legal challenges and congressional action). Breyer, "Legislative Veto," at 793–94. William Niskanen offers another variation. Instead of requiring that agency

regulations be enacted by Congress, he suggests that all members of Congress be empowered to get a floor vote within sixty legislative days on any new regulation. William A. Niskanen, "More Lonely Numbers," 26 *Regulation* 3, 22 (2003). The result would be that there would be no floor vote on truly minor or noncontroversial rules but that all members would be responsible for all the rules issued by federal agencies.

8. For examples of pushing pollution control, see the discussion in chapter 5. For Krupp, see John J. Fialka, "Senate Rejects Mandatory Curbs on Gas Emissions in 55–43 Vote," *Wall Street Journal,* Oct. 31, 2003, at B2. See also Christopher Drew and Richard A. Oppel Jr., "Air War—Remaking Energy Policy; How Power Lobby Won Battle of Pollution Control at EPA," *New York Times,* March 6, 2004, at A1.

9. One recent example of the importance voters place on the environment issue: 23 percent of independent voters say that President Bush's environmental policies are his main shortcoming. Two-thirds of all voters oppose relaxing environmental standards to deal with soaring energy prices. See Jackie Calmes, "A Special Weekly Report from the *Wall Street Journal*'s Capital Bureau," *Wall Street Journal,* June 29, 2001, at A1.

10. See *Breaking the Vicious Circle,* at chs. 1 and 2. Sunstein, *Risk and Reason,* at viii.

11. *Breaking the Vicious Circle,* at 72, 60–61.

12. The Delaney clause in the Federal Food, Drug, and Cosmetic Act states, "No additive shall be deemed to be safe if it is found to induce cancer when ingested by man or animal, or if it is found, after tests which are appropriate for the evaluation of the safety of food additives, to induce cancer in man or animal." See 21 U.S.C. § 348(c)(3)(A). For saccharin, see Pub. L. No. 95–203, § 3, 91 Stat. 1452 (1977).

13. See the discussion in chapter 1.

14. *Congressional Responsibility Act of 1995,* H.R. 2727, 104th Cong., 1st sess. (1995). An alternative, as mentioned, would be William Niskanen's proposal summarized in note 7. U.S. Constitution Art. I, § 5, ¶3.

15. The Constitution deals with federal lands under a separate provision. The Supreme Court has long and rightly held that this provision allows Congress to leave federal land management to agencies. See *Power without Responsibility,* at 186–89. John D. Leshy, "Is the Multiple Use/Sustained Yield Management Philosophy Still Applicable Today?," in *Multiple Use and Sustained Yield: Changing Philosophies for Federal Land Management?,* House Committee on Interior and Insular Affairs, 102nd Cong., 2nd sess., Committee Print No. 11 (Washington, D.C.: Government Printing Office, 1992), at 107, 117.

16. Muskie & Cutler, "A National Environmental Policy: Now You See It, Now You Don't," 25 *Maine Law Review* 163, 188 (1973).

Chapter 17. The Rights of Citizens

Epigraph: Curt Meine, *Aldo Leopold: His Life and Work* (London: University of Wisconsin Press, 1988), at 430.

1. Agency rules normally do not take effect for thirty days after they are promulgated, but may provide for delayed compliance. Administrative Procedure Act, 5 U.S.C. § 553(d). National Primary Drinking Water Regulations; Arsenic and Clarifications to Compliance and New Source Contaminants Monitoring, 66 *Federal Register* 6976, 7027 (2001) (hereinafter cited as Browner's Final Arsenic Rule). For press reaction, see, e.g., Anthony Lewis, "Abroad at Home: The Feeling of a Coup," *New York Times,* March 31, 2001, at A15. Maureen Dowd, "Liberties: The Asbestos President," *New York Times,* April 1, 2001, at § 4, p. 17 ("Being witty about poisoned drinking water isn't easy. It requires a certain obtuse savoir-faire."); Robert K. Musil, "Arsenic on Tap," *New York Times,* April 24, 2001, at A18. See also Sunstein, *Risk and Reason,* at 156–57 (commenting on press coverage). For Bush ruining the environment, see, e.g., Melinda Henneberger, "Despite Appearances, Whitman Says She and Bush Agree on Environment," *New York Times,* April 17, 2001, at A12 (quoting Dan Weiss, former political director of the Sierra Club: "Another day, another environmental standard wrecked. This is worse than under Reagan."). See also Gregg Easterbrook, *Everything You Know about the Bush Environmental Record Is Wrong* (Washington, D.C.: Brookings Institution Press, 2002). For Whitman's rule, see 66 *Federal Register* 28,342 (2001) (codified at 40 C.F.R. Parts 9, 141). The new decision did, however, make some changes. Through grants and loans, the federal government would provide some financial assistance to the hardest-hit municipalities, but it would still be the public who would pay. Also, Administrator Whitman concluded that new evidence made the health case against arsenic stronger than it had been when Administrator Browner made her decision on January 17, 2001.

2. 1974 Drinking Water Act. U.S. Public Health Service, 58 *Public Health Service Report* 69 (Jan. 1943); 27 *Federal Register* 2151 (1962). For limiting arsenic, see 40 *Federal Register* 59,566 (1975).

3. *Safe Drinking Water Act 1986 Amendments,* Pub. L. No. 99–339, § 101(b)(1)(C), 100 Stat. 666 (1986) (codified as amended at 42 U.S.C. § 300g-1(b)(1)(C)) (1994)). *Safe Drinking Water Act 1996 Amendments,* Pub. L. No. 104–182, § 109(a)(12)(A)(v), 110 Stat. 1615, 1616 (1996) (codified as amended at 42 U.S.C. § 300g-1(b)(12)(A)(v) (1996)). Natural Resources Defense Council, "White House Yields to NRDC Suit; Lets EPA Release New Arsenic-in-Tap-Water Standard" (press release; May 24, 2000). Browner's Final Arsenic Rule, at 6976. On March 25, 2003, the EPA published a "Minor Clarification" to make clear that 10 ppb was equivalent to 10 micrograms per liter or 0.010 milligrams per liter. See 68 *Federal Register* 14,502 (2003). For occurring naturally, see EPA, *Fact Sheet: Drinking Water Standard for Arsenic* (2001), available at www.epa .gov/safewater/ars/ars_rule_factsheet.html.

4. For preventing cancer, see Browner's Final Arsenic Rule, at 7009, 7012. Gina Kolata, "Putting a Price Tag on the Priceless," *New York Times,* April 8, 2001, at § 4, p. 4; Beth Daley, "Report May Prompt Tougher Rules for Water: EPA Requested Study of Arsenic and Cancer Risk," *Boston Globe,* Sept. 22, 2001, at A15; Floyd Frost, "Poisonous Decision: A Low Arsenic Standard Carries a High Cost," *Washington Post,* Sept. 16, 2001, at B5; Deborah Schoch, "Even Minute Levels of Arsenic Could Cause Cancer, Study Says," *Los Angeles Times,* Sept. 15, 2001, at § 2, p. 1. For speculative cancer prediction, see Browner's Final Arsenic Rule, at 7006–9, 7012. See also Cass R. Sunstein, "The Arithmetic of Arsenic," 90 *Georgetown Law Journal* 2255, 2272 (2002). For Taiwan data, see Toshihide Tsuda et al., "Ingested Arsenic and Internal Cancer: A Historic Cohort Study Followed for 33 Years," 141 *American Journal of Epidemiology* 198, 206 (1995); see also National Academy of Sciences, National Research Council, Subcommittee on Arsenic in Drinking Water, *Arsenic in Drinking Water* (Washington, D.C.: Government Printing Office, 1999), at 3. See also Browner's Final Arsenic Rule, at 7001–3. For difficulties with calculations, see Browner's Final Arsenic Rule, at 7003–4, 7005–6.

5. Office of Congressman Bernard Sanders, "Sanders to Introduce Legislation to Force President to Uphold Drinking Water Standards" (press release; March 21, 2001). For eight to twenty more lives, see Browner's Final Arsenic Rule, at 7006. NAS Subcommittee, *Arsenic in Drinking Water*; National Academy of Sciences, National Research Council, Subcommittee to Update the 1999 Arsenic in Drinking Water Report, *Arsenic in Drinking Water: 2001 Update* (Washington, D.C.: Government Printing Office, 2001) (hereinafter cited as *Arsenic Update*).

6. The papers favorably covered calls from environmental advocacy groups for stronger arsenic standards. See, e.g., "N.M. Water Sometimes Unsafe, Consumer Watchdog Group Says," *Albuquerque Tribune,* June 7, 1995, at A6; Chris Wingenroth, Campaign Director of PIRG, said, "Congress shouldn't be in the business of road-blocking efforts by the EPA to update safe drinking water standards." See Mike Taugher, "Report: Toughen Water Standards," *Albuquerque Journal,* Oct. 27, 1995, at C2; Tania Soussan, "Arsenic Study Nearly Finished," *Albuquerque Journal,* Jan. 21, 1997, at C1. For public costs, see, e.g., Carolyn Appelman, "Town Works to Tackle Arsenic Problem," *Albuquerque Journal,* July 19, 2000, at 1; Juliet Casey, "Vote to Keep Limit Will Be Urged," *Albuquerque Journal,* July 19, 2000, at 1; Juliet Casey, "Arsenic Removal Costs Estimated," *Albuquerque Journal,*" Aug. 15, 2000, at 5; Richard Benke, "Arsenic Standards Would Cost N.M. $400 Million," *Santa Fe New Mexican,* April 20, 2001, at A1. For cost to Los Lunas, see Tara King, "Arsenic Rules Concern Village," *Albuquerque Journal,* Sept. 19, 2002, at A1. This reflects the current estimate in order to meet compliance by 2006. Interview with Betty Behrand, Utilities/Public Works Director, Los Lunas, New Mexico, Sept. 3, 2003. New Mexico actually ranks forty-eighth among the fifty states and the District of

Columbia. See National Cancer Institute, *SEER Cancer Statistic Review 1975–2000* (2003), at ch. 26, p. 11. See also Lowry McAllen, "City Argues EPA Used Bad Science in Setting Rules for Arsenic in Drinking Water," *Albuquerque Tribune*, Sept. 19, 2000, at A3. For cancer and arsenic, see Brent Israelsen, "EPA Toughens Water-Systems Arsenic Limits," *Salt Lake Tribune*, Feb. 2, 2001, at A1; Lowry McAllen, "City Official Wants More Time to Review Arsenic Rule," *Albuquerque Tribune*, May 7, 2001, at A1. The study is D. R. Lewis et al., "Drinking Water Arsenic in Utah: A Cohort Mortality Study," 107 *Environmental Health Perspectives* 359 (1999).

7. *Safe Drinking Water Act 1996 Amendments*, 42 U.S.C. § 300g-1(b).

8. Browner's Final Arsenic Rule, at 6994.

9. Browner's Final Arsenic Rule, at 6995.

10. Sunstein, *Risk and Reason*, at 177.

11. *Safe Drinking Water Act 1996 Amendments*, 42 U.S.C. § 300g-1(b)(3)(C)(I), (VI). The House and Senate bills were passed unanimously, and the conference report passed unanimously in the Senate and passed 392–30 in the House. See 142 *Congressional Record* H 98–2-H9877 (1996); 142 *Congressional Record* S 94–5-S9498 (1996).

12. Sunstein, *Risk and Reason*, at 165–66. For a critique of the $6.1 valuation of a human life, see Jim Holt, "The Human Factor," *New York Times*, March, 28, 2004, at § 6, p. 13.

13. Bernard W. Bell, "*Marbury v. Madison* and the Madisonian Vision," 72 *George Washington Law Review* 197, 204 (2003). The scholars who argue that delegation undermines democracy include Douglas Arnold, Robert Dahl, John Ely, Morris Fiorina, and David Mayhew, all discussed in *Power without Responsibility*, at 84, 89, 99, 104. Editorial, "The Court Vetoes Line Item," *New York Times*, June 26, 1998, at A22; Editorial, "Paralysis on Clean Air," *New York Times*, Jan. 4, 2004 at § 4, p. 6; Editorial, "Silence on the Hill," *Washington Post*, Jan. 5, 2004, at A16; Editorial, "Once Again, Regulatory Reform," *Washington Post*, Aug. 26, 1997, at A14. Among the scholars who argue that delegation does not undermine democracy are Dan Kahan, Jerry Mashaw, and Peter Schuck. Jerry Mashaw, *Greed, Chaos, and Governance: Using Public Choice to Improve Public Law* (New Haven: Yale University Press, 1997), at 139–47; Dan Kahan, "Democracy Schmemocracy," 20 *Cardozo Law Review* 795 (1999); Peter Schuck, "Delegation and Democracy: Comments on David Schoenbrod," 20 *Cardozo Law Review* 775 (1999). Mashaw, Kahan, and Schuck take issue with my previous book on delegation. I deal with their major arguments in the text, but I urge those interested in the subject to read both their contentions in full and my reply in Schoenbrod, "Delegation and Democracy: A Reply to My Critics," 20 *Cardozo Law Review* 731 (1999).

14. New Mexico's representatives opposed the measure by 2 votes to 1, while both of New Mexico's senators supported the parallel measure in the Senate. *House Roll No. 288 HR 2620* (July 2001); *Senate Vote No. 265, HR 2620* (Aug.

2001). The Congressional Review Act of 2001 was included as Subtitle E of the *Small Business Regulatory Enforcement Fairness Act of 1996*, Pub. L. No. 104–121, 110 Stat. 857, 868 (1996). See also David Schoenbrod, "Politics and the Principle That Elected Legislators Should Make the Laws," 26 *Harvard Journal of Law and Public Policy* 239, 271 (2003). For Congress's voting on agency laws, see Morton Rosenberg, "Whatever Happened to Congressional Review of Agency Rulemaking? A Brief Overview, Assessment, and Proposal for Reform," 51 *Administrative Law Review* 1051 (1999); Morton Rosenberg, *Congressional Review of Agency Rulemaking: An Update and Assessment after Nullification of OSHA's Ergonomics Standard*, Congressional Research Report for Congress (2003), at 6 (ergonomics disapproval); Yochi J. Dreazen, "Senate Votes to Scrap New Media Rules," *Wall Street Journal*, Sept. 17, 2003, at A3.

15. For example, "Status of Outstanding Requirements for FY 2000 and Prior Years," attached to letter from Associate General Counsel James C. Nelson to David Schoenbrod, Nov. 21, 2003, in response to Freedom of Information Act Request No. HQ-RIN-02107–03, EPA, 2003.

16. Katharine Q. Seelye, "Whitman Dispels Talk That She Wants to Quit," *New York Times*, Dec. 14, 2002, at A17.

17. *Power without Responsibility*, at ch. 7; Joseph Sax, "The (Unhappy) Truth about NEPA," 26 *Oklahoma Law Review* 239, 239 (1973).

18. When challenged as facially unconstitutional, the EPA's arsenic rule was upheld on the basis that some of the water systems it regulates transport water across state lines. See *Nebraska v. EPA*, 331 F.3d 995 (D.C. Cir. 2003). Yet my concern, as I made plain in chapter 13, is not with the letter of the Constitution, as read by the courts, but rather with its spirit, which calls for the federal government to leave to the states issues that they are institutionally competent to resolve. For increase in cancer deaths, see Browner's Final Arsenic Rule, at 7006.

19. I am thus taking issue with Edward Rubin and others who argue that support for a limited national government is based on misplaced nostalgia. See Edward L. Rubin, "Puppy Federalism and the Blessings of America," 574 *Annals of the American Academy of Political & Social Science* 37 (2001). Professor Rubin mistakes waxing national power for the absence of good reasons to limit the national government. For voters and governments, see Hamilton, "Federalism," at 311, 320–23.

20. For New Mexico newspapers, see, e.g., Tim Archuleta, "Easing Arsenic Standard Will Save City Millions," *Albuquerque Tribune*, March 21, 2001, at A1; Tania Soussan, "Arsenic Standard on Hold," *Albuquerque Journal*, March 21, 2001, at A1. For newspapers elsewhere, see, e.g., Douglas Jehl, "EPA to Abandon New Arsenic Limits for Water Supply," *New York Times*, March 21, 2001, at A1; Katharine Q. Seelye, "Arsenic Standard for Water Is Too Lax, Study Concludes," *New York Times*, Sept. 11, 2001, at A20 ("wave of protest that it was more sympathetic to the chemical industry than to consumers."); Elizabeth Shogren,

"EPA Revokes New Arsenic Standards for Drinking Water, Health; Opponents Say It Is the Most Recent Move by the Bush Team That Favors Industry Over Public Safety," *Los Angeles Times,* March 21, 2001, at A1.

21. Don McKay, "City Chokes on Arsenic Proposal," *Albuquerque Journal,* Sept. 20, 2000, at B1.

22. Behrend, interview with the author, Sept. 3, 2003. For harming public health, see Floyd Frost, "Poisonous Decision: A Low Arsenic Standard Carries a High Cost," *Washington Post,* Sept. 16, 2001, at B5.

23. Hamilton, "Federalism," at 311, 320–23.

24. Mary Graham, *The Morning after Earth Day: Practical Environmental Politics* (Washington, D.C.: Brookings Institution Press, 1999), at 36–45; DeWitt John, *Civic Environmentalism: Alternatives to Regulation in States and Communities* (Washington, D.C.: Congressional Quarterly Press, 1994), at 7–18; Edward P. Weber, *Bringing Society Back In: Grassroots Ecosystems Management, Accountability, and Sustainable Communities* (Cambridge, Mass.: The MIT Press, 2003). *Bringing Society Back In* illustrates a deeply felt interest in participating in environmental decisions. Weber shows how local environmental groups, local businesses, and officials from all levels of government worked together to agree on local environment issues. Despite initial misgivings that businesses might run roughshod over environmental concerns, he comes out strongly favoring the results and the process. Weber suggests that national environmental laws do not inhibit such participation. That may sometimes be true in the natural-resource context from which his examples are drawn because national natural-resource laws tend to confer broad discretion on national officials. But in the pollution-control context that is the focus of my recommendation, national laws grant less discretion. The statute required EPA to make a national law on arsenic in drinking water, and, once made, the law restricted the discretion of national, state, and local officials. So, the participants at the town meeting in Los Lunas could discuss how to meet the 10 ppb standard, not whether to do so.

25. Charles C. Mann & Mark L. Plummer, "New Approaches to Conservation: Grass-Roots Seeds of Compromise," *Washington Post,* Oct. 11, 1998, at C3. For Evans, see Jane Braxton Little, "A Quiet Victory in Quincy," *High Country News,* Nov. 9, 1998.

Chapter 18. The Boon of Liberty

1. 116 *Congressional Record* 42,386 (1970). E.g., Friedrich A. Hayek, "The Use of Knowledge in Society," 35 *American Economic Review* 519 (1945). The application of this literature to environmental policy is discussed in Jonathan H. Adler, "Let Fifty Flowers Bloom: Transforming the States into Laboratories of Environmental Policy," available at www.federalismproject.org/masterpages/environment/flowers.pdf. For reinventing government, see Steve Lohr, "Washington Takes Leaf from Business Manuals," *New York Times,* Sept. 8, 1993, at B10.

2. Wallace E. Oates, "The Arsenic Rule: A Case for Decentralized Standard Setting?" 147 *Resources* 16, 17 (Spring 2002).

3. William D. Ruckelshaus, "Toward a Sustainable World: Government and Industries Policies Necessary for Sustained World Development," 261 *Scientific American* 166 (1989). Similarly, the NAS recommends that Congress amend the environmental statues to allow the EPA to consider such interconnections. See National Research Council, *Air Quality Management in the United States* (Washington, D.C.: National Academies Press, 2004), at ch. 7. See also Elliott, "Environmental TQM"; Richard B. Stewart, "A New Generation of Environmental Regulation?" 29 *Capital University Law Review* 21, 27–38 (2001). For integrated approaches, see Stewart, at 158–62.

4. Howard Klee Jr. & Mahesh Podar, *Amoco/USEPA Pollution Prevention Project: Executive Summary* (Amoco & EPA, May 1992), at v.

5. Paul R. Portney, "Market-Based Approaches to Environmental Policy— A 'Refresher' Course," 151 *Resources* 15, 17 (Summer 2003). He also describes the alternative of taxing emissions. Problems of enforcement could be dealt with by requiring the source to report what is supposed to come out of each pipe or stack. Filing a report is a lot easier than securing a permit. The cap could be set in proportion to present emissions (which is called "grandfathering") or the quantity of goods produced (for example, tons of steel).

6. See, e.g., Robert N. Stavins, "Lessons from the American Experiment with Market-Based Environmental Policies," in *Harnessing the Hurricane: The Challenge of Market-Based Governance* (ed. John Donahue & Joseph Nye; Washington, D.C.: Brookings Institution Press, 2002), available at www.ksg.harvard.edu/cbg/research/r.stavins_brookings_lessons.from.american.experiment.pdf.

7. For liberal scholars, see, e.g., Bruce A. Ackerman & Richard B. Stewart, Comment, "Reforming Environmental Law," 37 *Stanford Law Review* 1333 (1985). For dominance of rigid approach, see Stavins, "Lessons," at 10. For an example of emission trading to control water pollution, see John J. Fialka, "EPA Hashes Out Emissions Plans to Cut Pollution," *Wall Street Journal,* Jan. 10, 2003, at C10B.

8. The flexible programs include Project XL, the Common Sense Initiative, and the Environmental Leadership Program. National Academy of Public Administration, *Resolving the Paradox of Environmental Protection: An Agenda for Congress, EPA & the States* (1997), at 35. For a detailed case study of a failure to put the high-sounding objectives of Project XL into practice, see Alfred A. Marcus, Donald A. Geffen & Ken Sexton, *Reinventing Environmental Regulation: Lessons from Project XL* (Washington, D.C.: Resources for the Future, 2002). National Academy of Public Administration, at 35. For a later study on the impediments to EPA's allowing flexibility, see Marcus et al., *Reinventing Environmental Regulation.* Peder Larson, Commissioner, Minnesota Pollution Control Board, interview with the author, Sept. 18, 1997. As described in chapter 5, the deadlines for achieving the air quality standards forced the EPA to adopt

emissions trading in order to avoid having to stop the opening of new factories in much of the country, but the agency has circumscribed that trading in ways that have severely limited its usefulness. Stavins, "Lessons," at 6 (prior approval required for trades and the "20% rule"). In addition, the program limited trading to showing compliance with the attainment requirements and not other Clean Air Act requirements. A force alien to EPA, the Reagan White House instructed the EPA to institute emissions trading for lead in gasoline in the early 1980s. Trading saved $250 million a year in direct pollution-control costs. For acid-rain emissions, see 1990 Act. Congress also legislated trading for chlorofluorocarbons. See 42 U.S.C. § 7671f.

9. National Research Council, *Air Quality Management in the United States* (Washington, D.C.: National Academies Press, 2004), at 172. See also Dallas Burtraw & Erin Mansur, "The Environmental Effects of SO_2 Trading and Banking," 33 *Environmental Science & Technology* 3489, 3489 (1999) ("Geographic consequences are not consistent with the fears of the program's critics."). For modifying cap-and-trade, see NRC, *Air Quality Management*, at 206. See also Jonathan Remy Nash & Richard L. Revesz, "Markets and Geography: Designing Marketable Permit Schemes to Control Local and Regional Pollutants," 28 *Ecology Law Quarterly* 569, 610–16 (2001).

10. Stavins, "Lessons," at 11. Beginning in 1999, the EPA launched a market-based emissions trading program in order to reduce nitrogen oxide emissions from power plants and other large combustion sources in the northeast. Nine northeastern states and the District of Columbia teamed up with the EPA and set a regional ozone season "budget" or cap on nitrogen oxide emissions. See EPA, "Report Demonstrates Nitrogen Oxides Emission Trading Program Achieves 60 Percent Reduction of Emissions in Northeastern States" (press release; March 7, 2003, available at yosemite.epa.gov/opa/admpress.nsf/b1ab9f485b098972852562e7004 dc686/77ee9ea221afbb2a85256ce20077dfa5?OpenDocument. For tightening the EPA's control, see for example 42 U.S.C. §§ 7501–15.

11. The EPA agrees. See *Benefits and Costs 1970–1990*, at ES-2, available at www.epa.gov/air/sect812/copy.html ("Ultimately, these higher costs of production [referring to all direct pollution-control costs] were borne by stockholders, business owners, consumers, and taxpayers.")

12. Environmental Law Institute, *Endangered Environmental Laws Program: Background Paper* (undated), at 6.

13. EPA, *Environmental Investments: The Cost of a Clean Environment* (a report by the administrator to Congress; Washington, D.C.: Government Printing Office, 1990), at xvii (hereinafter cited as *Environmental Investments*). Under duress of statutes and presidential orders, the EPA does estimate the cost of individual statutes.

14. Michael Hazilla & Raymond J. Kopp, "Social Cost of Environmental Quality Regulations: A General Equilibrium Analysis," 98 *Journal of Policy and Economics* 853, 867 (1990). For other studies, see Cross, "Paradoxical Perils" 53

Washington & Lee Law Review at 916 (collecting studies). For negative consequences accumulating, see James C. Robinson, "The Impact of Environmental
and Occupational Health Regulation on Productivity Growth in U.S. Manufacturing," 12 *Yale Journal of Regulation* 387, 416 (1995) ("The cumulative effect
through 1986 on the manufacturing sector as a whole . . . was to reduce multifac-
tor productivity by 11.4% from the level it would have achieved absent EPA and
OSHA regulation."). Maureen L. Cropper, Chair, Advisory Council on Clean
Air Act Compliance Analysis, Science Advisory Board, to Administrator Carol
Browner, Nov. 19, 1999, at 3 (on file with author). The tax interaction effect is
distinct from, and on top of, the indirect effects described by Hazilla and Kopp,
according to an economist upon whom the advisory council and the EPA relied.
Dallas Burtraw, telephone interview with the author, Aug. 28, 2003. For the
EPA's minimizing effects, see EPA, *The Benefits and Costs of the Clean Air Act:
1990–2010, EPA Report to Congress* (1999), at ch. 3. For criticism, see Cropper to
Browner, at 2–3.

15. The relationship between indirect costs and the savings in direct costs
that can come from flexible market mechanisms is complicated. Dallas Burtraw
and Matt Cannon summarized the literature on this topic in "Heterogeneity in
Costs and Second Best Policies for Environmental Protection," Resources for
the Future, Discussion Paper 00–20, April 20, 2000, available at www.rff.org/
methods/cost_benefit.htm. Previous studies concluded that the savings in direct costs are outweighed by indirect losses if the market mechanism employed
gives the emission rights to existing entities. The upshot of such "grandfathering" would be that new entrants would need to buy or rent emissions rights
from existing entities. Burtraw and Cannon showed that this conclusion does
not hold when the costs of pollution control are heterogeneous rather than
homogeneous. In so doing, they made the point that the reason that such
"'grandfathered' tradeable permits" produce losses despite savings in direct
costs is that this approach "generates rents associated with the asset value of
permits that exacerbate pre-existing distortions resulting from the labor tax.
These rents . . . are not available [to government] to reduce the pre-existing tax.
The rents accrue over all emissions, while abatement costs accrue only over
reductions. For an incremental initial reduction, the permit rents swamp other
components of cost, making permits more expensive than the command and
control policies." "Heterogeneity," at 17. I oppose grandfathered tradeable permits. See the discussion of the bias against new sources in chapter 20, which
explains that the likelihood of such a bias is greatly reduced if regulation is at the
state rather than the federal level. Competing states have less inclination than
does the national government to grandfather companies in and less ability to
deliver large benefits by this means. The propensity of the national government
to use regulation to confer benefits on existing stakeholders may be one reason
that leaders of many major corporations favor national control. For a better
deal, see *Benefits and Costs 1970–1990*. See also discussion in chapter 5, note 25.

Chapter 19. The Appeal of Law

1. Aldo Leopold, "Thinking Like a Mountain," in *Sand County Almanac,* at 129.

2. Leopold, "Thinking Like a Mountain," at 130.

3. In December 1947, Aldo Leopold submitted a revised book manuscript titled "Great Possessions." "Great Possessions" was published in 1949 as *Sand County Almanac.*

4. Oliver Wendell Holmes, *The Common Law* (Boston: Little, Brown, 1923), at 41.

5. See, e.g., Lon L. Fuller, "The Forms and Limits of Adjudication," 92 *Harvard Law Review* 353, 373 (1978).

6. Friedrich A. Hayek, *Law, Legislation, and Liberty, Vol. I: Rules and Order* (Chicago: University of Chicago Press, 1973), at 88–89.

7. See Federal Water Pollution Control Act Amendments of 1972, 33 U.S.C. § 1251(a)(1).

8. *Brown v. Board of Education,* 347 U.S. 483 (1954). For the aftermath of *Brown,* see Gerald N. Rosenberg, *The Hollow Hope: Can Courts Bring About Social Change?* (Chicago: University of Chicago Press, 1991), at ch. 2. See Robert V. Percival, " 'Greening' the Constitution—Harmonizing Environmental and Constitutional Values," 32 *Environmental Law* 809, 857–59 (2002).

9. See Andrew P. Morriss, "Lessons for Environmental Law from the American Codification Debate," in *The Common Law and the Environment: Rethinking the Statutory Basis for Modern Environmental Law* (ed. Roger E. Meiners & Andrew P. Morriss; Lanham, Md.: Rowman & Littlefield, 2000), at 130–57 (hereinafter cited as *The Common Law and the Environment*).

10. Under many statutory provisions, such as those for setting ambient air standards, the EPA is barred from considering the practicalities. See *Lead Indus. Ass'n v. EPA,* 647 F.2d at 1149. Under others, it may consider practicalities, but may do so only in a limited fashion and while up against the legislative judgment that society really ought to be attaining the statutory ideal. For example, the 1974 Drinking Water Act's four-step process, which I outlined in the previous chapter, gave only a grudging nod to practicality. After deciding how much of a dangerous substance is safe to have in drinking water, the EPA was to decide whether it was feasible—that is, possible—to achieve that safe level. Possible, however, does not mean practical. It may be *possible* to sanitize a city's sidewalks with an antiseptic every night, but it is not practical. The EPA was also instructed to calculate the costs and benefits of various limits on the dangerous substance. Here, Congress permitted the EPA to consider practicalities but did not lend its authority to actually taking them into account in making the law. If the EPA had set the law above the lowest feasible level, it would have had to take responsibility for doing so, and it better have had a convincing

justification for exposing the public to any risk that could feasibly have been stopped.

11. More than half (57 percent) of Americans feel that "protecting the environment is so important that requirements and standards cannot be too high and continuing environmental improvements must be made regardless of the cost." *CBS News/New York Times Poll,* Nov. 20–24, 2002, available at www .pollingreport.com/enviro.htm.

12. Gregg Easterbrook, *Everything You Know about the Bush Environmental Record Is Wrong* (Washington, D.C.: Brookings Institution Press, 2002). Cass R. Sunstein, "The Arithmetic of Arsenic," 90 *Georgetown Law Journal* 2255, 2261–63 (2002).

13. J. B. Ruhl, "Working Both (Positivist) Ends toward a New (Pragmatist) Middle in Environmental Law," 68 *George Washington Law Review* 522, 523–24 (2000) (reviewing *Eco-Pragmatism*).

14. This question, along with the comparison to the abortion debate, was raised in Douglas Kysar & James Salzman, "Environmental Tribalism," 87 *Minnesota Law Review* 1099 (2003).

15. See *Power without Responsibility,* at 28–29.

16. Jim Carlton, "Many Voters Agree to Raise Money for Green Space," *Wall Street Journal,* Nov. 7, 2003, at A2.

17. Or Congress would enact common-law-like rules of the sort that Professor Thomas Merrill suggests for controlling interstate pollution. See, e.g., Merrill, "Golden Rules."

18. David Schoenbrod, "Protecting the Environment in the Spirit of the Common Law," in *The Common Law and the Environment,* at 3–24.

Chapter 20. The Joy of Doing

1. See Odwalla, Inc., "Odwalla Reintroduces Apple Juice" (press release; Dec. 5, 1996) (on file with author).

2. For proposed law, see 62 *Federal Register* 45,593 (1997). For warning label, see 63 *Federal Register* 37,030, 37,043 (1998).

3. Katy McLaughlin, "Hey, Buddy, Wanna Score Some Cheese?" *Wall Street Journal,* June 10, 2003, at D1.

4. R. Phillip Hartman, interview with the author, March 15, 2003.

5. Professor Randy Worobo, Associate Professor of Food and Microbiology, Cornell University, interview with the author, March 13, 2003.

6. Hartman and his colleague were partners in the beginning.

7. 66 *Federal Register* 6138 (2001).

8. Joseph Corby, Director, Division of Food Safety, New York Department of Agriculture and Markets, interview with the author, Aug. 8, 2003.

9. My research assistant and I called states that Dr. Randy Worobo had

preidentified as supportive or nonsupportive to ascertain the number of cider producers in 1997 and 2000. We got counts or reliable estimates from seven states. When asked for the reason for the decline, officials in nonsupportive states mentioned the FDA laws and economic conditions.

	1997	2000	Change	% Change
Supportive states				
New York	135	141	6	+4.4%
Ohio	115	108	−7	−6.1%
Wisconsin	35	33	−2	−5.7%
Total for supportive states	285	282	−3	1.1% decline
Nonsupportive states				
Indiana	40	15	−25	−62.5%
Illinois	113	85	−28	−24.8%
New Hampshire	48	30	−18	−37.5%
Vermont	30	12	−18	−60.0%
Total for nonsupportive states	231	142	−89	38.5% decline

Dr. Joanne Ingham, institutional research specialist at New York Law School, found that the decline in the number of cider producers in those states defined as nonsupportive was statistically significant. The results of a t-test showed a significant difference in the mean change in the number of cider producers between the supportive and nonsupportive states ($t = 4.02$, df $= 5$, p < 0.01).

10. For the rule on ultraviolet light, see 42 *Federal Register* 14,365 (1977). Hartman interview, March 15, 2003.

11. 65 *Federal Register* 71,056 (2000).

12. R. Philip Hartman, FPE, Inc., to Food and Drug Administration, Dec. 27, 2000 (on file with the author).

13. See, e.g., Winston Harrington et al., "On the Accuracy of Regulatory Cost Estimates," 19 *Journal of Policy Analysis and Management* 297 (2000), which found that the EPA underestimates the cost of removing a unit of pollution about as often as it overestimates that cost. It turns out, however, that industry usually has to remove fewer units of pollution than the EPA expects. This underestimation may mean that the EPA overestimates the benefits of regulation.

14. 63 *Federal Register* 20,450, 20,454 (1998); 66 *Federal Register* 6138 (2001).

15. Richard Breeden, "Small Talk: Ownership Values," *Wall Street Journal*, Nov. 18, 2003, at B9.

16. *Food Quality Protection Act of 1996*, Pub. L. No. 104–170, Title IV, 110 Stat. 1513 (1996). For support of farm organizations, see Kenneth Weinstein, Jeffrey Holmstead, William Wehrum & Douglas Nelson, "The Food Quality

Protection Act: A New Way of Looking at Pesticides," 28 *Environmental Law Reporter* 10555, 10560 (1998) (discussing letter from EPA assistant administrator Lynn Goldman). White House Chief of Staff Leon Panetta gave similar reassurances to the state presidents of the American Federation of Farm Bureaus at the White House during their summer 1996 meeting. Scott Rawlins, former American Federation of Farm Bureaus staff member, interview with the author, Dec. 3, 2003. For letter to Lugar, see 142 *Congressional Record* S 8928 (1996). For pesticide ban, see Weinstein et al. at 10559–60 (discussing margin of safety). EPA also tightened up other parameters of the safety decision. EPA, "Guidance for Submission of Probabilistic Human Health Exposure Assessments to the Office of Pesticide Programs" (Draft, Feb. 6, 1998). William O'Connor, interview with the author, Dec. 9, 2003.

17. E. Donald Elliott, "The Last Great Clean Air Act Book?" 5 *Environmental Lawyer* 321, 326–27 (1998). Editorial, "Paralysis on Clean Air," *New York Times,* Jan. 4, 2004, at § 4, p. 6.

18. EPA, *The Nation's Hazardous Waste Management Program at a Crossroads: The RCRA Implementation Study* (July 1990), at 36. Christopher Harris, Raymond C. Marshall & Patrick O. Cavanaugh, *Environmental Crimes* (Colorado Springs: Shepard's/McGraw Hill, 1994), at 8. For survey, see James Salzman et al., "Regulatory Traffic Jams," 2 *Wyoming Law Review* 253, 281 (2002). For Resources for the Future Study, see Davies, *Pollution Control* at 18.

19. James V. DeLong, *Out of Bounds, Out of Control: Regulatory Enforcement at EPA* (Washington, D.C.: Cato Institute, 2002), at 5. For civil penalties, see 42 U.S.C. § 7413(b) (emphasis added). For civil administrative penalties, see 42 U.S.C. § 7413(d)(1) (emphasis added). The EPA has the authority to levy fines regardless of whether any harm has occurred. See *Friends of the Earth v. Laidlaw Environmental Services,* 956 F. Supp. 588 (D.S.C. 1997), vacated on another issue by *Friends of the Earth v. Laidlaw Environmental Services,* 149 F.3d 303 (4th Cir. 1998), reversed by *Friends of the Earth v. Laidlaw Environmental Services,* 528 U.S. 167 (2000).

20. Email to his staff from Walter Mugdan, EPA Region II general counsel, Sept. 16, 1999 (on file with author). Testimony of Dr. Shelley H. Metzenbaum before the House Committee on Government Reform, Subcommittee on Energy Policy, Natural Resources, and Regulatory Affairs, Hearings on EPA and State Enforcement of Water Laws, Oct. 14, 2003, Ipswich, Mass. ("Even when enforcement targets are not formally established, agency staff tend to assume they must meet or exceed the previous year's enforcement levels. This can create a pressure to find enforcement cases just to meet the target, causing cases that might have been handled more appropriately without enforcement to get an enforcement response.") See also Jonathan H. Adler, "Bean Counting for a Better Earth: Environmental Enforcement at the EPA," 21 *Regulation* 2, 40 (1998).

21. For felony convictions, see 42 U.S.C. § 7413 (c)(1)–(3), (5). For the EPA's interpretation, see Daniel P. Riesel, *Environmental Enforcement: Civil and Criminal* (New York: Law Journal Press, 2001), at § 6.03. For subjective perceptions, see Riesel at § 7.01[1], at 7–2, 7–3. For incarceration, see Richard J. Lazarus, "Meeting the Demands of Integration in the Evolution of Environmental Law: Reforming Environmental Criminal Law," 83 *Georgetown Law Journal* 2407, 2529 (1995). See also Lois J. Schiffer & James F. Simon, "The Reality of Prosecuting Environmental Criminals: A Response to Professor Lazarus," 83 *Georgetown Law Journal* 2531 (1995); Richard J. Lazarus, "The Reality of Environmental Law in the Prosecution of Environmental Crimes: A Reply to the Department of Justice," 83 *Georgetown Law Journal* 2539 (1995).

22. Carol A. Browner, "Recent EPA Accomplishments" (Aug. 15, 1997), available at www.epa.gov/epahome/accomp.htm (on file with the author).

23. For lead in gasoline, see the discussion in chapter 4. For a summary of the literature on restricting competition, see Zywicki, "Environmental Externalities," at 856–67. See also the essays in *Environmental Politics: Public Costs, Private Rewards* (ed. Michael Greve & Fred Smith; New York: Praeger, 1992) and *Political Environmentalism: Going behind the Green Curtain* (ed. Terry L. Anderson; Stanford, Calif.: Hoover Institution Press, 2000). For stock prices, see Bruce Yandle, *Common Sense and Common Law for the Environment: Creating Wealth in Hummingbird Economies* (New York: Rowman & Littlefield, 1997), at 66, 70–71.

24. Byron Swift, "Electric Utility Regulation: Grandfathering, New Source Review, and NOx—Making Sense of a Flawed System," 31 *Environmental Reporter (BNA)* 1538, 1538–46 (2000). For pollution rights, see 42 U.S.C. §§ 7503(c), 7651b(e). See also Andrew P. Morriss, Bruce Yandle & Roger E. Meiners, "The Failure of EPA's Water Quality Reforms: From Environment-Enhancing Competition to Uniformity and Polluter Profits," 20 *UCLA Journal of Environmental Law and Policy* 25, 58 (2001/2002).

25. Matthew D. McCubbins et al., "Structure and Process, Politics and Policy: Administrative Arrangements and the Political Control of Agencies," 75 *Virginia Law Review* 431, 460–61 (1989).

26. W. Mark Crain & Thomas D. Hopkins, Office of Advocacy, Small Business Administration, *Small Business Research Summary: The Impact of Regulatory Costs on Small Firms* (Oct. 2001), at 3.

27. Peter Pashigian, "The Effect of Environmental Regulation on Plant Size and Factor Shares," 27 *Journal of Law & Economics* 1, 25–26 (1984).

28. For a discussion of lawyers and lobbyists as an interest group favoring the present system, see Zywicki, "Environmental Externalities," at 902–10.

29. See *Environmental Investments*, at 3–4.

30. See Food Quality Protection Act of 1996, § 408(b)(2)(A)(ii) (corresponding version at 21 U.S.C. § 346a(b)(2)(A)(ii)).

Chapter 21. Conclusion

Epigraph: In *God in the Dock: Essays on Theology and Ethics* (ed. Walter Hooper; Grand Rapids, Mich.: William B. Eerdmans, 1970), at 292.

1. James Scott, *Seeing Like a State: How Certain Schemes to Improve the Human Condition Have Failed* (New Haven: Yale University Press, 1998), at 19, 20, 193–261, 11–22. Such failures of course vary widely in terms of the culpability of the planners and the consequences for those upon whom the plans are imposed. "The most tragic episodes of state-initiated social engineering," Scott points out, "originate in a pernicious combination of four elements:" (1) "administrative ordering of nature and society," (2) "a high modernist ideology," by which he means "a faith that borrowed . . . the legitimacy of science and technology," (3) "an authoritarian state that is willing and able to use the full weight of its coercive power to bring these high modernist designs into being," and (4) "a prostate civil society that lacks the capacity to resist these plans." *Seeing Like a State*, at 4–5. Jane Jacobs, The Death and Life of Great American Cities (New York: Random House, 1961).

2. Scott, *Seeing Like a State*, at 343, 4.

3. For Congress's regulating emissions, see 42 U.S.C. §§ 7521, 7554. For authorizing the EPA, see, e.g., 42 U.S.C. §§ 7521(a)(3)(B), 7521(i).

4. Out of a nationwide poll of one thousand registered voters, "65% of respondents believe that state or local government would do a better job than the federal government in dealing with environmental concerns, and 72% said that state and local government should determine what pollution control measures are used to protect air quality." See Jonathan H. Adler & Kellyanne Fitzpatrick, "For the Environment, Against Overregulation," *Wall Street Journal*, July 29, 1996, at A12. E.g., American Farm Bureau Federation, *Farm Bureau Policies for 2003*, at 2, 6 ("[The legislature should avoid] delegation of broad, discretionary powers to the executive branch. . . ." "Public functions should be performed by the qualified unit of government closest to the people without coercion by administrative agencies of higher units of governments.").

5. For amending the Clean Air Act, see, e.g., National Research Council, *Air Quality Management in the United States* (Washington, D.C.: National Academies Press, 2004); Editorial, "Clarity on Clean Air," *New York Times*, Feb. 5, 2004, at A30. Many more legislators than the seventy representatives and dozen senators who sponsored the Congressional Responsibility Act would likely join in this demand for congressional responsibility. The Congressional Responsibility Act ran into the question of whether Congress could in fact process the quantity of regulations issuing from all the federal agencies. In a hearing on it, Professor Ernest Gellhorn suggested that Congress could inquire into this question empirically by taking responsibility for the laws issued by one agency. See *Regulatory Reform and Relief Act*, Hearings on HR 47 before the House Judiciary

Subcommittee on Commercial and Administrative Law, 104th Congress, 2d Session (1996) (testimony of Professor Gellhorn), at 64. The sponsors of the Congressional Responsibility Act were prevented from bringing it to a vote because the Republican leadership blocked it in committee. The demand for congressional responsibility would have no such difficulty, at least in the Senate, because it could be presented as an amendment to another piece of environmental legislation.

6. Jane Jacobs, *The Nature of Economics* (New York: Modern Library, 2000), at ix–x.

7. Eric A. Davidson, *You Can't Eat GNP: Economics as if Ecology Mattered* (Cambridge, Mass.: Perseus, 2000).

8. George Orwell, "Notes on Nationalism," in *The Collected Essays, Journalism and Letters of George Orwell: As I Please, 1943–1945* (ed. Sonia Orwell & Ian Angus; Boston: David R. Godine, 2000), at 379. Ronald E. Zupko & Robert A. Laures, *Straws in the Wind: Medieval Urban Environmental Law—The Case of Northern Italy* (Boulder, Colo.: Westview Press, 1996), at 1, 33. See also Robert M. Alison, "The Earliest Traces of a Conservation Conscience," 90 *Natural History* 72 (1981).

9. *The River,* at ix, 298, 300.

10. Leopold, *Sand County Almanac,* at 133.

Acknowledgments

The debts run up in writing this book began to accumulate shortly after the publication in 1993 of *Power without Responsibility: How Congress Abuses the People through Delegation* (Yale). In it, I argued that we lost something precious when members of Congress began to use agencies to evade their responsibility for the laws and that the Supreme Court ought to stop this practice. Not that I thought the Court would, at least not of a sudden and in the near term. I was writing to preserve a dream of government in which the laws governing the people were made by the representatives of the people. The book, however, got a more immediate response than I had expected.

The Cato Institute, a think tank in Washington, D.C., deserves some of the credit. Soon after *Power without Responsibility* was published, Cato's director of natural resources, Jerry Taylor, called to introduce himself. He and his colleagues had read the book, agreed with it, and wanted to work with me to spread its message in Washington. All I knew of Cato was that it called itself "libertarian," and that I liked. But I wondered whether its principles were a cover for more partisan interests. Jerry told me that I would have to judge for myself, but that we could work together on what we agreed upon. I have come to believe that the institute is, in fact, neither left nor right, Democratic or Republican, but rather "liberal" in the root sense of the word. The banner now on its Web site—"Individual liberty, limited government, free markets, and peace,"—fairly describes its stance on the divisive issues of today. Cato gave me the title "adjunct scholar," which brought a salary of zero and a platform in Washington. That platform got me involved in some of the litigation, legislation, and speeches described in this book. This experience has taught me that there is potentially broad public support for a government closer to home and accountable to people but that it is against the interests of the powerful in Washington, D.C., to lead the public this way. The courtiers will have to be driven to it, and that will happen, if at all, only if one speaks over their heads, directly to people.

To reach a broader audience, I had to learn a new way of writing quite different from that which had served me as a lawyer and law professor. My training ground was writing newspaper and magazine articles. Every editor was a writing coach, but the coaches who made the most difference were Neal Kozodoy of *Commentary,* Melanie Kirkpatrick of the *Wall Street Journal,* and Myron Magnet of *City Journal.*

Before I started to write differently, I had begun to think differently than I had at the NRDC. During this quarter-century-long intellectual journey, many veterans of the environmental movement provided suggestions and moral support. Angus Macbeth and Ross Sandler have been there for me always. So has Sergio Piomelli of the Columbia University College of Physicians and Surgeons, who was a star witness on lead poisoning in the 1970s. Bruce Adler, Douglas Blazey, and Carol Casazza gave me valuable insights in the course of our teaching seminars together at New York Law School. Barbara Bankoff, Louisa Spencer, and Richard Stewart were ever ready with advice. I owe a special debt to old colleagues still leading the NRDC today, especially John Adams, Richard Ayres, Frances Beinecke, Sarah Chasis, Eric Goldstein, David Hawkins, and George Woodwell. We have sometimes disagreed, but from our discussions I have always received moral support and better ideas. A high point was the opportunity to address the NRDC board of trustees in 1997. When it appeared many years into writing this book, which was interrupted by the publication of two others, that my teaching responsibilities would mean yet more delay, Edward Crane, president of the Cato Institute, and Richard Matasar, dean of New York Law School, worked out a way for me to get a semester off from teaching in order to bring the book to completion. New York Law School has, from beginning to end, generously supported my efforts.

Many people provided critically important information. E. Donald Elliott provided many valuable insights on how the EPA works. Gail Charnley and George Gray educated me on risk assessment. Lois Swirsky Gold shared her experience and knowledge of chemicals and cancer. Nadine Strossen and Anthony Romero explained how the ACLU organizes support for civil liberties at the state and local levels. Betty Behrend recounted the impact of the arsenic standard on Los Lunas, New Mexico. Dallas Burtraw, Alan Krupnick, Wallace Oates, and Raymond Kopp shared the vast collective knowledge of environmental economics at Resources for the Future. Philip Hartman, Randy Worobo, and Joe Corby elucidated the labyrinth of the FDA approval process. Joanne Ingham performed the statistical analysis of the cider producer data. David Boaz, Barbara Kahlow, Eric Lane, Gary Marchant, and Scott Rawlins were helpful on a variety of topics.

Dan Wilson and Susan Knapp educated me on the perils of growing apples in an administrative state. Jean Morrow reassured me that I had a faithful picture of her late husband, Everest Morrow. Mrs. Karen Tatko did the same in regard to her late father, William Hughes. My debt to my friends upstate is not only for specific information, but also for an education in a way of looking at a citizen's role in a republic. For this, I am indebted not only to those discussed in the book, but to many others as well, including (to name some chief examples) Ron Cadieux, Clifton and Jessie Fredette, Christian Hansen, John Sullivan, Dorothy Wilson, and John Winn.

Bruce Adler, Jonathan Adler, Barbara Bankoff, Douglas Blazey, Lynn Chu, Indur Goklany, Philip Howard, James Huffman, Edward Purcell, John Rademacher, Ross Sandler, Jan Selby, Richard Stewart, and Jerry Taylor took the time to read the entire manuscript in its unpolished state and provided many valuable suggestions.

I also learned from speaking, not only at the NRDC, Cato, and the American Farm Bureau Federation but also at Case Western School of Law, Georgetown University School of Law, the Mont Pelerin Society, the Northwestern College of Law at Lewis and Clark University, the Political Economic Research Council, Resources for the Future, and especially the Foundation for Research in Economics and the Environment where I met scholars, scientists, and judges of diverse perspective who informed my thinking.

Many research assistants at New York Law School lent their time and intelligence to the project as it evolved through the years. Those who helped most recently are Samantha Burd and Christi Wilson, class of 2003, and Mohammed Adel Akbik and Stephanie Trager, class of 2004. They helped with particular chapters. Nathan Ajiashvili, class of 2005, helped with every last thing. They were all wonderful. My students in the Environmental Law and Policy course at New York Law School provided many useful suggestions. William Mills of the New York Law School library turned over many remote rocks to satisfy my diverse requests for information. Gemma Jacobs, my faculty assistant, always got it done.

And then there is Deborah Paulus-Jagric. She was my research assistant on *Power without Responsibility* and has since come back to my aid, despite an ongoing, successful career of her own, to turn several other tortured manuscripts, the present volume included, into ones that can be presented to a respectable press. Then, too, she did the index.

When the idea of writing a book in the new manner coalesced in my mind, John Covell of Yale University Press convinced me that I could pull it off. In recent years, my editor at Yale has been Jean E. Thomson Black. Armed with training in environmental science and native sense, she kept me focused on the critical issues. Everyone at the press was very helpful, but I especially want to thank Nancy Moore, Margaret Otzel, and Sharon Rose, whose copy editing made such a difference.

My agent, Lynn Chu of Writers Representatives, Inc., saw some promise in this project long ago and has provided sage advice ever since.

Most fundamentally, there is the rock on my home front, Jan Selby.

Index

Also by David Schoenbrod:

Democracy by Decree: What Happens When Courts Run Government
(with Ross Sandler)

Power Without Responsibility: How Congress Abuses the People
Through Delegation